2

The Development and Growth of the Cruise Industry

The Development and Growth of the Cruise Industry

Roger Cartwright and Carolyn Baird

OXFORD   AUCKLAND   BOSTON   JOHANNESBURG   MELBOURNE   NEW DELHI

Butterworth-Heinemann
Linacre House, Jordan Hill, Oxford OX2 8DP
225 Wildwood Avenue, Woburn, MA 01801-2041
A division of Reed Educational and Professional Publishing Ltd

R A member of the Reed Elsevier plc group

First published 1999

British Library Cataloguing in Publication Data
Cartwright, Roger
   The development and growth of the cruise industry
   1. Cruise lines   2. Cruise ships
   I. Title   II. Baird, Carolyn
   387.5'42

Library of Congress Cataloguing in Publication Data
A catalogue record for this book is available from the Library of Congress

ISBN 0 7506 4384 6

Composition by Genesis Typesetting, Rochester, Kent
Printed and bound in Great Britain by
Biddles Ltd, Guildford and King's Lynn

Contents

Figures

Abbreviations

AMC	Armed merchant cruiser
B&B	Bed and breakfast
BVI	British Virgin Islands
CAA	Civil Aviation Authority
CATIA	Computer-graphics aided three-dimensional interactive application
CPD	Continuous professional development
DIY	Do it yourself
DST	Douglas Sleeper Transport
EPIC	Electronic pre-assembly in the CATIA
EU	European Union
GO	Gentile ordinaire
GPS	Global positioning systems
GRT	Gross registered tonnage
HAL	Holland America Line
IMO	International Maritime Organization
KD	Köln–Dusseldorf
KdF	*Kraft durch Freude* (Strength through Joy)
MEG	Maritime Evaluation Group
MSC	Mediterranean Shipping Company
NATO	North Atlantic Treaty Organization
NCL	Norwegian Cruise Line
NCV	Norwegian Coastal Voyage®
NDL	Nordeutsche Lloyd
P&O	Peninsular and Oriental
PSR	Passenger space ratio
QE2	*Queen Elizabeth 2*
RCI	Royal Caribbean International

RCCL	Royal Caribbean Cruise Line
RMS	Royal Mail Ship
SOLAS	(Convention on) Safety of Life at Sea
STUFT	Ships taken up from trade
USP	Unique selling point
WTO	World Trade Tourism Organization
WWW	World Wide Web

Map of the major cruise areas

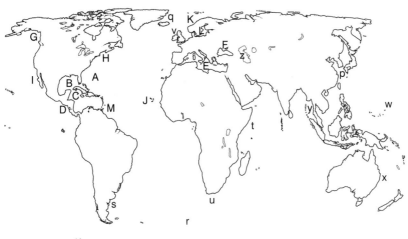

Key:

A	Eastern Caribbean	M	Amazon
B	Western Caribbean	p	China/Japan
C	Southern Caribbean	q	Iceland/Greenland
D	Trans-canal	r	Antarctic
E	Mediterranean	s	South America
F	Black Sea	t	East Africa/Indian Ocean
G	Alaska	u	South Africa
H	Eastern North America	v	Round Britain
I	Western USA & Mexico	w	Hawaii
J	Eastern Atlantic Islands	x	Australia/New Zealand
K	Norway	y	SE Asia
L	Baltic	z	Red Sea

Key:
A–M are traditional areas and p–z are developing areas.

Foreword

The cruise industry is the fastest developing sector of the leisure travel industry. More people are taking cruises than ever before and there is huge potential for growth in this dynamic industry.

Within the market there is great variance between the type of product offered by cruise operators. Individual ships also have their unique attributes which appeal to different people, thereby giving them their own 'personalities'.

The variety of cruise options available can be bewildering to potential buyers and to those who are trying to sell. This is complicated by the fact that cruising still has a stereotype image which is hard to overcome.

It is therefore becoming increasingly important for those involved in selling and promoting cruise holidays to have a greater understanding of the options available. This book will be an invaluable source of information for those wishing to improve their knowledge.

Operators will gain greater understanding of their position within the cruise market and this should help strengthen their relationship with the travel trade. In turn agents will be able to sell more confidently and consumers will benefit by being able to buy with confidence.

I believe this book will be a benefit to all those who are involved in, or are interested in, the cruise industry.

David Dingle
Commercial and Corporate
Development Director
P&O Cruises

Introduction

Late afternoon, over 1000 miles up the mighty Amazon River, so wide even this far up that the man needed binoculars to pick out details on the far bank. He watched in the humid heat as a native canoe propelled by an ancient outboard motor moved slowly upstream.

Pausing to wipe his brow, he turned and opened the door. The blast of the air conditioning engulfed his body and he moved slowly across the passageway.

There was just time for a shower before afternoon tea and a game of bingo, and he certainly didn't want to miss the show tonight; musical extravaganzas were one of his favourites.

Behind his back the river bank presented an unending view of trees and yet more trees; in front of him was a wide passageway, decorated in soothing pastel shades and hung with fine oil paintings of ships – the sound of a band could be heard in the distance . . .

Among the many advantages of cruise vacations is the ability to take your 'comfort zone' with you to exotic parts of the world. Playing bingo as the Amazonian rain forest glides by may not be everybody's idea of the perfect holiday but for an increasing number of late twentieth-century holiday-makers it has presented a viable alternative to the more conventional holiday package.

Cruising can be described as a multi-centre holiday where you take your hotel with you from centre to centre and for nearly 7.8 million people in 1998 (Ward, 1999) this was a type of holiday for which they were prepared to pay not inconsiderable sums of money. As will be shown in Chapter 1, cruising is nearly always at the top, in terms of cost, of the particular holiday price sector being considered by the customer. There are 'cheap' cruises but they are cheap compared to other cruises not in comparison with other holidays in that particular sector.

This book sets out to explore the reasons for the massive growth in the cruise industry in the 1970s, 1980s, 1990s and into the twenty-first century.

Why should an industry sector that many believe (we will show, falsely) is restricted to the wealthy merit a text to itself?

According to the Maritime Evaluation Group in 1998 nearly 7.8 million people worldwide undertook a cruise, the 1996 figure being 7.2 million with that for 1992 being 5.4 million, an increase of 44 per cent over the seven-year period. By nationality the figures are even more interesting (see Table I.1).

The US market comprised approximately 64 per cent of the total market in 1996 although this was down from 79 per cent in 1992. The figures are affected by the fact that it is the US market that is growing slowest of all.

It is no surprise to those who have followed the market that, since 1992, Airtours and Thompson Holidays have entered the UK cruise market with the use of three vessels each, and Peninsular and Oriental (P&O) increased their UK capacity by 82 per cent between 1992 and 1997 with another new vessel, the 76 000 ton *Aurora*, due to commence operations in 2000. Direct Cruises, a subsidiary of the Scottish-based Direct Holidays bought the 33 000 gross registered tonnage (GRT – see later for explanation) *Eugenio Costa* intending to launch her as the Edinburgh Castle in 1998. Advertising started in the summer of 1997, and in December 1997 the company announced that demand for berths was so high that they had acquired a second (28 500 GRT) vessel as a running mate. Direct Holidays sold the cruise operation to Airtours in the summer of 1998.

Table I.1 Increase in cruise passengers 1992–6

Nationality	1992	1998	Annual increase
USA	4 250 000	5.050 000	3%
UK	225 000	650 000	27%
Germany	190 000	283 000	7%
Canada	150 000	250 000	10%
Japan	20 000	225 000	146%

Source: Maritime Evaluation Group (Ward, 1999)

Similarly, there has been an increase in the number of vessels dedicated to the Japanese and German markets, the former showing the most potential for growth followed by the UK market.

On the basis of two people per cabin or stateroom, a high season day in 1998 will have had over 160 000 berths available.

Clearly, 7.8 million cruisers (the title we have given to those undertaking a cruise – see later) will inject considerable sums into the industry and thus the market is very competitive. It is, however, as will be shown later, a market that is showing increasing signs of both vertical and horizontal differentiation as described in Chapter 4.

As the market becomes more complex, those involved with it need to have a deeper understanding of the factors that influence the cruisers' buying patterns – this book is designed to examine such factors.

The reasons behind the degree of investment to meet an expanding customer base is worthy of study, hence this volume will examine the success factors that have allowed the sector to grow so spectacularly and those factors that will lead to continued success. As such this text will be of use to those studying travel and tourism, those working for tour/travel agents and those in the cruise industry who require a deeper understanding of their chosen field of work.

This is not a text that seeks to evaluate one cruise vessel against another, that task is performed well by Berlitz and Fodor, but one that seeks to look at the 'why' of cruising and why the sector has enjoyed spectacular success in the late 1980s and 1990s. As such the text will look at the history of cruising, the motivations of cruisers, the impact of cruising, the marketing concepts that have been applied by the sector and market differentiation within the cruise industry.

Chapter 1 looks at the cruise industry within the overall context of tourism and the growth of the tourist industry. Chapter 2 provides a history of the cruise industry from its early beginnings with the introduction of passenger steamships through to the mega-ships of the last years of the twentieth century. Chapters 3 and 4 consider the marketing aspects of the cruise industry. Chapter 5 is concerned with the areas cruised and the impact that the cruise industry has on local economies and infrastructures, and on people – both indigenous and cruisers alike. Chapter 6 centres on the design of cruise liners and the matching of design to function. Chapter 7 profiles the anatomy of a cruise, whilst Chapter 8 looks at the more esoteric types of cruising. The book concludes with Chapter 9, which considers the future of the cruise industry.

At the end of each chapter is a short case study:

Chapter 1 case study: A travel career
Chapter 2 case study: Norwegian Cruise Lines
Chapter 3 case study: Bolsover Cruise Club
Chapter 4 case study: Silversea Cruises
Chapter 5 case study: The Atlantic Islands
Chapter 6 case study: *Oriana*
Chapter 7 case study: *Royal Princess*
Chapter 8 case study: Hebridean Island Cruises
Chapter 9 case study: *Mistral*, Festival Cruises

Apart from Dickinson and Vladimir (1997) with their book *Selling the Sea* which concentrated almost exclusively on the US market, there has been little written about the industry. Those books which have considered cruising have tended to concentrate on the ships themselves, of especial interest to ship enthusiasts, or have sought to evaluate the products on offer, an outstanding example being the annual *Berlitz Guide to Cruising*. Edited by Douglas Ward, the guide is a mine of information and has provided an evaluation system similar to that used by the hotel industry. Ward's contribution is discussed in Chapter 8.

This is not a book about ships, only in so far as the vast majority of (but not as we shall see all) cruisers are waterborne. There is now a small but growing market in the rail and air 'cruise' sectors which is covered briefly at the end of Chapter 9.

That the ocean-going passenger-shipping industry, excluding car ferry operations, is booming is all the more remarkable as it has been pronounced 'dead' at least twice since 1945.

If we use as a barometer the number of vessels with over fifty passenger berths operating a scheduled passenger service between Europe and North America the figures in Table I.2 show a remarkable decline

Table I.2 No of vessels with berths for fifty or more passengers offering a scheduled Europe–North America service

Year	1939	1960	1969	1979
No of vessels	95*	58	32	1

Note: * includes *Queen Elizabeth* building

From 1979, only the *Queen Elizabeth 2* made the 'Grand Crossing'.

Chapter 2 examines the history of the renaissance: in 1999 there were 225 cruise liners evaluated by Ward (1999) and new and bigger liners were being introduced at a faster rate then ever before.

Nomenclature

There are a number of words and phrases used in this book that have their roots in the shipping rather than the tourist industry and an early explanation may make the text easier to follow.

Liner trade

Ocean-going ships whether passenger, passenger and cargo or cargo only that ran on a fixed route to a fixed schedule were traditionally called *liners*. Those cargo ships, which did not run to a fixed schedule or 'wandered' the seas as particular cargoes dictated, were known as *tramps*. In recent years, liner has come to mean a large passenger ship and by 1999 virtually all the large passenger ships in the world were *cruise liners*.

Cruise liner/ship

A cruise liner/ship is a passenger vessel operating for pleasure purposes only and not employed in the transportation industry. It is a matter of motivation, the passenger on a traditional liner wished to go from A to B. For the cruiser the voyage is just part of a holiday package.

Gender

It is normal to refer to ships in the feminine, and that convention is used throughout this book. As a matter of interest the Russian language refers to ships in the masculine.

Ownership

Throughout this book there will be references to cruise companies and the ships that they operate. The fact that a company has operated a ship, sometimes for a considerable period does not mean that they actually own the vessel outright. The business of ship ownership is complex and there are a number of ways in which a cruise company can acquire and operate ships.

Outright ownership

The capital costs of a new ship are very large indeed. The *Mistral* (47 900 GRT) of Festival cruises is estimated to have cost over $240 million (£150 million).

The major advantage to commissioning a ship from the builders (or taking over a recently started hull as in the case of *Mistral* – see case study at the end of Chapter 9) is that the company can build in their own designs and philosophy from inception. It is, however, a major investment requiring the acquiescence of bankers over a considerable period.

Second/third/fourth-hand etc. (or to use the parlance of the motor trade, 'pre-owned' vessels are cheaper but the company may be limited in making changes by the physical design of the ship. As will be shown in Chapter 2, many ships built for the liner trade were converted to cruise liners after the 1970s but were later restricted in competing with purpose-built cruise ships due to the nature of their internal layouts. A well-constructed ship has a long lifetime (twenty to forty years not being unusual) and thus ships may change hands a number of times in their careers.

Leaseback

The shipping industry in general, like other transportation sectors, makes considerable use of leaseback arrangements. The company commissions the ship and then sells it to a financial institution who then leases it back to the cruise company for an agreed period. For the financial institution this is a medium- to long-term investment opportunity with regular payments being guaranteed under the terms of the lease and ownership of the vessel at the end of the period if the lease is not renewed. For the cruise company there is an advantage of smooth cash flow at the beginning of a project for a new ship and they can still have the major say in the design philosophy if the vessel is a new build.

Mistral is actually owned by a consortium of French investors (Ward, 1999) and on long-term lease/charter to Festival (see the case study at the end of Chapter 9)

Chartering

While 'chartering' in the tourism industry has become almost synonymous with the charter flights used for package holidays, the concept is a very old one in terms of shipping operations.

Charter flights originated in the UK as a means of avoiding government restrictions on pricing. In the 1950s and 1960s the UK government regulated air fares; the only method of obtaining cheap tickets was for people to demonstrate that they belonged to a defined group and then they were allowed to charter an aircraft for their exclusive use. One of the earliest uses of this was for the families of those who had emigrated to Australia to form a group and then to charter an aircraft to visit their loved ones. Once such restrictions were removed, package holiday companies began to charter aircraft to fly their customers out to their chosen resorts. Many of the current 'charter' flights used by the package holiday companies involve only a paper transaction as the airline is, in many instances, part of the same group as the holiday company, e.g. Airtours who have their own airline and Thomson/ Britannia.

Cruise companies still charter aircraft in the conventional sense for a number of their cruises, especially where they can be assured that there will be a large number of cruisers travelling from just one or two destination airports. P&O have used charters for Victoria cruises in the Caribbean based on departures from London Gatwick and Manchester and Princess operate charters to and from a number of Caribbean cruises for UK cruisers.

In Chapter 3, the concept of barriers to entry will be considered and one of the biggest barriers to entry into the cruise industry is the cost of ships (see above).

One method of avoiding a high initial cost is to charter a vessel from its owners and then operate it under the cruise companies logo, or even to arrange for the owning company to operate it for you. One advantage of this is that the cruise company can operate a seasonal product; Thomson increased their capacity by chartering Premier Cruise's *Island Breeze* during their peak periods and Page and Moy chartered the *Ocean Majesty* specifically for the UK market during the spring and summer.

There are degrees of chartering. A bareboat charter will provide just a vessel, but it is also possible to acquire a ship and most of the crew, as a number of companies do, using company staff for the customer interface roles and contracting entertainers who will appeal to the specific market.

Ships may change owners but not operating companies, or remain under the same ownership but operate for different cruise companies. As such, in this book, actual details of ownership are not given. To the customer it is the operating company that is most important. They have booked a cruise on a certain ship, operated by a certain cruise company and it is their interaction with that company and either its staff or the staff contracted to it that is all important. National registries of ships and specialist volumes, e.g. Kludas (1992), give details of ownership etc.

Former names

Where a name is shown as ex ... this indicates that it was the previous name(s) of a vessel, e.g. *Norway* (ex *France*).

Size

In order to have a common denominator when discussing the size of ships we have chosen to use the GRT. Gross registered tonnage is not a measure of weight but of capacity and is the total enclosed volume of the ship in cubic feet divided by 100. The word 'tonnage' comes from the medieval 'tun' meaning a barrel. This is the normal method of describing the size of a merchant vessel and is measured in accordance with the International Convention on Tonnage Measurement that came into force on 18 July 1982.

A comparison of the *Olympic* of 1911 and her ill-fated sister ship, *Titanic* of 1912, show an example of how this is used. Although almost identical, *Titanic* had the forward part of A deck enclosed and, thus, the GRT figure of 45 224 for *Olympic* increased to 46 328 for *Titanic*.

Adding an extra deck with enclosed spaces can dramatically increase the GRT. When the *Norway* (ex *France*) had two decks added during her 1990 refit, her GRT increased from 66 343 to 76 049)

The size of warships, on the other hand is measured by the amount of water they displace (known as the displacement) on Archimedean principals.

As over two-thirds of the world's cruise ships operate in the US market and North America still operates using feet and inches, most measurements are given in feet with the metric equivalent in brackets if appropriate.

Currency

Two-thirds of the cruises sold in the world are sold in US dollars and this is the currency used on over two-thirds of the world's cruise ships. Even Italian companies such as Costa (part of the Carnival Group) use the US dollar on all but European-based cruises where the lira is used on board. In this book amounts of money are provided in pounds sterling and US dollars converted at £1 = $1.60.

About this book

The concept of this book is to give those interested in the cruise industry for either academic or employment reasons an overall picture of the industry at the end of the twentieth and the start of the twenty-first centuries. Details change all the time – companies start up, companies go into liquidation, ships change hands and the economies of the areas visited by the cruise industry change. In order to avoid becoming dated we have tried to give a general picture and to avoid confusing data, especially statistical information that may change rapidly. Thus we have not delved in detail into the economic statistics of any one company or any particular destination. Up-to-date information can be found on the World Wide Web (WWW). Just searching under cruise ships with any INTERNET search engine will bring up a large number of general and company-specific web pages. In a similar vein, information about tourist numbers and economic impact can be found by searching under the name of the location. This information will be the most up to date generally available and it seems that the WWW and the information it contains will be complementary to this book. Virtually all of the major cruise companies have web pages, many giving considerable detail about the ships, prices and itineraries.

In addition to referring to the sources quoted throughout the volume we also interviewed customers and staff of the cruise companies, and those whose lives are bound up with the industry. We visited a number of cruise destinations to see the effects of the industry on those destinations and also sampled the cruise product from Airtours, Cunard, Princess and P&O Cruises. The latter was carried out as full-fare paying passengers booked through an independent travel agent.

We were fortunate in that we were able to identify a sample of fifty-eight UK, thirty-five US and seven Canadian cruisers who were willing to assist us and who are referred to as 'the sample'. We are aware that this sample should have many more US members in it to be truly representative.

We spoke to people who would never consider a cruise, believing that it would be claustrophobic, not suitable for children or that they would be overcome with seasickness. We also met those who were addicted to cruising, taking one, two or even three cruises per annum (the record for our sample was nine cruises in one year). We also encountered incredible company and even ship loyalty. There were those loyal to P&O/Princess, to Cunard, to Fred Olsen, to Holland America, to Norwegian Cruise Lines etc., and those loyal to *Oriana*, *Black Prince*, *Vistafjord* etc. We discovered that this loyalty was most marked with UK cruisers, North Americans being more likely to cruise with a variety of companies although it must be admitted that there is more choice in the North American market.

We also discovered that UK cruisers were more at home in a maritime environment than their North American counterparts, perhaps a factor of history and culture. UK cruisers were more likely to refer to a ship as 'she' and to decks and cabins whilst the North Americans spoke of floors and rooms. Indeed UK (and other European) brochures are more likely to refer to the accommodation as cabins whereas North American parlance speaks of staterooms. These and other differences will be explored within the text.

Any opinions we quote are either those of the individuals concerned or our own unless specifically ascribed to a company.

We are grateful for the information made available to us by P&O Cruises, Princess Cruises, Norwegian Cruise Line, Bolsover Cruise Club, Star Clippers, Festival Cruises, Silversea Cruises, Hebridean Island Cruises and Cruise Scotland. We are especially grateful to the late Captain Tompkins of the *Royal Princess* and Purser Alessandro Bologna who provided unconditional access to both officers and crew in order to see the behind the scenes operation of a modern cruise vessel.

We are also grateful to Margaret Robinson from Cheshire, Carol and Leonard Gosling from Bath and Mary and Ken Bogas of Vancouver, British Columbia, who have provided valuable insight into those for whom cruising is more than just a once in a lifetime activity.

There are four major constituencies with an interest in the cruise industry:

1 Those who work (or wish to work) for cruise companies.
2 Those studying travel and tourism as part of a college, university or in-house course.
3 Those wishing to undertake a cruise.
4 Those interested in ships.

This book is intended for the first two. The book does not set out to be a general text on tourism. It is assumed that readers will have an interest in tourism in general and be seeking to see how the cruise industry fits into the greater whole. There has been little written about the general cruise industry and it receives only scant mention in any of the generic texts on tourism. The only specific book that has been available is

Dickinson, R. and Vladimir, A. (1997). *Selling the Sea*.
New York: Wiley.

This is a useful text but deals exclusively with the US market. Dominant as the US market has been up to the twenty-first century, there are, as will be shown, growing cruise markets in the UK, the rest of Europe and Asia, and it is right that these receive consideration. *Selling the Sea* is an excellent complementary text and gives a good indication of how the US market operates and what life is like on board a cruise liner designed for that market.

P&O commissioned a text for the introduction of the *Oriana* which contains not only details of the ship but a history of the company and valuable information on the industry:

P&O (1995). *Oriana – From Dream to Reality.* London: P&O Cruises.

There is also a company video to accompany the above text.

In addition to the brochures provided by the cruise companies, there are two main guides to cruising for those wishing to undertake a cruise. Fordor guides to the best cruises (Fodor, 1999, published annually) profile the cruises available to the US market but cover the markets in the rest of the world in just a few pages. They do contain, however, excellent details of the places visited on US market cruise itineraries. The *Berlitz Guide to Cruising and Cruise Ships* edited by Douglas Ward (Ward, 1999, also an annual publication) covers the vast majority of cruise ships operating across the world and, in addition to useful background reading, provides an independent, comparative evaluation of each ship complete with a star rating (see Chapter 8). We have found the *Berlitz Guide* to be very useful as it gives a fairly detailed description of the facilities on board each vessel, and an annual purchase should be considered by all those working in the industry and those planning a cruise.

Ship 'buffs' are exceptionally well served by the book trade. There are any numbers of texts, from company-specific histories to descriptions of ships. Useful ancillary reading to this text (for those interested specifically in ships) are:

Kludas, A. (1992). *Great Passenger Ships of the World Today.* Sparkford: Patrick Stephens.
Miller, W. H. Jnr (1992). *Modern Cruise Ships, 1965–1990.* Toronto: General Publishing.
Miller, W. H. Jnr (1995). Pictorial Encyclopaedia of Ocean Liners, 1860–1994. Toronto: General Publishing.

This book does not seek to describe ships nor does it endeavour to evaluate the product offered by the large number of cruise companies in the marketplace;

that is a task better carried out by others. It does seek to put the cruise industry into both a tourism and marketing context in order that the product knowledge of those involved in the industry will be enhanced.

> ... with a loud blast of her whistle the great white liner moved slowly to starboard and inched her way towards her berth below the Galata Bridge. Out of the early morning mists the minarets of Istanbul pricked the dawn sky. The bustle of dis-embarkation was already beginning and for the complement of cruisers another adventure had ended leaving memories and a desire to plan the next cruise just as soon as possible.

1

Cruising in context

This chapter includes:

- a brief history of tourism
- the railway revolution
- air travel
- package holidays
- holiday camps
- the leisure society
- tourism
- motivation
- typologies of tourists
- the tourist gaze
- the tourist career ladder
- reasons for cruising
- reasons for not cruising
- case study: one person's tourist career ladder

The cruise sector is a small but growing sector of the general tourist industry. Tourism, as an industry has been growing steadily since the middle of the nineteenth century although the need for some form of break from daily labours is as old as humanity itself.

A brief history of tourism

Tourism grew out of religious piety. One means of showing faith and piety has been the undertaking of a pilgrimage. In medieval times this really was a sacrifice involving long journeys with considerable danger. The world's major religions have always had great reverence for the pilgrim, making it almost mandatory in many cases, e.g. the Islamic hadj to Mecca.

It is not surprising, therefore, that commercial centres grew up alongside religious ones. If people were travelling to Winchester or York, Santiago de Compostela, Mecca or Amritsa for religious purposes, then they would need to eat and sleep, and where people gathered together markets and fairs would develop.

In medieval Britain only the richest could travel on long pilgrimages but the poor could use their holy day to visit the nearest religious centre. Associated with these religious festivities would be a fair. Indeed towns vied for the charter to hold a fair, as this was a guaranteed source of civic income.

It is interesting to speculate on the difference in origin between the British word 'holiday', from holy day and the North American, 'vacation' from 'to leave'. Today they are synonymous but their roots are very different. By the time North America entered its period of rapid growth after the Civil War (1861–5), the emphasis in Europe had shifted from holidays being a religious occasion to being a time for recuperation from work, and the concept of 'going away for a break' was gaining ground. Modern political correctness in the USA has replaced Merry Christmas with Happy Holiday, a supposedly non-religious greeting. There is some irony in that this is derived from holy day!

The industrial revolution of the early 1800s had a dramatic effect on the social fabric of both Europe and North America. Two aspects especially have impacted upon the development of tourism: the growth of large organizations leading to considerable urban development and the building of an efficient transport infrastructure.

The rich have always been able to take a break, indeed in the UK many wealthy families would own at least two homes, one in the city (normally London or Edinburgh) and one in the country. From the sixteenth century onwards many of the wealthier in European society would undertake the 'Grand Tour' of the classical sights of European civilization (tours which exist as coach or cruise holidays today). Such tours began as scholastic ventures but later became more 'romantic' in nature with the tourist undertaking an emotional engagement with unfamiliar landscapes and cultures. It had long been recognized, certainly after both the Black Death (*circa* fourteenth century) and the Great Plague of London (1665) that country air was healthier than that of the city. As the industrial revolution increased, so did the size of cities. Manchester (UK) had a population of 50 000 in 1775, and the combined population of Manchester and Salford (the city on the other side of the River Irwell) had increased eightfold by 1830 when the Liverpool and Manchester Railway commenced commercial operations, and had doubled again by 1850 (Hall, 1995).

The railway revolution

The railway revolution which commenced with the passenger operations using steam traction by the aforementioned Liverpool and Manchester Railway in the UK and the Charleston and Hamburg railroad in the USA in December 1830 (Holbrook, 1947). The Baltimore and Ohio railroad was built earlier but did not commence steam operations until later. Railways allowed much bigger organizations to be developed as the size of previous organizations had been limited by the distance people could walk to work. From the 1830s onwards not only did housing grow up around factories, but also as ribbon development alongside first the railway lines and then the tramways (streetcars in the US). By 1914 not only had cities like London, Manchester (UK) and New York developed efficient suburban steam railways, but the railways themselves were beginning to be electrified (Hall, 1995) and it was actually possible, albeit with changes, to travel from Stockport (to the south of Manchester) to Liverpool by tramcar (Yearsley, 1962).

As early as 1841, Thomas Cook, a printer from Leicester, had organized the first 'package holiday', a day excursion using the recently built local railway (Laws, 1997). Cook's name lives on not only in the Thomas Cook company but also in the saying 'taking a Cook's tour'. Such tours provided a safe way to travel, especially for females, given the views of society at the time. Both coach holidays and cruising still provide a safe physical and social environment for the modern-day traveller of increasing years.

Close-packed housing and pollution led to a near breakdown in public health in urban areas in both Europe and North America during the latter part of the nineteenth century and the concept that bracing sea or mountain air could act as a cure began to be popular. The upper and middle classes had long valued the benefits of sea and mountain air, although the journey to such areas could be long and tiresome as roads were only fit for slow-moving carriages. These classes were the first to use the railways for holidays in the true sense, to get away from the city. Weekends and the grouse shooting season saw massive (by the standards of the times) excursion trains leaving Euston and King's Cross for Scotland or Waterloo and Victoria for the South Coast.

The owners of the mills and factories could be benevolent and, in any case, soon came to realize that there was a limit to the length of day and indeed the number of consecutive days and weeks an employee could work. In the UK various Acts of Parliament were passed protecting the workforce, and the idea of time off for rest other than Sunday began to become a right, e.g. the Holiday with Pay Act (1938). This right has been further protected in the European Union Working Time Directive (1998). There was also a need to maintain plant and machinery, and a concept developed in the northern mill towns of England of a complete cessation of much of the commercial activity for a week so that such maintenance and improvements could be carried out. Using an old term for a public holiday, these 'Wakes' weeks where a whole town would effectively shut down except for essential services, became common and the population began to travel to the seaside. Each town had a different 'Wakes week' and resorts such as Blackpool in Lancashire developed as working-class holiday destinations. The railways were able to service the travel requirements and whilst the wealthy might go to Scotland, the mill and factory workers from the early 1900s onwards began to take a week's holiday by the sea, especially where this was a mere hour or so's train journey away.

Blackpool, together with other northern English and southern Scottish resorts developed quickly. Even if a full week away was unaffordable, the railway companies ran day excursions to the resorts, a practice that continued until well after the Second World War. At the start of Hall's book on Manchester's railways (1995) is a splendid photograph taken in 1960 of an eleven-coach Goole to Blackpool excursion passing the Dunlop Cotton Mills in Castleton (Lancashire). Fairlie (1989) has written of standing near Dalgety in central Scotland in the 1950s on the opening Saturdays of the Glasgow or Edinburgh trade holidays and watching a progression of excursion trains from Glasgow and Edinburgh to the Fife coastal resorts, trains which often comprised the oldest carriages and veteran locomotives, he writes: 'often with children at the carriage windows, their faces full of anticipation. They (the trains) would swing over central junction and go barking away up the hill, small wheels spinning purposefully. Then the process would repeat itself a few minutes later'.

Huge cities could not shut down completely and in these, different trades had different holiday periods.

Towns like Blackpool, just as in the current cruise industry (Chapter 4), developed a whole range of types of accommodation ranging from extremely large hotels to the boarding houses set in the backstreets. The stories of the typical boarding house landlady are legion but as a type of accommodation it developed into the guesthouse and B&B (bed and breakfast) of today and gave many of today's cruisers their first taste of a holiday.

Lavery and Van Doren (1990) have provided a detailed background to railway generated seaside holidays, and their schematic of a typical seaside resort in the Victorian era is still recognizable in many of today's UK holiday resorts.

Developments post-Second World War were incremental rather than revolutionary during the 1950s and early 1960s. Car ferries were in their infancy, the first major UK car ferry operation being that of Captain Townsend with the *Halladale* (converted from HMS *Halladale*, a River Class frigate of the Second World War) and flying was for the few.

The growth in air travel

When, between 1933 and 1935, the Douglas Aircraft Corporation introduced the DC 1, 2 and 3 – the latter to become the Dakota in the UK and one of the most successful commercial aircraft ever – the world of air travel began to open up. But it was not until the introduction of the Sud-Est Caravelle in 1959, the Boeing 727 in 1963 and the BAC 1-11 in 1965 that there were inexpensive to operate, short- to medium-haul jet aircraft able to fly holiday-makers to more distant destinations on a charter basis (see Introduction). Previous jets, the Comet, the Boeing 707 and the DC 8 were essentially long-haul aircraft. Laws (1997) has profiled the introduction of charter operations linked to package holidays and, from the 1960s onwards, increasing prosperity in the UK and other European countries coupled with the opportunities offered by the introduction of jet airliners led to a huge growth in affordable foreign package holidays.

Growth in package holidays

Vladimir Raitz, founder of Horizon Holidays, organized the first package holiday by air in 1950 and by 1970, 2.7 million inclusive holidays were undertaken outside the UK (Laws, 1997).

One of the results of this expansion was the development of a series of large resorts especially in Spain, resorts that were often isolated from the original

5

village communities where a homogenized experience could be obtained by the holiday-maker (Krippendorf, 1987) – in effect Blackpool with sun and sangria!

For the first time holiday-makers from the UK came to share their experience with those from other European countries and the residents of the resorts (plus an increasing number of expatriot entrepreneurs) began to modify their commercial behaviour to cater for the huge numbers of tourists (Pi-Sunyer, 1989). British pubs and German *bier kellars* began to open, each catering for their national groups. From the 1980s onwards concerns began to be expressed that many of the resorts were being ruined by a combination of cheap holidays attracting a younger and younger clientele and the effects of cheap alcohol leading to unruly behaviour.

According to the UK Civil Aviation Authority (CAA), the three market leaders in the UK package holiday business – Thomson, Airtours and First Choice – took over 5.5 million holiday-makers on package holidays in the summer of 1994 (CAA, 1994). Shortly thereafter all three companies – first Airtours, then Thomson and latterly (1999) First Choice – entered the cruise market (see Chapter 2).

The very nature of an inclusive or package holiday (and cruises fall into this category) requires interdependence between partners. Travel agents, aircraft operators, hotels, cruise ship operators, local excursion companies and food and beverage suppliers are linked much more closely than when a tourist travels independently. These interdependencies have been profiled by Laws (1997) and provide an interesting view of the balance between competition and collaboration.

In 1939 few Europeans or second generation plus North Americans had travelled outside their own national boundaries, and even fewer had been on an aircraft. By 1985 US citizens were spending in excess of $8 billion per annum on foreign travel and over 10 million Britons were undertaking an annual foreign package holiday (Lavery and Van Doren, 1990). The same authors quote figures showing that tourism and leisure accounted for over 1 million jobs in the UK and approaching 5 million in the USA.

The early developments in foreign package holidays were to regions within easy flying distance of North America and Northern Europe, giving Mexico, Spain, Portugal and Greece a head start in the development of mass tourism. Longer-haul tourism, especially to less developed countries, has been less quick to develop although the latter half of the 1990s saw Thailand become the most popular UK long-haul destination. In 1950, 66 per cent of the international tourist market share was held by Europe, with the Americas accounting for 30 per cent. Europe had maintained its position still accounting for 64 per cent in 1990 but the Americas had slipped to 20 per cent, whilst Africa held 3.3 per cent and with Asia and the Pacific Rim having grown from virtually zero in 1950 up to 12 per cent (Harrison, 1992).

Holiday camps

In 1936 the British entrepreneur, Billy (later Sir Billy) Butlin established his first holiday camp in the English east coast town of Skegness, the camp opening in 1937. This was the forerunner of the modern package holiday. Butlin and his competitor (Fred Pontin) established camps throughout the UK, maximum popularity being in the 1950s and 1960s. All-inclusive, and with nightly entertainment, the camps not only provided a family atmosphere but also launched a number of variety entertainment careers. Many of the later stars of the UK light entertainment and music scenes commenced their careers as Butlin's Redcoats or Pontin's Bluecoats.

In 1971 Thomson introduced weekend short break trips to Majorca for £13 ($21) and by 1974 the UK holiday companies of Thomson, Intrasun and Horizon had their own charter airlines. In 1970, 2.7 million UK holiday-makers took a holiday involving a charter airline, by 1980 the figure had grown to 6.25 million. The restrictions on UK citizens taking sterling currency abroad (see Chapter 2) were lifted in 1969 and the holiday camps began a slow decline. Both Butlin and Pontin experimented with camps in the main foreign resorts but without much success. The holiday camp appears to have been an institution that was successful for a time for UK-based holiday-makers on a UK holiday but did not appeal when placed in a foreign setting.

Whilst the UK holiday camp industry may have declined (although it is still catering to a specific market), there are echoes of it, albeit much more up-market in the all-inclusive resorts operated by some hotel groups and as pioneered by Club Mediterranean.

The modern European cruise market can trace its ancestry back to both the liner trade and the original holiday camps. What has never been seen, however, is the development of self-catering facilities on cruise ships, although such facilities were a part of the holiday camp ethos which also included restaurants and still remain popular in many European holiday resorts. The entertainment on many budget cruises has a certain similarity to that provided by holiday camps, Ward (1999) referring to entertainment on

7

some ships as being of 'the end of the pier variety' – an allusion to the type of entertainment provided in many UK holiday resorts and holiday camps.

The introduction by the Travel Savings Association of the cruise liner *Reina del Mar* (20 234 GRT) in 1964, later operated by Union Castle, was an attempt to take the holiday camp ethos to sea. The *Reina del Mar* introduced many to cruising but, as will be discussed in the next chapter, the facilities and the entertainment were rudimentary and amateur by today's standards.

By 1980, the package holiday trade was well established and moving from short-haul destinations to medium- and even long-haul packages. Prices were coming down quickly compared to average earnings and a foreign holiday was no longer a once in a lifetime event but an annual experience.

The study of how leisure and recreation form an integral part of human behaviour is, however, relatively new. The concept of leisure as both an academic and professional discipline only really emerged in the 1960s. In the UK the Institute of Leisure and Amenity Management and the Leisure Studies Association were formed as late as the 1970s (Haywood et al., 1989).

The leisure society

Genesis (11:1–2) and Exodus (20:9–11) both stress the importance of resting on the 'seventh' day, and this commandment has a firm root in physiology. Abraham Maslow's (1970) hierarchy of motivation stresses that the need for sleep and rest is one of the most basic of biological needs. Maslow proposed that needs, which are basic necessities, as opposed to wants which are the way we wish needs to be delivered, are hierarchical in nature.

The most basic needs are *physiological* – food, drink, sleep, rest etc. Only when these are satisfied do we and other animals, in general, move on to the next step in the hierarchy – *safety*. This explains why shipwrecked sailors will drink seawater despite the fact that they know this will do them considerable harm, the need to drink is more basic than safety. After safety comes *belonging*, followed by *esteem* with what Maslow termed self-actualization, i.e., the need to fulfil potential is the highest need. The model is simple and sometimes in fulfilling potential, e.g. the artist or poet starving in a garret, basic needs may be suppressed but it does help explain a great deal of animal behaviour.

It is generally agreed amongst economists that disposable incomes are increasing and this allows the individual to spend more money on leisure activities. There has also been a parallel increase in what we describe as 'disposable time', time that the individual can do with as he or she wishes. Such time can be used for social obligations, overtime (to increase pay) or for leisure. Paradoxically in a situation where jobs are in short supply, many will choose to (or feel under pressure to) offer their disposable time to their employers in order to increase stability of tenure, thereby leading to a time famine for a large number of people (Shaw, 1990). It is interesting that the European Union Working Time Directive as applied by the UK in 1999 sets maximum hours of work but allows the employee to work longer if they so wish. Many do not, perhaps, wish to work longer but feel obliged to do so in order to protect their employment.

Individuals need to balance often competing demands of work and leisure. Zuzanek and Mannell (1983) postulated four hypotheses on the relationships between work and leisure.

The trade-off hypothesis

Individuals choose between using time for work or leisure dependent on their particular circumstances at the time. Working longer hours may produce more income but there will be less 'disposable time' (see later) in which to spend the money. Working less hours increases disposable time but provides less financial resource.

Ryan (1991) makes the point that as income increases, the demand for tourism (being income elastic) increases at a greater rate, thus a small increase in income may lead to a disproportionate demand for either more holidays or more expensive holidays, or indeed both. This could well account for the boom in cruise holidays from the 1970s onwards.

Economists use the term 'opportunity costs' for the alternatives that could have been achieved with the available financial resource but cannot now be achieved as the resource has been spent. Time is also a finite resource and thus has opportunity costs. Based on Toffler's (1970) forecast on working patterns becoming more flexible, Ryan (1991) argues that the opportunity costs for higher earning groups would become greater and greater, and that they would take less leisure time. This has happened and has led to an increase in time famine and work-related illnesses, especially those connected with stress.

The compensation hypothesis

McGregor (1960) put forward the idea that there were two competing views about how humans approached work. Theory X, he suggested, stated that:

9

1 The average human dislikes work and will avoid it if at all possible.
2 Employees need constant supervision and control.
3 The average human does not seek responsibility.

On the other hand, his theory Y, which he believed was much closer to the human condition, stated that:

1 Work is a natural part of life.
2 Humans seek responsibility.
3 Rewards at work are more motivating than punishments.
4 Not all rewards are financial.

The compensation hypothesis appears rooted in theory X in that it states that leisure is the compensation for the drudgery of work and therefore leisure activities, especially holidays, provide a means of escape. Such a view may have been correct at one time but seems overly simplistic for the twenty-first century.

The spill-over hypothesis

Routines shaped by work patterns and relationships spill over into leisure time, thus determining the nature of the leisure activity. The hypothesis suggests that those with passive work styles will indulge in passive leisure activities and vice versa. The traditional view of cruising was closely linked to the employment patterns of those who took a cruise; in effect becoming a sea-going version of their work and domestic styles. Modern cruisers come from all walks of life, the industry no longer being as exclusive.

The neutralist hypothesis

According to this hypothesis there is no definable connection between work and leisure. As mentioned above, the modern cruise industry displays many aspects of this hypothesis which denies the causal relationship between work and leisure, with work being the underlying determinant. This is in contrast to the other three hypotheses.

As with all hypotheses and analytical tools there is not a mutual exclusivity and behaviour is likely to exhibit factors from each.

Parker (1983) has suggested a similar approach to Zuzanek and Mannell (1983), talking about possible relationships between work and leisure:

- extension
- opposition
- neutrality.

That is, leisure might be an extension of work, involving one's work colleagues, or it might be completely different on a conscious or subconscious basis or, indeed, there might be no link at all.

Leisure means different things to different people in different cultures and, as will be shown later, at different times in history. Haywood et al. (1989) have described four different conceptions of leisure within Western society:

1 Leisure as residual time (the time left over after work and domestic obligations are fulfilled).
2 Leisure as activities (the non-economic use of time).
3 Leisure as functional (performing a useful physiological or psychological function).
4 Leisure as freedom (an end in itself, the capacity to be oneself).

Haywood et al. (1989) further divide leisure into 'active production' or 'passive consumption' – ideas which are self-explanatory and are of great importance to the cruise industry which, by its very nature, is able to meet the needs of the cruiser for both activity and passivity by providing a safe haven for such behaviour.

For all those who pay and participate in a cruise, the cruise and the planning for it constitute part of their leisure activity and, as such, compete in terms of time and money with other leisure activities.

Leisure is big business. Not only sporting activities but hobbies, be they gardening, DIY or model railways, support large commercial sectors, one of the largest being the tourism industry.

Tourism

At the Ottawa Conference (1991), the World Tourism Organization defined tourism as 'The activities of persons travelling to and staying in places outside their usual environment for not more than one consecutive year for leisure, business and other purposes'.

The British Tourist Authority (as quoted in Ryan, 1991) defined a tourist trip as 'A stay of one or more nights away from home for holidays, visits to friends or relatives, business conferences or any other purpose, except such things as boarding education or semi-permanent employment'.

It is clear from the above that tourism, by definition, involves moving away from home and sleeping somewhere else for at least one night. For the purposes of this book, day trips are excluded.

The relationship between leisure and tourism

'Tourism represents a significant, often prolonged leisure activity' (Haywood et al., 1989). Ryan (1991) has considered the relationships between tourism and work (tourism/work ratio) and between tourism and other forms of leisure (tourism/leisure ratio). By 'ratio' Ryan is referring to the percentage change in hours spent in tourism as opposed to work or in tourism as opposed to other, competing forms of leisure. Unless an increase in the tourism/work ratio is accompanied by a corresponding increase in disposable income then the individual will, effectively, have less money to take a holiday and may well choose a less expensive leisure pursuit. As cruising requires both considerable financial and time resources *vis-à-vis* other forms of tourism/leisure, as a sector it is more vulnerable to any decrease in disposable income or time. In part as an antidote to time famine, cruises have shifted from being two to three weeks long to seven days. However, a fourteen-day cruise does not cost as much as two seven-day cruises, an example of the trade-off between disposable income and disposable time.

Motivation

Push–pull factors

Burns and Holden (1995) put forward the concept of factors which 'push' the individual into a form of escape linked to those which 'pull' the individual to a particular place or type of vacation. Each holiday is in effect a combination of push and pull. The initial motivation is the push and the actual choice the pull.

Holy days and vacations

Employers have realized that they cannot expect people to work twenty-four hours, seven days a week, and nearly all religions have a version of the 'seventh' day. The derivation of the word holiday is 'holy day', those days including the Sabbath, which were set aside for religious worship.

Belonging, as defined by Maslow (see earlier), is a middle-order need that increasingly requires those with similar interests or beliefs to travel in order to come together. Whilst this book is not the place to discuss whether the human species has a need for a deity, it is true that the vast majority of the world's religions are social in nature, they involve groups of people coming together to worship. It is hardly surprising, therefore, that certain hotels and, indeed, particular cruise ships cater for particular national groups – belonging being such a basic need. In effect the 'escape' is for many tourists an escape from geography and not from their normal society. Tourists wish to escape from normality but as normality often equates to security, holiday destinations need to perform a delicate balancing act in providing just enough difference but enough reminders of normality. Hence the ambiguity of a bacon and egg breakfast in a Greek taverna. By the enclosed nature of the product, the cruise industry has a considerable advantage in this respect.

Typologies of tourists

In Chapter 4, a typology of cruisers will be introduced. Various authorities have considered models for describing tourists. Cohen (1972) provided four categories for describing tourists:

- the organized mass tourist
- the individual mass tourist
- the explorer
- the drifter.

Cohen's mass tourist likes to travel in a fairly large group of similarly minded companions and is happy to trade off safety for individuality. Somebody else makes all the arrangements and the tourist plays a fairly passive role. Such tourism maintains the maximum possible psychological and social distance between the tourist and the host community.

The individual mass tourists go to the same places as the organized mass tourist but gain some personal satisfaction in making some of their own arrangements. It is likely that they will only wish to make their own peripheral arrangements, car hire, excursions etc. and will be passive when it comes to transportation to the resort, relying on the mainstream package operators.

Both types exhibit features of the spill-over hypothesis covered earlier in this chapter.

A key factor in all mass tourism is the apparent need for tourists to maintain an environmental and cultural bubble around themselves. In effect they seek an environment similar to that at home for their main base, whether a hotel or cruise ship, and are thus cocooned from too great an interaction with the host environment (Boorstin, 1964). Holiday hotels and cruise ships that maintain an image of home are an important factor for this huge, segment of the tourism market. In effect these are people who have little wish to leave their comfort zone except for relatively short periods of time – and even then only in a controlled and regulated manner.

Explorers and drifters arrange their own travel. Explorers want to visit less developed destinations but still wish to retain their comfort zone. Chapter 8 on niche cruising is almost entirely devoted to this type of cruiser. Drifters do not see themselves as tourists and wish to identify with the host community. Cruising is probably their least preferred holiday unless it is as a deckhand on a tramp steamer!

Plog (1987), researching in the 1970s divided tourists into:

- Allocentrics, who equate to drifters (above).
- Psychocentrics, who are concerned primarily with safety and fit into the mass tourist categories covered above and who form the vast majority of cruisers.
- Midcentrics, who are likely to want to retain some home comforts and thus equate to the explorers above.

Based on these ideas, in Chapter 5 we shall be introducing a set of categories specific to cruising but rooted in the more generic tourism typologies.

Ryan (1991) has looked at the importance of the psychological determinants in the tourism industry, quoting from Crompton (1979) and Mathieson and Wall (1982:

- Escape
- Relaxation
- Play
- Strengthening family bonds
- Prestige
- Social interaction
- Sexual opportunity
- Education
- Self-fulfilment
- Wish fulfilment
- Shopping.

The tourist gaze

Urry (1990) developed the concept of the tourist gaze to explain the effect upon the tourist of that which he or she goes to see. Every tourist approaches a new destination or experience with a set of preconceptions. Much of the pleasure of a holiday is in the anticipation; indeed the anticipation may be more pleasurable than the reality. Urry believes that tourists perceive that they go away to experience something new and that they do not want to 'gaze' upon the familiar unless it is in a different context. If tourism is about escape, it is difficult to rationalize 1700 UK tourists embarking upon the *Oriana* which is in itself quintessentially British. However, set that British quintessentiality on the Atlantic Ocean and one has the familiar in an unfamiliar guise and thus the need of the tourist to gaze is satisfied. There has been familiarity coupled with an escape from the humdrum. Perhaps the *Oriana* is life, not as we know it, but as it might be if the day-to-day routines were removed. The need for a sufficient comfort zone and enough of the unfamiliar to satisfy the gaze gives a major challenge to those promoting tourism products. There is a need to provide new horizons within the safe familiarity of home.

Urry (1990) considers that the capturing of memories is an important part of tourist psychology. Photographs and souvenirs are tangible reminders of brief moments in time. They cannot in themselves convey the full ambience of a place but looking at them can actually evoke memories that are not only visual but can subconsciously re-create the sights, smells, sounds and emotions associated with that particular spot at that moment in time. In turn, this reinforces the motivation to either return or to undertake a similar vacation.

Is the deck of a cruise liner a romantic place? The rational answer should be that it is just a collection of wooden planks. However, our upbringing etc. has reinforced a romantic notion of ships and the sea, and thus this becomes self-perpetuating. It is romantic because people believe it is romantic and behave accordingly. While behaving in such a way people are viewed by others and thus the perceptions are reinforced and become, in effect, reality.

Tourist career ladder

Pearce (1988) introduced the concept of tourists following a career ladder. The ladder is similar to a work career ladder and is influenced by upbringing, education, peer influence, past experience and lifestyle. Burns and Holden

(1995) suggest a model whereby the relationship between individual motivation and the image of any destination or mode of holiday is influenced by a series of factors, including past experience, occupation, lifestyle, the individual and social environment, the available means of travel, disposable income and disposable time. These factors combine to generate a personal demand for tourism rooted in the needs of the individual. The case study at the end of this chapter shows such a ladder for one of our sample. As people become older and (hopefully) their disposable income increases, so the type of vacation they require changes; in effect they progress, if not up a ladder, along a sloping continuum. Research using our sample suggests that there are a number of stages to an individual's tourism career, stages that the majority of tourists actually go through:

■ family holidays arranged by parents etc.
■ budget holidays with peers, often in a group
■ budget holidays with partner
■ family holidays**
■ post-family holidays*
■ Single or mature group holidays.*

Note: * = traditional cruise market; ** = 1990s cruising growth area

Cruising has traditionally been seen as a vacation for the older tourist whose children have grown up. A major development in the 1990s has been the entry into the market by companies who have targeted families by providing facilities for children. Thomson and Airtours in the UK are good examples and the entry of Disney into the cruise market in 1998 shows that this is indeed an area with considerable growth potential.

Earlier the link between age and disposable income was stated. The 1980s and 1990s saw the emergence of a new market for the tourism industry – younger people with considerable income but no families. The term DINKYs was coined for these younger people who were often couples but not necessarily married – Double Income, No Kids Yet. Carnival Cruises (the Carnival Group is the largest cruise operation in the world) has provided a product that is deliberately targeted at this market with ships that are designed to appeal to a much younger customer base than the traditional image of cruising.

In March 1999 it was possible to obtain a seven-day cruise from the UK for £399 ($640) per person. This cruise would be based on an inside cabin shared by at least two people. In terms of the price charged by many cruise companies £399 is cheap, but compared with the price of an equivalent land-based holiday it is at the high end. Dickinson and Vladimir (1997) make the point that cruising always appears at the top end of any comparable holiday price range. To somebody undertaking a £2000 cruise, £400 is cheap. To those used to paying £200 for an all-inclusive holiday (and there are a number advertised at this price in March 1999), £400 is expensive. Cruising appears, for many of those who have undertaken it, to be a step up on their particular tourism career ladder.

Reasons for cruising

People take holidays for a variety of reasons, motivation having been considered earlier in this chapter. They may wish to relax, to explore, to socialize etc. Cruisers form part of the general holiday market but like the main market the constituents show considerable variation according to age, lifestyle, previous experience, disposable income, disposable time etc.

The sample of cruisers referred to in the introduction was asked to list their reasons for cruising. There were considerable differences between younger (under 50) and older (over 50) cruisers as shown in Table 1.1.

Climate was more important to the under 50s as were entertainment and, not surprisingly, children's facilities. The latter were very important to the under-35 age group, a potentially huge growth market for the industry. The

Table 1.1 Reasons for cruising (by age)

Reason	Under 50	Over 50
Culture	3	4
Entertainment	21	11
Children's facilities	17	0
No/few children	1	9
Safety	12	31
Pampering	7	12
Special Occasion	12	0.5
Romance	0	0.5
Climate	15	6
Food	6	7.5
Ease of travel	5	12
Recuperation	0	0.5
Social	1	6
	100	100

third place given for climate may seem surprising. Many of the newer cruising areas, however, e.g. Alaska, Iceland, Cape Horn and around Britain, are not renowned for their climate.

In general terms the main factors quoted by the sample for cruising as opposed to other forms of vacation fell into three main categories:

1 *Relaxation*. Cruising offers not just the ability to lie in the sun, but more the convenience of arriving at the ship, unpacking once and then having the 'hotel room' move with you from place to place. The fact that entertainments were close at hand and included was also a major factor.
2 *Safety*. Cruising was seen as a safe method of seeing the world. Older people also appreciated the ability to be entertained at night without having to take any risks. The self-contained aspect of cruising was important to them.
3 *Social*. Cruising was seen as more exclusive than other package vacations. This is both a strength and a weakness. Those who do cruise claim to appreciate the exclusivity in both the type of fellow cruisers and the social cachet of being a cruiser. Exclusivity was quoted as a major factor for not taking a cruise package by non-cruisers.

All of these reasons fit into the Ryan (1991) categories although his analysis does not really mention the safety aspect which the sample rated as fairly important. As a subsector of the tourism industry, it is to be expected that cruising will show some distinctive motivational factors.

Reasons for not cruising

It is as important to consider why 98 per cent of the population have never taken a cruise as to consider the reasons why 2 per cent (approximate figures) have.

Discussions with people who had not considered cruising or had rejected the concept revealed five main reasons, all of which were in line with the findings of Dickinson and Vladimir (1997):

1 *Expense*. Cruising was seen, rightly, as being at the expensive end of any holiday price range. There was not a general awareness of the range of prices on offer and when asked to estimate the cheapest cruise, the majority of those questioned (n = 75) overestimated the minimum cost of a UK cruise by nearly 100 per cent.
2 *Exclusivity*. Cruising was seen by many as being socially exclusive. Many thought that it was for wealthier people. The idea of taking a cruise appears

to be one use for large-scale lottery winnings. It was clear that the cruise companies still had some way to go to ensure that holiday-makers were made aware of the fact that cruising could (and does) cater for a wide variety of market segments.

3 *Family*. Cruising is seen by many as a holiday for couples and not suitable for children. The newer entrants to the market and many of the latest ships from traditional cruise companies have facilities for children. The fact that Disney has entered the cruise market provides evidence of a major market initiative to cater for the family market.

4 *Claustrophobia*. There was little appreciation of the size of modern cruise ships. Claustrophobia was mentioned frequently but when asked to conceptualize the space on board an in excess of 100 000 GRT ship the awareness was lacking. People believed that there would be no quiet spaces.

5 *Seasickness*. Often quoted, seasickness appeared to be a major factor in not taking a cruise. Modern, stabilized ships and new drugs can mitigate against the effects of this ancient malaise (Nelson was a frequent sufferer) but the fear of discomfort appeared to be very marked.

Cruising is part of the general tourism industry. The chapters of this book will consider cruising in depth but it is important to remember that it is part of a greater whole. As will be shown throughout the book, cruising depends on other sectors of the industry, especially air transport and resort hotels, to grow and develop.

Tourism is a major world industry and next to the purchase of a house and motor car forms one of the major items of Western recurrent expenditure. Whilst small as a percentage of holidays undertaken, the cruise industry has been growing throughout the last three decades of the twentieth century and has received massive capital investment. Cruisers form part of the overall tourism market but are a segment with their own clearly defined wants and needs – areas that this book will examine.

Case study

One person's travel career

In order to demonstrate the concept of a travel career ladder (Pearce, 1989), details are provided of the travel career ladder of one member of our sample. The subject, a UK citizen aged 50 in 1999, displays a typical progression from family boarding house holidays through to a current 'career' in cruising.

Within the cruise section of the career can be seen a movement both up market and to different areas of cruising:

1949–60: UK boarding house based holidays with parents
1962: School trip – The Nederlands
1963–5: UK hotel-based holidays with parents
1966: Standard cruise – Mediterranean, with parents
1967: Standard cruise – Mediterranean, with parents
1968: Standard cruise – Mediterranean, with parents
1969–72; UK hotel-based holidays
1972: Premium cruise – with wife and parents
1973–83: Motoring holidays in Europe
1984: Coach holiday – Eastern Europe
1985: Package holiday – Crete
1986: Package holiday – North Africa
1987: Coach holiday – Eastern Europe
1988: Land holiday – Western USA
1988: Package holiday – North Africa
1989: Coach holiday – Central Europe
1990: Package holiday – Minorca
1991: Package holiday – North Africa
1992: Premium cruise – Caribbean
1993: Premium cruise – Amazon and Caribbean
1994: Premium cruise – Black Sea
1995: Premium cruise – Panama Canal and Caribbean
1995: Land holiday – Canada
1996: Standard cruise – Eastern Mediterranean
1996: Premium cruise – Atlantic Islands
1997: Premium cruise – Mediterranean
1997: Land holiday – Canada
1998; Premium cruise – Caribbean
1999: Premium cruise – Mediterranean
1999: Premium cruise – Atlantic Islands
2000: Premium cruise – Far East

2

A history of cruising

This chapter includes:

- the development of the cruise industry from its origins in the liner trade until 1999
- early cruises
- developments in the North Atlantic liner trade
- US Prohibition and 'booze' cruises
- the use of cruise ships by the Nazi Party in Germany
- the use of redundant tonnage post-Second World War and British government currency restrictions
- the demise and rebirth of the UK cruise market
- the expansion of the US cruise market and the development of the Asian market
- case study: Norwegian Cruise Line

This is an important chapter, if one wishes to understand the current state and future direction of the cruise industry and to understand how it developed. History cannot be changed but it can reveal pointers to the future. A summary of the major developments in cruising will be found in Appendix 1.

As the history of the industry has become extremely complex due to a series of mergers in the late 1990s, this chapter has been 'frozen' at the end of 1998/beginning of 1999. Appendix 2 provides a list of the vessels owned by the major cruise companies (the 'Big Four') during 1998–9.

Whilst humanity has always used seas and rivers as trade routes, until the coming of steamships even the shortest coastal voyage was hazardous relying as it did on either brute strength using oars or the vagaries of the wind.

After numerous experiments in the UK, the USA and France, the first practical steam-driven vessel, the tug *Charlotte Dundas*, went into service on the Forth–Clyde Canal in Scotland in 1801. She was followed in 1807 by Foulton's *Cleremont* built in New York. The Royal Navy were loathe to give up their sail heritage and whilst the USA completed a steam warship, the *Demologos*, just too late for the 1812 war with Britain, it was not until 1822 that the Royal Navy acquired a steamer in the form of the paddle-driven *Comet*. Early steam ships used simple beam engines to drive paddles, the screw propeller not coming into vogue until 1844 with the launch of the USS *Princeton* (MacIntyre and Bathe, 1974). These early steamers were wooden vessels, only carrying enough fuel for short coastal voyages. In January 1818 the 424 GRT sailing ship *Savannah* of the Black Ball Line left New York with eight passengers and, despite it being the worst time of year for crossing the North Atlantic, reached Liverpool and completed the first scheduled passenger sailing across the Atlantic taking nearly twenty-eight days (663 hours) to make the crossing. The engines were used for only eighty hours (McAuley, 1997). The Black Ball Line was intended to run to a timetable!

Atlantic crossings by steam-powered ships in addition to voyages to South Africa and India became more frequent, and in 1839 the British Admiralty awarded the UK–North America mail contract to a Canadian, Samuel Cunard, and on 4 July (in honour of the USA) the *Britannia* sailed from Liverpool arriving at Halifax (Nova Scotia) on 17 July, and Boston (Massachusetts) on the 20 July. Ships such as the *Britannia* and Brunel's earlier *Great Western* (1838) had made the North Atlantic crossing much safer for passengers than the sailing packets, in addition to slashing the journey times.

When Brunel launched the *Great Britain* (3270 GRT) in 1843, the world's first iron hulled, propeller-driven passenger vessel, the pattern for future developments was set. Sail was dispensed with as beam engines gave way to reciprocating ones and then to turbines. By 1901, the UK White Star Line had placed the *Celtic* (20 904 GRT) in service; by 1907 Cunard's *Mauritania* and *Lusitania* were over 30 000 GRT (31 938), and in 1911 White Star introduced the 46 329 GRT *Olympic* to be followed in 1912 by the *Titanic*. At that time it was considered that ocean travel was completely safe but pride came before a fall, as the loss of the *Titanic* on 12 April whilst on her maiden voyage showed (Davie, 1987: Eddy, Potter and Page, 1976).

Cruising, as defined in the Introduction and as distinct from ocean voyages designed to transport an individual from one place to another (the liner or ferry trade), made a fairly early entry into the shipping industry after the advent of steam because the ability to run scheduled services that did not rely on the wind was greatly enhanced. Given that the first steam crossings of the Atlantic by the *Sirius* and the *Great Western* were made in 1838, it may come as a surprise to discover that the first ocean 'pleasure' cruise was as early as 1881 when the Oceanic Yachting Company bought P&O's *Ceylon* and refitted her as a full-time cruise ship for the European market. The first 'advertised' cruise had been a dummy advertisement for a cruise around the Orkney and Shetland Islands in 1835. A cruise that never took place, although in 1886 the North of Scotland and Orkney and Shetland Steamship Company commenced £10 ($16) cruises on their St *Rognvald*. Similar cruises are still offered today by their successors, P&O Scottish Ferries.

By the early 1900s, White Star Line, P&O in their own right and the Hamburg Amerika Line were offering regular cruises. Since the late 1890s, Orient Line had been offering regular Caribbean, Mediterranean and Scandinavian cruises on board three of its vessels. For British passengers the Norwegian Fjords and the Mediterranean were the major cruising areas, a not too dissimilar situation to today. In 1912, Cunard introduced the *Laconia* and the *Franconia* (traditional Cunard names) as their first dual-purpose cruise/ line vessels. At this stage cruising was still an ancillary affair to the main business of regular voyages between fixed points and was an expensive holiday only open to a privileged few. The 16 502 GRT *Victoria Luise* was converted as a purpose-built cruise ship from the liner *Deutschland* in 1911 by Hamburg Amerika Line who experimented with cruising right up until 1939. The *Victoria Luise* survived the First World War but never returned to cruising, being converted to an immigrant ship and subsequently broken up in 1925.

Following the end of the First World War, the shipping companies had a major shortage of tonnage for their core liner business and even vessels taken in reparations from Germany were insufficient to meet the increased demands of traffic, especially on the North Atlantic. Emigration from Europe to North America resumed after the war and the geopolitical changes to borders after the peace settlement of Versailles in 1919 caused major population displacements, especially in Eastern Europe, and the USA received many of the displaced refugees (Fisher, 1935). Between 1892 and 1924 over 12 million immigrants arrived in New York alone (McAuley, 1997). In addition most of the liners in service were unsuitable for pleasure voyages due to their design. Perceived wisdom for the time was that passengers did not wish to interact with their environment and thus views of the ocean were few and far between.

It was only in the 1930s that larger windows began to appear on ships (see Chapter 6). Orient Line resumed cruising in 1922 but it is to the USA that we must look for the major expansion of cruising, and that came about because of a bizarre political decision that is perhaps better known for the rise of gangsters such as Al Capone.

At midnight on 16 January 1920, the Eighteenth Amendment to the Constitution of the USA, prohibiting 'the manufacture, sale or transportation of intoxicating liquors' came into force. This measure had been under discussion for some time in an attempt to combat a belief that alcohol consumption was affecting the moral and economic well-being of the USA. In 1870 there were 100 000 saloons in the USA, one for every 400 citizens. Only wines prepared for personal use in homes were exempted. All of a sudden, America could not drink. Gangsters soon developed ways to process and supply alcohol and the Federal Bureau of Investigation was tasked to prevent the trade – an impossible job but for many law-abiding Americans illicit drinking was not the answer.

This was the time of the 'roaring twenties' and it soon became apparent to shipowners that there was a market gap they could meet. Whilst US-flagged vessels were unable to serve alcohol, once out of US territorial limits there were no restrictions on non-US flagged vessels. Indeed, Hamburg Amerika who had been operating the *Resolute* and the *Reliance* under the US flag soon transferred their registry to Panama and began the move to flags of convenience, which will be discussed later in this chapter.

'Booze' cruises alone would not have led to the first great growth of the cruise industry but coupled to the flamboyant style of the age, cruising became a more intense experience than the leisurely pre-war operations and one, for Americans at least, where you could enjoy a legal drink. Prohibition registered cruising on the consciousness of the holidaying public (still a small minority) as an acceptable, fun method of the annual getaway.

In the UK, cruising was still very much a minority experience, although it is reported that 175 000 British people cruised in 1931 and Moss Brothers (the gentleman's outfitters) had already produced an 'All at Sea' brochure (P&O, 1995). As an interesting aside, each cruise cost approximately £30 ($48) per head for a fortnight. With the fare and onboard spending added, the 1998 figure is nearer to £2500 ($4000)! (authors' own figures).

Prohibition lasted until 1933 and cruises out of US ports provided a good way for shipping companies to gain a few more years out of tonnage that might have been sent to the breakers yard. The new luxury liners with their better facilities, windows with sea views and art deco designs came into service in the 1930s.

Entry of the Germans

The 1930s were the heyday of the liner trade; ships such as the *Normandie*, the *Queen Mary*, the *Bremen* and the *Rex* became household names and brought a degree of luxury hitherto unknown to sea travel. For the first time, ships were airy and light with huge public rooms for all classes. As such they were also well equipped to undertake periodic pleasure cruises in addition to their liner trade duties. In 1938 the *Normandie*, 83 000 GRT of the French Line (and considered by many to be the most beautiful ship ever built), undertook a twenty-two day New York–Rio de Janeiro–New York cruise with the cheapest ticket being $395 and the dearest $8600; not a holiday for the ordinary person especially given the $48 (£30) for two weeks available to UK cruisers as quoted earlier.

The German government, under Adolf Hitler, used cruising as a political measure to reward their workforce. The KdF (*Kraft durch Freude*) 'Strength through Joy' cruise operation was directly controlled by the propaganda ministry of the Third Reich. The organization ran an all-German cruise operation that offered inexpensive holidays for workers and especially Nazi Party members. Whilst the organization commenced using recently constructed German tonnage from the recognized German shipping companies, by 1938/9 they had placed in service two ships both over 25 000 GRT, the *Wilhelm Gustloff* and the *Robert Ley* (both sunk with great loss of life towards the end of the Second World War). These two were the first specially commissioned cruise vessels of any nationality to enter service. As quoted in Maddocks (1983): 'These ships were, in fact, remarkable in many respects. They became the pacesetters for construction of special cruise ships even down to the present day. All 1465 passengers were allowed to have outside cabins.'

These cruises were also important in the history of the industry as, for the first time, cruising became available to the middle and working classes as

25

opposed to just the rich. Slower than regular liners and carrying no cargo they became the prototype for ships such as the *Royal Princess* that ushered in a later expansion of the industry.

Prior to the outbreak of the Second World War, a number of companies had experimented with offering cruises to complement their liner trade. The famous Cunard liner *Mauritania* (holder of the Blue Riband) spent her last five years (1930–5) primarily engaged on cruising. The UK Blue Star line rebuilt the 12 847 GRT *Andorra* as the *Andorra Star* for cruising in 1928, a function she fulfilled until the outbreak of the Second World War in 1939, the ship being sunk in 1940. In 1935, Panama Pacific Line purchased the 24 578 GRT *Belgenland* (ex *Belgic*) of the Belgian Red Star Line (part of IIM) completed in 1917 and rebuilt as a passenger ship in 1923. She was renamed *Columbia* and used solely for cruising but the venture lasted less than a year, the ship being sold for scrap in 1936.

The Second World War brought an end to pleasure cruising, but before September 1939 the basics of the cruise industry were in place:

- the use of surplus tonnage to generate extra income
- defined cruising areas, Bahamas and the Caribbean for the USA and Norway and the Western Mediterranean for Europe
- specialist ships for the cruise industry as noted above
- an expansion into a younger market segment.

Post-Second World War

By 1945 much of the pre-war passenger tonnage had been sunk, was worn out or was needed for the bringing home of troops and the repatriation of refugees. The nations of Europe and North America embarked on a massive programme of passenger-ship building unaware of the impact that air travel was likely to make on the industry.

That ships might now be built for the dual liner/cruise trade became apparent when Cunard launched the *Caronia*, (34 274 GRT) in 1948 and she was especially fitted out for cruising as well as the Southampton–New York service. Indeed Cunard claimed that her multi-toned green colouring was designed to offset the heat of the tropics.

It would take too long to detail the large number of vessels built between the launch of the *Caronia* in 1948 and the last of the traditional type lines, the *QE2* in 1968, but Table 2.1 shows the number of passenger vessels launched for the North Atlantic trade during those years (excluding vessels whose main

Table 2.1   Major passenger vessels in North Atlantic service post-Second World War

Country	Service	Vessels surviving Second World War	New vessels
UK & Canada	Europe–USA	7	3
	Europe–Canada	5	7
USA	Europe–USA	1	3
Italy	Europe–USA	7	7
Germany	Europe–USA	1	6*
France	Europe–USA	2	3
The Netherlands	Europe–USA	2	4
Greece	Europe–USA	1	6**
Sweden	Europe–USA	1	4
Norway	Europe–USA	1	3
Israel	Israel–USA	0	4

Notes: * Includes four ships bought second hand and the reacquisition of the *Bremen*, ex *Pasteur*, ex *Bremen*; ** five of the six were second hand.

trade was cargo with just a few passengers, but including vessels built during the Second World war but which did not enter passenger service until after the conflict).

As the world recovered from the ravages of global warfare, sea travel was booming again. Demobilized troops were returning home and a series of voyages taking GI brides to the USA were undertaken. In addition to the new tonnage on the North Atlantic, P&O, Orient Lines and Shaw Saville were rebuilding the routes to India and Australia, traffic having been given a boost by the £10 ($16) assisted passages scheme designed to encourage immigration to Australia from the UK. Union Castle/SafMarine were also building new ships for the South Africa service. There were a large number of nearly new ships on the seas, most of which had been designed with an eye to cruising if the liner trade suffered a decline, although such declines were presumed to be temporary – the war was over, people wanted to travel and there was apparently no alternative to the ocean liner. Propeller-driven aircraft were slow, noisy, uncomfortable and, to the eyes of many, unsafe.

Yet when Boeing introduced the 707 jet airliner into commercial service with Pan Am on 26 October 1958, the future looked poor for shipping companies. Whilst the British-built Comet introduced in 1952 was the world's first commercial jet aircraft, the 707 was the first successful model, carrying over 150 passengers compared with the Comet's initial forty-four (later stretched to ninety-four) in the Comet 4B. Cunard and the other shipping companies found that they were no longer in the shipping business; they were in the mass transportation over a long distance business, and competitors in the form of the new jet airliners could do the job much faster. A classic example of substitution, a concept we will consider when we look at marketing in Chapter 3. The shipping companies looked for new markets within the cruising market, but ships designed for the liner trade were not really suitable for the holiday market. Many of the companies collapsed and their vessels, consequently laid up. The Boeing 707 and its main competitor, the DC8, destroyed the liner trade and the advent of the larger Boeing 747 (the 'jumbo jet') in December 1969 dealt it the final death blow. However, as we shall see later, the advent of the large commercial jet aircraft was just what the cruise industry needed to move it into a mass market.

British currency restrictions

Just as a political decision, Prohibition, launched the US cruise industry, it was a political decision by the British government in the 1960s that brought the UK cruise sector to a wider market. No sooner had Briton's begun to abandon their traditional British seaside holiday in favour of the shores of the Mediterranean, in particular Spain, than for economic reasons, the government stepped in to curtail foreign holidays by restricting UK passport holders to taking only £50 ($80) in foreign currency or traveller's cheques out of the country. Credit cards were virtually unknown in those days and demand for foreign holidays consequently slumped.

However, British-registered ships used sterling as the currency on board and thus passengers needed to use their £50 foreign currency allowance only whilst ashore.

Companies such as P&O and Cunard were able to switch tonnage, rapidly outliving its usefulness due to the inroads of air travel, into the UK cruise market, as did Shaw Saville whose *Southern Cross* and *Northern Star* operated cruises out of Liverpool and Southampton. Originally built for the £10 assisted passage scheme from the UK to Australia, the *Southern Cross* and the *Northern Star* (21 000 GRT) built in the early 1950s were of a revolutionary design with their funnels situated well aft thus providing considerable deck space for soaking up the tropical sun. The design has stood the test of time and, indeed, the *Southern Cross* was still operating cruises in 1998 as the SS *Ocean Breeze* (after a number of name changes) for Dolphin Cruise Lines in the Caribbean. In the 1960s it was the Royal Mail Line's

Andes, 24 689 GRT (420, 'first class' passengers, displaced from the UK–South America service by jet aircraft), which became the first UK full-time cruise liner. Both the *Andes* and the ex Pacific Steam Navigation line *Reina del Mar*, 21 234 GRT (*Queen of the Seas*) also from the UK–South America run that introduced many of today's UK frequent cruisers to this form of holiday. Originally chartered by the Travel Savings Association set up by Max Wilson who also chartered the Empress of Britain (25 516 GRT), the *Reina del Mar* was then leased to Union Castle who added extra accommodation and offered relatively inexpensive Mediterranean cruises from Southampton during the 1960s, remaining in service until 1974. Many of the older regular UK cruisers interviewed for this book, took their first cruise on the *Reina del Mar* during the 1960s and early 1970s.

Air transport decimated North Atlantic passenger shipping in the first instance and this left a large number of relatively new vessels lying idle. Canadian Pacific, who had suffered large losses in the Second World War had commissioned three semi-sisters, *Empress of Britain* (1955), *Empress of England* (1956), *Empress of Canada* (1961) all of approximately 25 000 GRT for the Liverpool–Montreal service. Cunard had introduced the *Saxonia* (1954, renamed *Carmania* in 1963), *Invernia* (1955, renamed *Franconia* in 1963), *Carinthia* (1956) and *Sylvania* (1957) also of approximately 25 000 GRT and designed for the UK–Canada service. These vessels were two-class (first and second) ships and thus needed considerable adaptation once 'classless cruising' became the norm, but they were available to the cruise industry relatively quickly. The history of the *Empress of Britain* illustrates the complex history of this generation of vessels:

SS *Empress of Britain*, 25 516 GRT

1956: Launched at Fairfield Shipping and Engineering Glasgow for Canadian Pacific
1956: April, maiden voyage Liverpool–Montreal
1964: Chartered to Travel Savings Association
1964: November, sold to Greek Line as *Queen Anna Maria*
1964: March, placed on Greek Line Piraeu–New York service and cruising
1975: Sold to Carnival Cruise Lines and renamed *Carnivale*
1993: October, renamed *FiestaMarina* (*sic*) for Carnival's Latin American marketplace, the product being named FiestaMarina Cruises
1994: September, FiestaMarina Cruises ceased operation, ship sold to Royal Olympic Cruises
1994: Renamed *Olympic*

The *Empress of Canada* became the first ship of Carnival Cruises, the *Mardi Gras*, in 1972, where she distinguished herself by running aground off Miami on her maiden voyage. She became Direct Cruises' *Apollo* in 1998 and thus with the sale of that company to Airtours re-entered the Carnival family. The *Empress of England* became the *Ocean Monarch* of Shaw Saville in 1970, lasting only a couple of years until the company left the passenger market.

The Cunard vessels also became early vessels for fledgling cruise operations. The *Carmania* (ex *Saxonia*) became the *Leonid Sobinov* of the Soviet Union's State Shipping operation in 1973, to be joined by the *Franconia* (ex *Ivernia*) both operating until the break up of the Soviet Union in the mid-1990s. The *Carinthia* and the *Sylvania* were acquired by Sitmar Cruises in 1968 as the *Fairsea* (originally *Fairland*) and the *Fairwind* respectively. When P&O acquired Sitmar in 1988, they were transferred to the Princess operation to become the *Fair Princess* and the *Dawn Princess*. By 1998, two of the ex Cunarders were still operating, the *Albatross* of Phoenix Seereisen (ex *Sylvania/Fairwind/Dawn Princess*) operating for the Northern European, predominantly German market and the *Fair Princess* for the Australian market.

Not only the UK had surplus Atlantic passenger tonnage; so had the Scandinavian countries, France, The Netherlands and Italy. Many of the vessels were acquired by cruise companies, often after the original owners had tried to run a cruise operation. The reasons for the failure of traditional shipping companies to make a success of their cruise operations are complex but amongst the factors mitigating against them were:

■ use of more expensive indigenous nationals as crew members
■ reluctance to transfer to cheaper 'flags of convenience' for reasons to be discussed below
■ lack of investment to convert two- and three-class ships to one class
■ a lack of understanding that the cruise industry was different to the traditional liner trade in respect of facilities, customer expectations etc.

Flags of convenience

In the years up to and immediately following the Second World War it was the norm for passenger ships (and indeed most freighters) to operate with crews drawn from the country of ownership where the ship would also be registered. Many countries laid down strict criteria for crews of ships registered with them. Criteria were much less strict for ships registered under 'flags of convenience' especially as related to the nationality of crews. British seamen needed to be paid more than many from Third World countries and whilst the traditional companies clung to their national registrations, new companies such as Carnival registered their ships under 'flags of convenience', notably Panama and Liberia and, recently, the Bahamas. There was a perception in the 1960s that such ships were less safe than those registered and inspected by the UK, Germany, Italy, France, Scandinavia, The Netherlands etc. but, even if that were true then, it is not so today as far as the passenger side of shipping goes. Companies and insurers cannot afford anything less than the highest standards. The switch to 'flags of convenience' has meant that most of the world's cruise ships are registered in only a few countries, many not known for their maritime heritage as Table 2.2 shows.

The high position of Norway and The Netherlands indicates the role played by Scandinavian countries in the development of Caribbean cruising and of the importance of Holland America Line (HAL), now part of Carnival in the US marketplace. The current trend appears to be for new tonnage to be registered in either Liberia or the Bahamas unless there are compelling reasons not to do so. National considerations and customer perceptions may take precedence over purely financial ones and, as will be shown in Chapter 4, political considerations may be important. In January 1999, the Deputy Prime Minister

Table 2.2 Cruise ship registrations by country, number and approx. tonnage, 1997 (arranged in tonnage order)

Country	No. of ships	Approx. tonnage
Liberia	45	1 772 000
Bahamas	43	1 120 000
Panama	17	549 000
Norway	18	535 000
The Netherlands	8	381 000
Great Britain	10	352 000
Italy	5	131 000
Ukraine	8	122 000
Greece	10	106 000
Germany	4	104 000
Japan	5	100 000
Russia	12	77 000
USA	4	63 000
Cyprus	5	59 000

Source: Ward (1997).

of the UK, John Prescott asked Cunard (by then owned by Carnival) not to break with tradition and to register the proposed *Queen Mary* in the UK. The USA has never been a major shipowning nation, there having ever only been nine US-registered liners of over 20 000 GRT on the North Atlantic compared with thirty-eight flying the British Red Ensign. The USA was mainly serviced by European-registered vessels, albeit owned by US companies' such as the Morgan empire which had massive financial stakes in many of the operations. Thus US cruisers appear less reluctant to cruise on 'foreign vessels' whilst their UK counterparts have been slower to undertake cruises on non-British ships. When P&O transferred the *Star Princess* from the Princess operation to the P&O Cruises' UK fleet following the scrapping of the *Canberra*, they not only changed the name to *Arcadia* but the registration from Liberia to the UK. Direct Cruises, the cruise operation of Direct Holidays, who operated in the UK during 1998 prior to the sale of the cruise operation to Airtours, made great play in their brochure that their first vessel, the *Edinburgh Castle* was registered in the UK and flew the Red Ensign, stating 'you will be setting sail under the Red Ensign, under the care and guidance of a British Captain and his forty British officers' (Direct Cruises Summer 1998 brochure: 7). Their second vessel, the *Apollo* was registered in Greece but even then the company stressed the British nature of both ships: 'we are proud to say that the connections with Britain are part of the history of both ships. The *Edinburgh Castle* sails under the Red Ensign [Authors' note: the *Edinburgh Castle* was built in Italy as the *Eugenio Costa* in 1966] and the *Apollo* was actually built in Britain, at the Vickers Armstrong shipyard in Newcastle-upon-Tyne' (Direct Cruises 1998 preview brochure: 8).

The newer UK cruise operators, Airtours, Thomson etc., have not registered ships in the UK especially where, in the latter case the vessels are operated on their behalf by a third party.

The figures for Russia and the Ukraine (which would have been considered as one prior to the 1990s break up of the USSR) reflects a fairly successful attempt by the USSR to tap the European market from the late 1960s onwards. Offering budget cruises to holiday makers from the Western democracies gave the USSR a valuable source of hard currency and an opportunity to show a more positive side of communist philosophy. Using both the second-hand former Cunard tonnage mentioned earlier in this chapter and new vessels mainly from German yards, the operations continued until the break-up of the Soviet Bloc. From the late 1990s the Ukraine has been trying to regain a share of the market, especially given the increased popularity of the Black Sea as a cruise destination. However, customer expectations have changed, and both new tonnage and a new approach will be needed if this is to prove successful.

Much of the tonnage, whilst still owned by Russia and the Ukraine, is operated by Western concerns on their behalf in an attempt to meet Western customer expectations. The Russians also offer specialist cruises to the Polar regions using the 20 000 GRT nuclear-powered icebreaker *ib Yamal* (see Chapter 9).

By the mid-1960s there was the beginnings of a thriving European cruise industry, mainly centred on the UK. As a product, it was very unsophisticated compared with today's cruising. Entertainment was mainly dancing and 'crew shows' with fancy dress competitions and other passenger-derived amusements popular. Many of the ships either operated a two-class system or had difficult passenger flows due to their previous two- and three-class nature. Passenger numbers were climbing and new areas for cruising had been opened up especially in the Eastern Mediterranean and the Aegean where Greek companies, Epirotiki and Chandris Lines being a good examples, began to operate fly-cruises based on the Greek Islands.

Many of the ships were old. Chandris acquired the 16 435 GRT *Queen Frederica* in 1965 for the UK–Australia service but the ship was used almost exclusively on cruising in the Mediterranean carrying a large number of UK cruisers. The *Queen Frederica* had been built as early as 1926 as the *Malolo* for the Matson Navigation Company of San Francisco and placed on the US West Coast–Honolulu (Hawaii) route. Renamed *Matsonia* in 1937 she served as a troopship in the Second World War, being sold to Home Line for the Italy–New York service in 1948 and renamed *Atlantic*. She was transferred to a subsidiary, National Hellenic America Line in 1954 and renamed *Queen Frederica*, retaining the name when bought by Chandris and refitted to carry over 1000 cruisers. This veteran of fifty years was finally withdrawn at the end of 1973 and broken up in 1977, a remarkable record for a ship which like the *Reina del Mar* gave many UK cruisers their first taste of this type of vacation (*Sea Breezes*, 1977).

Such was the demand for ships that even small passenger ferries displaced by more modern car-carrying vessels were converted to cruise vessels. In addition to their larger ships, Chandris (the company rebranded as Celebrity in the 1990s and acquired by RCI in 1998) had a number of such vessels. The 4325 GRT *Fantasia* of 1964 had commenced operations in 1935 as the *Duke of York* for the London, Midland and Scottish Railway service from Heysham to Belfast. Rebuilt in 1950, Chandris fitted her out for 381 cruisers paying from £49 ($79) to £119 ($190) for two-week cruises in the Eastern Mediterranean and Aegean operating out of Venice. She was joined by two other former UK passenger ferries, *Fiesta* (ex *Mona's Isle*) and *Fiorita* (ex *Amsterdam*), finally being broken up in 1974 after thirty-nine years of service including war service as HMS *Duke of Wellington* (the name Duke of York being in use on a King George the Fifth class battleship). Epirotiki Lines also used former UK passenger ferries for their Mediterranean Cruise operations (Isherwood, 1977).

Chandris was a major player in the European market through its various subsidiaries with three large vessels, *Queen Frederica* (above), *Britanis*, 18 655 GRT (ex *Monterey*, ex *Matsonia*, ex *Lurline*) and the *Australis*, 26 485 GRT (ex *America*) originally acquired for the Europe–Australia service but later switched to cruising, plus a fleet of smaller, converted vessels as mentioned above. For the UK market, Chandris was at the lower end of the price range but the rebranding into Celebrity Cruises in 1989 brought the company into Premium operations (see Chapter 4)

The Spanish ferry company, Naviera Anzar SA of Bilbao operated a brief cruise operation from Liverpool to the Canary Islands and back using two 13 500 GRT car ferries between 1975 and 1977. Whilst the operation drew praise the availability of package holidays using flights to the Canaries prevented it from being commercially viable. However, as will be shown in Chapter 5, the Atlantic Islands have become a very popular cruise area for UK cruisers in the 1990s so that although Anzar's operation was hit by rising oil prices and a falling pound, it could have been successful but for the general economic climate.

The decline of United Kingdom operations

A seamen's strike in 1966 and the massive oil rises of the early 1970s brought this expansion to an end and the UK sector began to go into decline. Once currency restrictions for UK citizens were removed, the Mediterranean package holiday boom, assisted by the availability of cheap jet aircraft charters (see later), began and the UK cruise industry shrank dramatically. This can be seen by the fact that until the *Oriana* was put into service by P&O in 1995 no new vessel for the UK liner/cruise market had been built since the *Cunard Countess* in 1977, and this despite the disposal of a large number of UK registered and operated vessels. The US market, however, was beginning to boom and between 1965 and 1995 no fewer than fifty-seven newly built vessels of over 15 000 GRT entered the US market.

By the 1970s the requirements of UK and other northern European holiday-makers were changing. The removal of currency restrictions and the successful operation of the 119-seat BAC 1-11 in 1965 (of which 230 were built making it one of the most successful UK built jet airliners) and similar products from French and US manufacturers, especially the Boeing 727 and 737 models, brought about relatively cheap foreign package holidays and led to the boom in hotel and apartment building in Spain, Portugal, the Atlantic and Mediterranean islands and Cyprus. Cheaper than cruises and providing the traveller with a seamless web plus a holiday that commenced a mere two to three hours after leaving home without having to cross the Bay of Biscay, these holidays and the companies that provided them boomed. The boom also led to a massive expansion of regional airports in Europe, mainly to cater for the holiday charter traffic. As an example, the charter arm of Thomson Holidays, Britannia Airlines, had departures from a large number of UK airports (London Gatwick, Luton, Stanstead, Norwich, Bristol, Cardiff, Birmingham, East Midlands, Manchester, Liverpool, Leeds/Bradford, Tees-side, Newcastle, Glasgow, Edinburgh and Belfast) with other operators flying out of these plus Bournemouth, Exeter, Humberside and Aberdeen.

Mediterranean-based cruise companies, especially those operating around the Greek Islands, developed partnerships with the package companies to operate early cruise and stay holidays but these were only marginally successful. The British and Germans forsook the seaside boarding houses of the previous generation, with their shared facilities, for the hotels and apartments of the Costa del Sol etc. which had private facilities, swimming pools and an all-inclusive deal; the ingredients of cruising but at a fraction of the price. Even in the late 1990s, cruising is still a more expensive option than a land-based stay.

Also in the 1960s, British India (a P&O subsidiary) converted some former troopships, first the *Dunera* and the *Devonia* and then the larger *Uganda* and *Nevasa* into educational cruise vessels, carrying mainly schoolchildren but with some ordinary cruisers. The British government was withdrawing its military presence from east of Suez and there was no longer the demand for troopships. The educational schoolship market survived until the end of the 1970s and finally collapsed when the *Uganda* was requisitioned for the Falkland's conflict in 1982.

In 1963 Home Lines launched the 26 000 GRT *Oceanic* intended for the Cuxhaven (Germany)–New York service, but the ship was switched almost exclusively for cruising after its maiden voyage, a similar change of use occurring to the 19 800 GRT *Ivan Franko*, a Russian vessel again originally intended for the North Atlantic liner service. When the *QE2* entered North Atlantic service in 1969 she became the last vessel to be built and used on that service, and in the late 1990s was the only vessel operating even occasional

North Atlantic crossings as opposed to positioning voyages where cruise ships are moved from one operating area to another (see Chapter 5).

By the early 1980s the major UK companies had shrunk to:

- P&O: two ships, *Canberra* (44 807 GRT) and *Sea Princess* 27 670 GRT (now *Victoria*)
- Cunard: three ships, *QE2* (66 451 GRT), *Cunard Countess*, *Cunard Princess* (each 17 495 GRT)
- Fred Olsen: one ship, *Black Prince* (11 209 GRT).

Famous names from established companies, *Chusan*, *Orsova*, *Carmania* etc. had been scrapped or sold and the Ocean terminal at Southampton had become a shadow of its former self (Appendix 3 provides a list of the major UK and European tonnage displaced by the advent of the passenger jet aircraft). Revival, however, as we shall see later was on its way.

P&O merged with Orient Lines in 1960, *Canberra*'s semi-sister, *Oriana* (42 000 GRT) was transferred to the Australian market to commence cruises out of Sydney in the 1970s.

The 1960s had also seen the Greek Chandris Group commence Mediterranean operations, as did the Italian Costa Line; both companies using second-hand surplus tonnage later reinvented themselves with innovative new ships to tap into the lucrative North American market.

North American growth

The North American market began to expand rapidly in 1966. In that year Ted Arison (later of Carnival Cruises fame) and the Norwegian company, Kloster Reederei, formed a partnership to offer Caribbean cruises from the then little known port of Miami. Kloster provided the *Sunward* which had been built as a passenger ferry designed for the UK–Spain service and Arison marketed the package. The *Sunward* had been a sufferer from the UK currency restrictions that had caused a drop in demand for foreign holidays. Thus was Norwegian Caribbean Line (renamed Norwegian Cruise Line [NCL] in 1987) formed, a company that still has a strong position in the US market and which forms the case study at the end of this chapter. Disagreements between Knut Kloster and Arison led to a parting of the ways in 1972 and Arison set up Carnival Cruises, a company which by 1998 had also acquired Holland America Line and Cunard, plus a stake in the new British operator, Airtours to gain, as we shall see in Chapter 5, the major market share in the industry.

Following the success of NCL, two other Scandinavian companies entered the Caribbean market – Royal Caribbean Cruise Line (still operating in 1999 as Royal Caribbean International) and Royal Viking Line (acquired by Kloster in 1984 and Cunard in 1994 and thus eventually in 1998 by Carnival) – and the Scandinavian influence has remained strong within the US-based marketplace.

Sunward was followed by a distinctive design of vessels, *Starward* (1968), *Skyward* (1969), *Southward* (1971), of between 12 000 and 17 000 GRT for fourteen-day Caribbean cruises out of Miami. Miami was then a little known Florida port, not easily accessed from the continental USA but the growth in jet air transport brought it within a few hours flying from the majority of US and Canadian cities. Between 1963 and 1987 Boeing sold no less than 1832 Boeing 727 medium-range aircraft. Between 1967 and 1987 over 2300 shorter-range Boeing 737 shorter-range aircraft plus excellent sales of the replacement for the 727, the 757 (also the mainstay of the UK charter operators) introduced in 1982 (Green, Swanborough and Mowinski, 1987). Reaching the Miami area was no longer a problem for North Americans seeking a cruise vacation, medium-range jets were well able to operate out of the extensive US regional airport network.

From 1969 to 1971 Royal Caribbean Cruise Line (RCCL) now Royal Caribbean International (RCI) introduced three approximately 18 500 GRT, 700–880-passenger vessels with distinctive lounges placed halfway up their funnels (*Song of Norway, Nordic Prince* and *Sun Viking*), the first two being later lengthened to accommodate over 1190 passengers. Royal Viking Line followed suit with their trio of ships, albeit to a slightly different philosophy. *Royal Viking Star* (1971), *Royal Viking Sky* (1972) and *Royal Viking Sea* (1973) were bigger at 21 800 GRT but carried only 550–60 passengers. They too were lengthened later to become over 28 000 GRT and carry 812 passengers. Differentiation based on passenger/space ratio was already beginning within the US market, a concept we will be delivering in depth in Chapter 4.

When Carnival Cruises' first ship, the 18 000 GRT *Mardi Gras* (ex *Empress of Canada*), went aground off Miami in 1972 on her maiden voyage it seemed an ill omen for Ted Arison's new enterprise but, by acquiring second-hand tonnage then taking over existing companies including HAL and Cunard, Carnival was able to succeed. By building their own mega-ships Carnival has become the market leader in the cruise industry with over 27 per cent of the world's cruise ship tonnage controlled or partially owned by the Carnival Corporation in 1999. An excellent account of Carnival's growth is given in Dickinson and Vladimir (1997).

The USA led growth in the cruise industry in the 1970s and 1980s, with new companies being formed each year (as well as ones leaving the market or being bought up).

The Love Boat

In 1965 Stanley B. McDonald had founded Princess Cruises on the western seaboard of the USA. In 1974 the company was purchased by P&O, although it still operated under the Princess brand. As we shall see later this provided P&O with an easy entry into the US market where the P&O brand was less well known. During 1974 P&O purchased the *Pacific Princess* (20 636 GRT) and *Island Princess* (19 907 GRT) from the defunct Flagship Cruises who had ordered the vessels in 1970. In 1977 both ships were made available to Aaron Spelling Productions and became the stars of *The Love Boat*, a highly successful television series. So successful was *The Love Boat* that even in the 1990s Princess were still saying, 'It's more than a cruise, it's the Love Boat' ©.

Americans became entranced with the fun, sun and romance depicted in the series and it was just as successful when shown to UK audiences. German audiences had their own long-running show *Traumshiffe* (*Dreamship*) which started in the 1980s and featured the 9570 GRT MV *Berlin* of Deilmann Reederie.

In 1974 RCL introduced the 10 500 GRT *Golden Odyssey*, unique in that her 425 passengers equalled the maximum capacity of a Boeing 747 and thus allowed a chartered 'jumbo' to bring a full shipload of passengers to the vessel.

One can see just how cruising expanded worldwide by considering the number of vessels and total tonnage brought into cruising each year from 1963 until 1997 (Table 2.3). The figures for each year include both newly built and adapted ships that entered cruising service that year and, in the case of the converted vessels, their tonnage after conversion.

In 1996 and 1997 over 1 million GRT of new build entered the industry and whilst there had been withdrawals of older tonnage, they were few and far between. What the figures represent is a massive re-equipment by the major companies and the emergence of new companies using older vessels discarded by the major companies.

As will be examined later, much of the growth of companies such as P&O and Carnival has been achieved, especially within the US market, through horizontal integration, a concept formalized by Michael Porter (1980; 1985) in

Table 2.3 New build and conversions, 1963–97

Year	No. of vessels	Tonnage
1963	2	48 000
1964	0	0
1965	3	50 000
1966	3	78 000
1967	6	121 000
1968	3	33 000
1969	5	158 000
1970	4	72 000
1971	6	109 000
1972	8	142 000
1973	8	198 000
1974	5	78 000
1975	10	172 000
1976	4	70 000
1977	2	19 000
1978	2	39 000
1980	3	45 000
1981	1	19 000
1982	4	103 000
1983	3	66 000
1984	4	121 000
1985	4	105 000
1986	4	107 000
1987	3	83 000
1988	6	185 000
1989	5	205 000
1990	13	432 000
1991	4	243 000
1992	12	372 000
1993	6	279 000
1994	3	104 000
1995	6	408 000
1996	9	567 000
1997	9	545 000

his work on competitive strategies. Both companies have grown by acquiring other cruise operators. Carnival acquired HAL in 1988 and as HAL had acquired a 50 per cent stake in Windstar Sail Cruises in 1987 and the full company just prior to the takeover by Carnival. Carnival expanded its operations to include a premier operator, HAL, then Cunard in 1998 and a niche operator, Windstar. Further details of these types of acquisitions will be examined in Chapter 4 but the concept behind them has been to expand the operation by acquiring another operator with experience in a slightly different market segment. Interestingly, as we shall show in Chapter 3, the original brand names often carry with them considerable customer loyalty and are frequently retained.

In addition to its entry into the UK market through an almost 30 per cent acquisition of Airtours, Carnival also acquired the shares of Costa in 1997 and then, in 1998, acquired the Cunard operation from Trafalgar House. The latter acquisition included the new *Queen Mary* announced at the end of 1998 and the subject of an intervention by the UK government as a request for the ship to be registered in the UK (see Chapter 4).

By 1998 the major share of the US market was serviced by Carnival companies, P&O Companies (mainly Princess), RCI and NCL with Chandris rebranding, through Celebrity Cruises beginning to regain market share before being acquired by RCI.

The US market had begun to undergo major differentiation in the 1980s. Holland America Line were considered to be at the premier end of the market, Carnival were acquiring major market share in the 'family market', probably the most lucrative growth area and there were a number of smaller operators servicing the budget end of the market.

The Greek company, Chandris, had been in the cruise business for a long time, operating mainly second-hand tonnage for both US and European customers. Many of their ships were very old. In 1994 the 26 000 GRT *Britanis* (operating under the Fantasy brand) was the oldest passenger ship still in service having been built as the *Monterey* for the San Francisco–Sydney service as early as 1932. In 1983 Chandris had bought the ex Italian liner 28 000 GRT *Galileo Galilei*, and renamed her *Galileo*, and used her for cruising in the Caribbean. Chandris refitted the ship in Germany in 1989 to become the first vessel for their new, premier cruise company, Celebrity Cruises and renamed her *Meridian* (sold to Sun Vista Cruises as the *Sun Vista* in 1998) in 1990 when she was joined by the newly built 47 000 GRT *Horizon*, a very striking looking ship. Horizon's semi-sister *Zenith* followed in 1992, with the 70 000 GRT *Century* in 1995, and the 74 000 GRT *Galaxy* and *Mercury* in 1996 and 1997 respectively. (The entertainment staff on the *Galaxy* were the feature of a British television documentary in 1998.) This totalled 342 000 GRT for a new brand in seven short years all designed for the Premium (see Chapter 4) end of the market. At the same time Chandris continued to operate the Fantasy brand for the budget market. In 1998, Celebrity Cruises was acquired by RCI, bringing that company into the number two slot in the market.

Mega-ships

The first of the 'mega-ships' was the 73 000 GRT RCI *Sovereign of the Seas* in 1988 followed, in 1990, by the *Norway*. In 1979 Norwegian Caribbean had bought the last of the Atlantic liners, the 66 300 GRT *France* (1962) for cruising, renaming her the *Norway* and in 1990 she had two extra decks added and her tonnage increased to 76 000 GRT in order to carry 2400 passengers (to date the Norway remains the world's longest passenger ship at 315.5 m/1 035 ft). Carnival introduced the 70 367 GRT *Fantasy* also in 1990, followed by her sister, *Ecstasy*, in 1991 with six more sisters being delivered up to 1998 making a class of eight vessels. Not to be outdone, P&O/Princess introduced 69 845 GRT *Crown Princess* in 1990. The first of the mega-ships for Costa was the 74 000 GRT *Costa Victoria* of 1996, by which time all of the major companies had vessels over 70 000 GRT in service. The 100 000 GRT barrier was broken in 1996 by the 101 353 GRT *Carnival Destiny* followed in 1998 by P&O/Princess's 109 000 GRT *Grand Princess* with no fewer than 2600 berths available for each cruise. The plans for these ships had been in gestation for some time as it takes years to plan and build a ship of this size. A provisional decision to build the 69 000 GRT *Oriana* for the UK market was taken by P&O in 1988 with the ship being ordered in 1991. The keel was laid on 11 March 1993 with the ship entering service for her maiden cruise in the spring of 1995. The *Oriana* is covered as a case study at the end of Chapter 6.

Whilst the mainstream trend was for larger ships, a niche market in smaller, yacht-like vessels was developing. Sea Goddess Cruises had entered the market in 1984/5 with two 4260 GRT, ninety-passenger ships (the company acquired by Cunard in 1988). It was followed by Seabourne Cruises (originally called Signet Cruises) who put three 9900 GRT vessels carrying 140 passengers into service from 1986 (25 per cent of Seabourne was acquired by Carnival in 1991). In 1992 Silversea Cruises, whose lineage could be traced back to the Sitmar Line commenced operation and placed two luxury 16 800 GRT vessels, *Silver Wind* and *Silver Cloud* into operation, each carrying 296 passengers (compare this with Airtours' *Seawing* (16 600 GRT) which carries a maximum of 976 passengers). In August 1998, Silversea announced that they had ordered two more vessels, each of 25 000 GRT, with options on two more vessels which would have an even higher passenger to space ratio that the original two. (More information about Silversea Cruises can be found in the case study at the end of Chapter 4.)

In 1984 P&O/Princess had introduced the 44 000 GRT *Royal Princess* which, whilst large for the mid-1980s, was important in that she introduced new standards of passenger comfort for the mainstream US market. Not only were all her 600 cabins outside but she also had two complete decks of cabins that feature a veranda. As will be shown in Chapter 6 when design is considered, introducing a veranda entails a fundamental rethink of the design of a ship where previously cabins had been in the hull and public rooms in the superstructure. The *Royal Princess* was effectively built 'upside down', but set the trend for much future building.

Whilst traditional cruising had been mainly for couples, the family market was waiting to be tapped. In its early days Carnival had a partnership with Disney whereby Carnival Cruises could form part of a Disney package and later Carnival ships were designed to be family friendly. In 1993, American Family Cruises was launched by Bruce Nierenberg who intended to use the 32 750 GRT *Engenio Costa* and the 31 500 GRT *Costa Riviera* as the *American Adventure* and *American Pioneer* respectively to operate seven-day family-oriented cruises out of Miami. The venture did not succeed, but 1998 saw the debut of the two-funnelled, 85 500 GRT *Disney Magic* (with another vessel building) designed to put the Disney experience afloat and provide the family package for which Disney had become a benchmark. In the UK as will be shown later in this chapter, family considerations have been an important factor in the rebirth of the cruise industry.

When Carnival Cruises introduced the 101 353 GRT *Carnival Destiny* in 1996, another record was broken. This was the first ship unable to transit the Panama Canal and thus confined the ship to Caribbean operations. She was followed the next year by the 109 000 GRT *Grand Princess* of Princess Cruises destined for Caribbean and Mediterranean cruises. By the year 2001, Princess intend to have three of these mega-ships in operation, whilst the first of the RCI 'Eagle' class, the lead ship of which is the 137 000 GRT *Voyager of the Seas*, is due to debut before the year 2000.

The introduction of such huge ships is leading to further differentiation within the marketplace.

Rebirth of the United Kingdom cruise industry

As was shown in Chapter 1, by 1998 the growth in the US market was slowing but the UK market was about to expand dramatically and was to be met in part not by horizontal integration but by vertical integration. Companies that operated in the traditional holiday market were about to add cruising to their portfolio and greatly increase the supply of cruise holidays for the UK market.

As quoted earlier, the UK cruise market was in the doldrums in the 1970s and 1980s. The 'sea, sun and sand' package holiday had introduced many Britons to the concept of foreign holidays but the majority of these were Mediterranean bases using package charters out of UK regional airports. As holiday-makers sought to widen their travel experience (see Chapter 3) and as the disposable incomes of those in work increased, so longer-haul destinations became more popular. Florida was no longer just a dream, and British holiday-makers were frequently to be found on the beaches of Kenya, Thailand and the Indian Ocean.

There was a sizeable market of people looking for a different form of holiday but modern social trends mitigated against the 'stuffy' image of cruising with its dressing for dinner etc. There continued to be a loyal residual market and P&O's 44 000 *Canberra*, 'The Great White Whale' veteran of the Falkland's campaign, still drew respectable repeat business and new cruisers but, equipped with many cabins that still had no private facilities, the experience could not compete with ships such as the *Royal Princess*. By the 1990s up to 15 per cent of the passengers on a P&O/Princess ship could be from the UK and research showed that there was still an active UK market.

In planning for the future, P&O showed that UK cruisers in 1987 had numbered 128 500 with 1988 figures showing a further increase to 152 000 of which over 50 per cent undertook fly cruises (Source – *The Ballad of Oriana*, P&O Cruises). By 1992 there were 225 000 UK cruisers, a figure that rose to 480 000 by 1996 (Ward, 1994; 1997) as shown in Chapter 1.

It was these figures that led P&O to order the 69 000 GRT *Oriana* as stated earlier but they also led to new companies coming into the market and operating in a totally different manner. By 1998 P&O Cruises (the UK cruising arm of P&O) and their Swan Hellenic operation using the *Minerva* was in the position shown in Table 2.4.

Table 2.4 P&O United Kingdom position, 1998

Ship	Date	GRT	No. of passengers	Notes
Oriana	1995	69 000	1975	
Victoria	1966/ 9	29 000	743	ex *Kungsholme*, ex *Sea Princess*
Arcadia	1989/97	63 500	1621	ex *Star Princess*
Aurora	2000	76 000	2000	Building
Minerva	1996	12 000	456	Swan Hellenic

As the major holder of the UK market share, P&O were in a very strong position but the withdrawal of the veteran *Canberra* in autumn 1997 left a hole in the market. Whilst P&O hoped that *Canberra* passengers – *Canberra* was a ship which attracted a very high degree of repeat business – would transfer their affections to the other vessels in the company, others were quick to exploit a perceived market gap.

In 1997, Direct Cruises was set up by the UK-based Direct Holidays to operate the 32 700 *Eugenio Costa* as the *Edinburgh Castle*. Although slightly smaller than *Canberra*, the ship had something of the looks of the much loved favourite and the company's initial brochures actually made direct comparisons with the *Canberra*, their quoted savings being directly linked to Canberra fares. It seems that Direct Cruises had their eye on the *Canberra* market hence two mentions of a competitor's vessel in their brochure.

Ward (1999) likens the operation to that of the now defunct Union Castle company operating between the UK and South Africa. Union Castle became the operators of the *Reina del Mar* (see earlier) and in many respects the Direct Cruise operation resembled that of the *Reina del Mar*, being aimed at a particular UK segment. It is our view, however, that the marketing was directed particularly at former *Canberra* cruisers.

Unfortunately for Direct Cruises, whilst their initial uptake was enough to need a second ship, the *Apollo*, for the first season, they had a start reminiscent of that of Carnival and the *Mardi Gras*. Press reports indicated that the *Edinburgh Castle* was not fully complete in time for the first cruise, although this was related to only a few cabins; the *Apollo* was late out of refit and cruises had to be cancelled and then in the summer of 1998 the *Edinburgh Castle* was the subject of a legionnaires disease scare. Later in the summer of 1998 Direct Holidays sold the Direct Cruise operation to Airtours, although the cruises continued to be operated and branded separately. On the 24 February 1999, the company actually owning the *Edinburgh Castle* (Direct Cruises being the operators) went into liquidation putting the future of the vessel in doubt.

As mentioned in the Direct Cruises brochure for 1998, there had been three other new entrants to the UK market. Like Direct Holidays all three had their antecedents in the package holiday business and two of them were adept at vertical integration, a concept to be covered later in this book.

Thomson and Airtours not only put together and delivered package holidays, they also sold them through their related high street retail outlets and operated their own charter airlines. Thus it made sense to offer cruises to the emergent family market who may have been tiring of the standard beach package but wished to remain with the package concept. Page and Moy, a well-known UK travel operator commenced operations with the 10 400 GRT *Ocean Majesty* under long-term summer charter in 1997.

Airtours and Thomson commenced cruise operations in 1995 using displaced tonnage from the US market and both grew quickly by offering a low-cost, family package linked to beach holidays. By 1998 both had expanded from the Mediterranean and the Atlantic Islands into the Caribbean markets. In 1996, Carnival purchased a stake of just under 30 per cent in Airtours.

In 1998, First Choice Holidays, another of the major UK operators, announced that from 1999 they would be offering cruises under their own brand in addition to selling those of other operators. Like Thomson, they contracted the services of the Louis Cruise Line in Cyprus to assist with much of the operation and chartered the *Bolero* from Festival Cruises.

In late 1998, Festival Cruises (known for many years in the US as Azur-Bolero Cruises) announced that they would be bringing the newly built French-registered *Mistral* (47 900 GRT) into service in 1999 to add to the European market in the Mediterranean (see the case study at the end of Chapter 9). This followed the rebranding of StarLauro as the Mediterranean Shipping Company (MSC) and further increased the choice for European passengers.

These new entrants offered a very different package to the traditional cruise, although still retaining its best ingredients. Their ships (as shown below) were older and the emphasis was on family fun. They also made cabin selection easier by allocating cabins on boarding and offering fewer categories of cabin. Thomson's *Island Breeze* (38 000 GRT) has eight categories of cabin whilst the Princess vessel, *Sky Princess* (46 000 GRT) has no less than eighteen. This simplification is more in line with the way hotel accommodation is sold in the package holiday business. We will be examining the different nature of the markets served by these companies in later chapters but they have become major players, albeit using vessels that were 'getting on in years' and which will need replacing if the companies are going to continue operations – a not dissimilar story to that of Carnival in its early days. Indeed a number of former Carnival vessels feature in their fleets.

The Asian market

The late 1990s saw a massive expansion in the Asian market. The growth started in Japan but as the economies of South-East Asia boomed, so did the expansion of the domestic cruising market. Star Cruises, which catered for the indigenous and the US/European cruiser according to Ward (1999) rapidly becoming the Carnival Cruises of Asia. In terms of capacity, the Asian market expanded by 46 per cent between 1994 and 1997 and by a similar figure (47 per cent) between 1997 and 1998. By that time Star Cruises had 3.7 per cent market share based on tonnage and 4.6 per cent when calculated on total capacity.

Cruising however is subject to the vagaries of economic recession and political instability. Awani Cruises was set up in 1996 to service the growing potential of the Indonesian cruise market. The recession in the South-East Asian economies of mid-1998, which led to political instability in Indonesia and the overthrow of the government, was a major factor in the company ceasing operations in the 1998. At the same time Carnival decided not to go ahead with a partnership with the South Korean company, Hyundai, using the *Tropicale* to launch Carnival Cruises Asia. Holidays are still a luxury item and are one of the first things to be affected when recession bites. By 1996 the Asian market including Japan formed 9.5 per cent of the market, this being on a par with the UK which provided just over 10 per cent.

Other growth markets

The German market grew at approximately 20 per cent per annum between 1994 and 1997 although the growth appears to have levelled out by 1998. Germans still formed 3.3 per cent of the total market, with France and Italy together forming 5.2 per cent. According to the UK Cruise Agency, Thornton's Cruise World, the Scandinavian market had grown over 300 per cent between 1995 and 1997, perhaps not surprising given the investment by Norwegian companies in the industry. Nevertheless, the USA and Canada still provide a massive 65 per cent of the global market and thus many of the design concepts etc. are still targeted at the North American market.

Festival Cruises are developing a 'European' product designed to appeal across the European Union (EU) which will be considered in the case study to Chapter 9.

Sail cruises

From the early 1990s a new feature began to appear in the Caribbean and the Mediterranean, that of the luxury sail-cruise ships. A far cry from the nineteenth century tea clippers or the spartan conditions of many military sail training ships, these vessels used the latest sail technology together with accommodation approaching that of a traditional cruise liner to provide something different. Large for sailing ships, up to 5000 GRT, these vessels and their market will be considered in Chapter 8.

Safety

Cruising has proved to be a very safe method of taking a vacation. Whilst there have been small fires at sea and ships have run aground, there have been very few major incidents that have resulted in major loss of life. Fire at sea is a very real danger and a number of cruise vessels have been lost this way, mostly either whilst alongside, under refit or on their way to the breaker's yard with only a skeleton crew. The *Brittany*, 16 335 GRT (ex *Bretagne*) of Chandris Lines was gutted by fire in 1966 whilst in Greece and the 18 739 GRT *Rasa Sayang* (ex *De Gras*, ex *Bergenfjord*) was heavily damaged by fire, also in Greece, whilst refitting in 1980 and later sank. One ship with a phoenix-like quality is the 25 000 GRT *Leeward* of NCL. In 1980, Rederii A/B Sally of Sweden launched a large car ferry named the *Sally Albatros*, which was converted to a cruise ship in 1988. In 1990 the ship was nearly totally destroyed by fire during an annual overhaul. The surviving parts were used to build a new *Sally Albatros* (25 000 GRT) which was launched in 1991 but was badly damaged by grounding in the Baltic in 1984. Repairs cost over £22 million ($36 million), the repaired vessel being acquired by NCL in 1995 and renamed *Leeward*. The 20 469 GRT *Pallas Athena* (ex *Carla Costa*, ex *Carla C*, ex *Flandre*) of Epirotiki Lines burned out in Piraeus in 1994, again whilst in port.

The worst disaster to befall a cruise liner on the open seas was the loss by fire in December 1963 of 19 040 GRT *Lakonia* (built in 1930 as the *Johan Van Oldenbarnevelt* and sold in 1962) of the Greek Line off Madeira with the loss of 128 lives. In July 1970 the 16 844 GRT *Fulvia* (ex *Oslofjord*) chartered by Costa was abandoned off the Canary Islands after being ravaged by fire.

In June 1981 the *Kareliya* 13 250 GRT of the Black Sea Shipping Co ran aground whilst on a cruise from the UK to the Canary Islands and was so badly damaged that passengers had to be flown home, but there were no injuries. In 1989 the *Maxim Gorkiy* (ex *Hamburg*), 25 000 GRT of the same company was found in drifting ice on an Icelandic cruise. Pressure from the ice resulted in leaks and the 575 passengers and 120 out of the 378 crew were forced to abandon ship in freezing temperatures. The skeleton crew managed to save the ship and all of those in lifeboats were rescued.

The worst disaster to befall cruise passengers was not at sea but formed part of the world's worst air disaster, which occurred on the ground at Tenerife

Airport. Because of a bomb at Las Palmas airport in the Canaries on 27 March 1977, flights were diverted to the nearby island of Tenerife. Amongst the diverted flights were two Boeing 747s, one belonging to the Dutch airline KLM and a chartered Pan Am aircraft carrying 378 passengers destined for an RCL (see earlier) cruise. In fog on Tenerife's runway the KLM aircraft accelerated into the path of the Pan Am machine due to an error by the KLM pilot. All 248 passengers on the KLM flight were killed and there were only sixty-one survivors from Pan Am.

In October 1985, terrorists seized the 23 600 GRT *Achille Lauro* off the Egyptian coast and murdered one US passenger before surrendering, and in late 1994 the same ship caught fire off the Horn of Africa but thanks to a massive rescue operation only three lives were lost.

In February 1986, the Soviet cruise liner, *Mikhail Lermontov* (19 872 GRT) built in 1971, struck rocks off New Zealand and was abandoned, later sinking.

On 3 August 1991 the 8000 GRT *Oceanos* developed a leak that led to a power failure whilst it was off South Africa. All 580 people on board were flown by helicopter to safety on 4 August, the ship sinking the same afternoon.

In December 1998, the *Monarch of the Seas* (RCL, 73 941 GRT) was holed on a shoal of St Maarten in the Caribbean and all the passengers were evacuated although with no casualties. Their cruise being cancelled, this incident followed on from the evacuation of all 2600 passengers from the 70 367 GRT *Ecstasy* of Carnival Cruises as a result of fire.

A more serious fire in May of 1999 led to the sinking of 30 440 *Sun Vista*. *Galileo Galileo* ex-Meridian of Sun Vista Cruises off the coast of Malaysia. The ship was only half full and all 1104 passengers and crew were able to abandon ship with no serious injuries. Luckily the weather was calm but Tom Otley and Stephen Bevan pointed out in the *Sunday Times* of 30 May, 1999, quoting the International Maritime Organization's (IMO) Roger Kohn, that, 'with thousands of people on board a large ship, half of them geriatric, how are they going to be able to leap out nimbly into a force 9 gale?' The 1992 Safety of Life at Sea (SOLAS) Regulations of 1992, prescribe very stringent standards for new ships but it remains to be seen how easily 3000 plus passengers can be evacuated. Both the *Sunday Times* and the previous day's *Daily Telegraph* raised questions about the ability of such a large-scale evacuation. In the Caribbean where there are always a number of large cruise ships within easy distance of each other this may present less of a problem than in the growing number of more remote areas.

By coincidence, BBC2's *Timewatch* programme of Saturday, 29 May, 1999 postulated that the success in rescuing the vast majority of the passengers and crew of the White Star liner *Republic* (17 378 GRT), after a collision off Massachusetts in 1909 and the part that radio played in the rescue (Gardiner and Van der Vat, 1995), may have led to a complacency about the ease of rescue that was sadly disproved three years later when the *Titanic* foundered.

The prize for the unluckiest ship must go to the *Edinburgh Castle* of Direct Cruises. In 1998 she was the centre of a legionnaires disease scare, broke down in Cadiz and was finally placed 'under arrest' in Southampton in December of that year being at the centre of a commercial dispute.

Another ship to be arrested was the *Pacific Princess*, which was impounded, together with her passengers, in Piraeus (Athens) in December 1998 following the apprehension of two of her crew for drug smuggling.

Considering the numbers carried, cruising is like flying – immensely safe– not surprising as both industries have to meet strict international regulations which are being revised at an increasing rate to make the dangers of loss, especially by fire, less and less likely. Given, however, that cruise ships may contain thousands of people, some of whom may smoke, and large quantities of electrical equipment etc., fire can never be entirely ruled out, hence the use of fire-retardant and fire-resistant materials in modern ships.

The history of cruising, especially in recent years, is also bound up with new design philosophies and an ever widening expansion of cruising areas. It is also reflective of social trends.

The chapters of this book will examine the design philosophies that have led to the current generation of purpose-built cruise ships, how cruising has reached previously little explored parts of the globe and how it has ceased to become a vacation pastime for just the wealthy.

Cruising began as one way to use surplus tonnage and then received a major boost with Prohibition in the USA. Non-US flagged ships could embark passengers for prohibition beating cruises. Similarly when, in the 1960s the UK government placed strict currency and exchange regulations on those citizens leaving the country, UK-flagged ships were exempt.

Mass tourism by air was believed to have sounded the death knell of the ocean liner but a symbiotic relationship leading to the fly cruise has developed which has allowed the passenger ship to make a huge comeback.

Case study

Norwegian Cruise Lines

Norwegian Cruise Lines was founded by Knut Kloster of the Norwegian shipping company Klosters Rederi in 1966. Reflecting the geographic nature of its operations, the company was originally named Norwegian Caribbean Lines.

Norwegian Cruise Lines was to the US market what the **Reina del Mar** was to the UK, for many Americans it was their first taste of cruising and even in 1998 the company still held fourth place as regards market share.

The **Sunward**, the first ship of the new company which had Ted Arison of later Carnival fame as a partner, was originally designed for the UK–Spanish Canary Islands market and included accommodation for vehicles. The expansion of charter air operations meant that UK holiday-makers did not need transportation for cars, and the ship was used to inaugurate cruise operations from Miami, then just a small Florida port.

Norwegian Cruise Lines was an overnight success in the US market and , although Arison left in the early 1970s to set up Carnival, the combination of purpose-built ships operating to the Caribbean from a port in the southern USA offered exactly what the fledgling US market required.

In 1968 the purpose-built for cruising 12 959 GRT **Starward** was delivered, followed by the larger 16 254 GRT **Skyward** in 1969. By 1971 the market had grown sufficiently for another Kloster company, Royal Viking Line, to be formed and at least two of their vessels were later transferred to the NCL fleet – **Royal Viking Star** of 1971 becoming the **Westward** in 1991 and the 1972 **Royal Viking Sky** becoming NCL's third **Sunward** also in 1991.

In 1979 NCL acquired the world's longest passenger ship, the 66 343 GRT ex **Atlantic** liner, **France**, which had been laid up since 1974, and renamed her **Norway**, She was then the largest ship to operate out of the now booming port of Miami. In 1984 the **Norway** had her steam engines replaced by diesels and in 1990 the Lloydwerft yard in Bremerhaven fitted two new decks to the top of the superstructure increasing her tonnage to 76 049 GRT and giving her a capacity of 2032 berths.

By 1994 the NCL fleet (the Norwegian Cruise Line name was adopted in 1987 to reflect the expansion into different cruising areas other than the

Table 2.5   NCL fleet, 1998

Built as	NCL name pre-1996	NCL name post-1996	Tonnage	Berths
Sally Albatros/ Viking Saga 1980	Leeward	Leeward	25 000	1150
France 1962	Norway	Norway	76 049	2370
Crown Odyssey 1988		Norwegian Crown	34 250	1221
Dreamward 1992	Dreamward	Norwegian Dream	41 000	1760
Crown Majesty/ Cunard Dynasty/ Crown Dynasty 1993		Norwegian Dynasty	19 069	916
Royal Majesty 1992		Norwegian Majesty	32 396	1501
Windward 1993	Windward	Norwegian Wind	41 000	1760
Seaward 1988	Seaward	Norwegian Sea	42 276	1798
Norwegian Sky 1999	Norwegian Sky	Norwegian Sky	76 000	2340
Royal Odyssey/ Royal Viking Sea 1973		Norwegian Star	28 000	1150

Caribbean) comprised seven ships with a total tonnage of 248 609 GRT and the provision of 9443 berths making it the biggest component of the twelve-ship, 12 989-berth combined Kloster fleet that comprised NCL, Royal Viking Line and Royal Cruise Line. In 1993 Kloster sold the Royal Viking operation to Cunard and merged NCL and the Royal Cruise Line. At the same time a series of name changes for ships commenced with current policy being to have a 'Norwegian' prefix to the name.

Norwegian Cruise Lines have expanded their operations far from the Caribbean, the 1999 programme featuring cruises based on Bermuda, New England and the eastern seaboard of Canada, Alaska, South America, the Pacific (Hawaii), Scandinavia, the Mediterranean and Northern Europe, in addition to the Caribbean. In order to cope with growth, many of the NCL ships have been stretched and the company appear to have taken the decision to keep a proportion of the fleet in the mid-size bracket of around 40 000 GRT.

Norwegian Star was re-named **Norwegian Capricorn** in 1999 and used on a joint venture operating out of Sydney for the Australian market.

In 1998 NCL acquired the Orient Line and its 20 502 vessel the **Marco Polo** which operates a series of worldwide cruises each year. The operation will remain separate for the foreseeable future.

Norwegian Cruise Lines intend to increase their capacity year on year and have announced new vessels carrying approximately 2000 passengers for delivery in 2000, 2001, 2002 and 2003 respectively which will provide the company with sixteen ships and over 24 300 berths by the year 2003.

Although the smallest of the 'Big Four' (Carnival, RCI, P&O and NCL) with approximately 6.5 per cent of the global market in 1998, the company are a major player in the cruise industry.

Norwegian Cruise Lines played a major role in the launch of the US market and the company has been both one of the survivors and also one of the success stories during the massive expansion of the cruise industry between 1968 and 1998. The design of NCL vessels has stood the test of time with many of their original ships still operating in the cruise market, albeit under new ownership.

3

Market aspects

This chapter includes:

- market concepts and their application to the cruise industry
- marketing mix
- core and supplementary products
- product life cycle
- Boston matrix
- quality equilibrium
- competition.

No company can exist without customers, and thus an understanding of the market in which the cruise companies operate is vital to an understanding of their operations.

Market concepts have their own language and set of concepts, and these are being introduced early in this book in order to use them in later chapters. This chapter will introduce a series of market concepts and models, which you can then use in succeeding chapters to examine the cruising industry. Chapter 4 continues the market theme by considering differentiation and segmentation in some detail.

A market is a place where exchange takes place. In medieval times, farmers, weavers, silversmiths etc. would bring their goods to a central point, normally the market square in a town, meet with potential buyers and an exchange of goods for money (or other goods in a barter system) would take place. Today's markets are considerably more complex and yet the same basic transaction occurs: the cruise company has ships and itineraries, and the potential cruisers have money to spend. There are a number of cruise companies, most with very similar basic products trying to attract new customers and to retain their existing ones. The cruise brochures are no different in concept to a row of barrows in a fruit and vegetable market. The customers examine the goods on offer and then make their choice depending on their requirements and budgets. Unless marketing has been carefully thought through, not only may one company lose the trade but so may the whole sector; the customer may decide on a villa holiday in Tuscany or Florida or may even decide to buy a new washing machine instead.

What is marketing?

There is a misconception that marketing is mostly about advertising and promotion. True they form part of what we shall examine as the marketing mix, but they are only a part. Cartwright and Green (1997) have described marketing as 'Finding out what your customers want and then supplying it at a profit'. Advertising tells your customers about what you have to offer but it is only useful in so far as the product or service matches their requirements. History records a number of products that were launched (because they seemed a good idea) without extensive customer research; the Ford Edsell, the Sinclair CV in the personal transportation sector are classic examples. They were technically revolutionary but not what the market required at the time, i.e., people would not pay money for them and if no one will buy it doesn't matter how good the product actually is.

It follows, therefore, that the first step in any marketing operation is to find out who are your potential customers, what kind of budgets they have, what they want and how much they are prepared to pay. A company then must examine whether they can provide that product at a price that is deemed value for money by the customer and allows the company to make sufficient financial margin to satisfy its shareholders. Finally, having delivered the product, the company needs to find out if it satisfied (or indeed, delighted) the customer and what lessons can be learned for future transactions with that or other existing or potential customers.

The cruise industry provides some really excellent examples of marketing concepts and this chapter examines these concepts with especial reference to the industry to show how cruise companies have used marketing ideas in order to position themselves to maximize customer take-up.

Market research

Organizations that produce products and services without much research into what the customer actually wants (as opposed to a vague idea) are known as *product-led* organizations, whereas those which produce products and services in response to customer demand are generally referred to as *customer-driven* organizations. In other than demand-led economies where monopolies are the norm, experience has shown that, as disposable income and choice increase, the more successful organizations tend to operate a more customer-driven approach. This section is designed to consider how the successful cruise companies find out about their customers and tailor their products accordingly.

Using their customer loyalty schemes and customer satisfaction surveys, cruise companies are well placed to find out what their customers actually want. Cruise ship entertainment staff also spend a considerable amount of time 'managing by wandering about' (Peters, 1987), a process that was profiled by Cartwright and Green (1997) when examining the work of a cruise director and a purser.

Cruise companies offer incentives such as free draws in order to encourage customers to complete rating forms, such forms being studied very carefully and even affecting the future contracts of performers.

After the first cruise with a company it is usual for the customer to be offered membership of the 'loyalty' club, which will provide company news via a newsletter, discounted fares and special offers on board subsequent cruises. The Captain's Circle (Princess), Venetian Society (Silversea), Cunard World Club, and NCL Masters are examples of these. Membership is usually free, although there is an annual charge for P&O's POSH Club but this does entitle members to discounts on many on-board purchases. Just like land-based loyalty schemes, the information that can be obtained about preferences, buying patterns etc. is invaluable and aids the market research process.

There is considerable skill required in drawing up an effective customer survey questionnaire and care must be taken to allow for cultural differences in allocating ratings. Our own research in 1996 indicated that US customers were three times more likely to rate an aspect of a cruise at the maximum (say 6) than UK customers who would rate that aspect at 5 despite being just as satisfied. The explanation we were given was that 'if we rate as a 6, they have nothing to aim for', another example of different national behaviour patterns. Phipps and Simmons (1995) have produced fifteen Golden Rules for questionnaire design in order to ensure that the questions are non-biased and provide effective information.

All of the cruise companies we spoke to kept logs of customer comments, made both during and after cruises, in order to see if there were patterns to complaints, suggestions and praise; they not only needed to know what was going wrong but also what they were doing right. One problem is that people are far more likely to complain than to praise (Cartwright and Green, 1997).

The marketing mix

The term 'marketing mix' was developed at Harvard during the 1930s and 1940s, and was initially known as the 4Ps, Product, Price, Promotion and Place. Kotler (1980) has refined this to the 4Cs, Product becoming Customer Value, Price replaced by Cost, Promotion by Communication and Place by Convenience. Other workers have added such items as People, Physical Attributes and Processes to the 4Ps, but the basic model is sufficient to explain how the mix works within the cruise industry especially as we relate the latter 3 Ps (People, Physical Attributes and Processes) to items within the 4Cs. Using the 4Ps and Cs we will show how the modern cruise industry achieves success through a careful use of the mix.

Product/customer value

A gleaming white cruise liner is anchored off a Caribbean island. What is the product that the customers have purchased? An easy question to answer is, they've bought a cruise, but is it that simple?

As part of the research for this book we asked a large number of cruisers (over 100) over a period of time, 'what is it that makes a cruise different from other holidays?' i.e., what is the product? After all, these people could have purchased a variety of types of answer. We found out first what the product was not, it was not an ocean voyage. The fact that the ship sailed the seas was almost incidental to the experience. The most frequent responses were:

- being looked after in luxury
- ability to travel to different places without packing and unpacking at each stop
- a total holiday/entertainment package

- safety
- interesting destinations.

Put together, the picture frequently painted was of a safe, luxurious, anxiety-free way to see the world with everything there at your fingertips within your comfort zone. Even the weather, especially the sun, was not necessarily a major factor, except in the Caribbean and Mediterranean, but calm seas were.

When the UK cruising market had its first boom in the 1960s (see Chapter 2) the operators were mainly companies who knew and understood the ocean liner business but whose experience of the holiday business was limited. The survivors, including P&O, Cunard and the Chandris Group, moved from being in the ocean liner/shipping business, where the aim was to move people from one continent to another (a task better undertaken by a Boeing 747 or an Airbus A340), into the floating package holiday business. In doing so they have reinvented themselves to a considerable degree. You have to be in the know to recognize that the sleek and luxurious MS *Galaxy* (73 850 GRT) of 1996, and featured in the UK television documentary *The Cruise*, was owned by the same company that operated low-cost Mediterranean cruises in the 1960s on board the *Australis* (ex *America*, ex *West Point*) – Chandris Group (now part of RCI) – the clue is the cross on the funnel.

In contrast many of the newcomers to the cruise market, Airtours, Thompson and Direct Cruises in the UK and Disney in the USA, were already household names in other sectors of the travel and tourism industry. They had the expertise and experience to put a good holiday product together and translated that to a seagoing experience with considerable success (in most cases) during the latter half of the 1990s.

Thus we can describe a mainstream cruise in terms of product as a total, seagoing holiday package that combines destinations and entertainment in a seamless package. Of course, this is not to everyone's taste and, as this book shows, there is a market, albeit smaller, for other types of cruise; expedition cruises, sailing ship cruises, coastal cruises etc. and these will also receive consideration in terms of the market they serve.

Kotler preferred the term *customer value* to product because it describes a more customer-oriented approach and the customer may see the 'product' in different terms. For example, a car is a product with many makes and models to choose from but to the customer its value may be in terms of convenient personal transportation or even image. It is the value that the customer places on the product or service that makes him or her buy it.

On a simplistic level a customer is somebody for whom you satisfy a want or need with some form of payment. The payment may be money, it may be time, it may be goodwill but there is some form of payment. Needs are usually described as being basic and wants refer to the concept of *added value*. A simple example will suffice to show the difference. It is early morning, you have just woken up in your stateroom, the Caribbean sun is shining and you are hungry. Your need is for food. A dietician could calculate the number of calories and the balance of food that you need to function for the day and it may be that some bread and butter with a glass of water would suffice to meet that need. However, you may desire bacon, eggs, hash browns, toast and coffee; that is your want (indeed *desire* may be an effective synonym for *want*). A *want* is a *need* that has had value added to it. Interestingly in the example given the basic need may be far more healthy for you than the want. If you make breakfast for yourself you would be your own customer, but you are on a cruise and as you can eat in your cabin, out on deck or in the restaurant, visit a cafe, diner or hotel for your breakfast, then another *added value* factor will come into play, that of *service*. Somebody else will cook and deliver your breakfast and you will be their customer. The value you place on the breakfast will then be composed of a number of items:

- the quality and quantity of the food itself
- the type of food offered
- the quality of cooking and manner of presentation
- the efficiency and friendliness of the service
- the ambience of the surroundings.

Each of the above will add a certain value to your breakfast and this will probably be reflected in both the price you were asked to pay by the cruise company and the price you were prepared to pay. If you have paid a large sum for your cruise you will expect room service to be free, if you are on a low-cost cruise this may be an added extra. P&O, Celebrity, Cunard, Costa, RCI etc. do not charge for room service for all but the most luxurious of items; Airtours, who charge less for their cruises, do. Of course the customer has paid overall because this will be reflected in the price.

Core and supplementary products

Most people can tell you what their core product is: for General Motors it is cars, for AMTRAK it is a train service, for Shell it is petroleum products, but what adds value are the more intangible supplementary products. Anybody can sail you around the Canaries and North Africa, that is a core product, but the standards of food, entertainment, shore excursions and service are supplementaries. These are vitally important because next to price supplementaries are an important aspect of customer choice. Indeed many products, e.g. airline tickets, cars and holidays, are sold on the supplementaries; the core product is a given. If you buy a car you assume that you will be provided with a defect-free means of transportation; what the advertisers concentrate on are sunroofs, power steering, air bags etc. We can illustrate this diagrammatically in Figure 3.1.

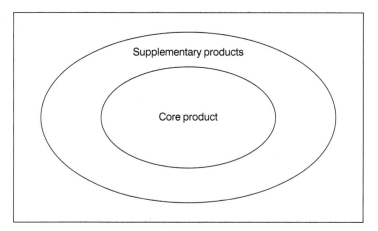

Figure 3.1 Core and supplementary products

If we consider what happens on a cruise (to be considered in detail in Chapter 7), it is clear that there are a large number of supplementary products including:

■ transportation to the vessel
■ pre- and post-cruise hotel stays
■ on-board shopping
■ on-board beauty treatments
■ on-board health/sports facilities
■ shore excursions.

In this section we are going to consider the implications for the overall impression of the first two of these and we shall return to them in detail in a later chapter. Transportation and hotel stays are important because what happens at the beginning and the end of a holiday may well be that which leaves a lasting impression. Our first impressions are psychologically very important because these set the standard against which we judge the rest of the experience. This is known as the 'halo' effect; good first impressions lead to positive feelings and views about what happens subsequently, whereas poor first impressions may lead to a negative attitude about the rest of the cruise. Similarly, even if the cruise has been superb, a bad experience on the way home may lead to a jaundiced view of the total package.

By definition, cruises leave from a port and the advent of fly cruises (as discussed in Chapter 2) has meant that airlines and hotel companies have become partners with the cruise operators.

The distances involved in travelling to the cruise ship can become enormous as shown in Table 3.1.

Table 3.1   Base port distances from London

Cruise base port	Distance from London
Southampton	82 miles (131 km)
Dover	82 miles (131 km)
Miami	4446 miles (7113 km)
San Juan	4800 miles (7680 km)
Acapulco	7100 miles (11 360 km)
Venice	640 miles (1024 km)

In order to ensure that the cruise gets off to a good start, the cruise operators take considerable care in making travel arrangements as smooth as possible. For the UK market, all cruises that involve flying are sold as a package, although the customer is free to make their own arrangements if they wish with a subsequent reduction in price. For the North American market, cruise fares are often quoted without the necessary flights although the companies do have arrangements with the airlines for customer transportation.

Many fly cruises rely on a close relationship with scheduled air carriers to get their customers to the ship. Whilst the cruise operator will want the very best service for their customers, they will be dependent on the service standards of the airline and yet if the customer has a complaint it will be the cruise operator that will stand to lose future business. If, for whatever reason, and especially at the end of the cruise, the air carrier suffers delays or splits up families on the aircraft, customers often believe that this reflects badly on the cruise operator even if they know that the cruise operator has relatively little control over this aspect of the holiday. After all, it is the cruise operator they have booked with and the cruise operator to whom they have paid their money.

Nothing causes greater problems than lost or delayed baggage. Despite anecdotal tales, very little baggage is lost for long. One of the authors of this book made over 160 scheduled and charter flights in an eight-year period and luggage was lost only once and then for only sixteen hours. However, customers have to join a ship that is likely to sail within a few hours of their arrival at the port of departure and if luggage has been delayed it needs to be transported to the next port of call as quickly as possible. Cruises normally involve packing casual, informal and formal clothes, and if the luggage has not arrived by the time of departure there is the danger of being inappropriately dressed for the traditional Captain's welcome cocktail party. Cruise operators make immense efforts to ensure that customers whose baggage has been lost or delayed are inconvenienced as little as possible – crew members even lending garments if required. However, as the BBC television programme *Watchdog* reported in March 1998, disasters can happen. A UK couple on a luxury Mediterranean cruise were left with only the clothes they stood up in and hand baggage for three days after their luggage failed to be transported from the pre-cruise hotel they had booked through the cruise operator. Unfortunately, the dress code on the ship prohibited them appearing in casual clothes after 6 p.m. and they were forced to miss several social events and even had to eat dinner in their cabin. They were offered a reduction on their next cruise but it is doubtful whether they would want to travel again with a company that had treated them so harshly. Cruise companies can and do change the airlines with which they contract if service standards slip below an acceptable minimum.

Where all or a fair percentage of the customers are travelling from a relatively small geographical area, it is possible for the cruise operator to use the services of a chartered aircraft. This has the advantage that the cruise operator has greater control of service levels and baggage can be shipped directly from the aircraft to the ship with less likelihood of delays. The disadvantages centre on the configuration of charter aircraft, with less legroom for passengers. A Boeing 757 in scheduled economy configuration will normally have a seat pitch of 34 inches whereas the charter configuration can have a seat pitch of 30 inches, and 4 inches can make a big difference on a long-haul flight. The differences between the capacity of scheduled and charter configurations can be seen in Table 3.2 and represent typical arrangements.

61

Table 3.2   Configuration of aircraft

Aircraft type	Configuration: scheduled	Configuration: charter
Boeing 737–300	8 Business class + 120 Economy @ 32" – total 128 passengers	149 @ 30"
Boeing 757	195 Economy @ 34"	239 @ 32"
Boeing 767	30 Business class + 184 Economy @ 33"	255–290 (if extra exits fitted) @ 30"

P&O Cruises used Britannia Airlines (part of the Thompson Holiday organization, themselves a new entrant into the cruise market) and the Dutch company Martinair for the 1998 Caribbean programme operated by the *Victoria*, 28 891 GRT. Operated mainly for UK customers each cruise had a charter flight from Manchester and London. With a total passenger capacity of 743 (all berths fully occupied), three Boeing 767s can transport all the passengers to and from the cruise departure and arrivals ports in the Caribbean. The Royal Cruise Lines' *Golden Odyssey* of 1974 was purpose-built for 425 passengers, the capacity of a fully loaded Boeing 747 in order to achieve a synergy between air and cruise operations.

Existing holiday companies like Airtours, who entered the cruise market in 1995, and Thomson are able to use their large fleets of charter configured (mainly Boeing) aircraft to support their cruise holidays. By using embarkation ports that are in areas where they already have an extensive hotel-based holiday operation, these companies are able to offer extensive pre- and post-cruise stays plus the ability to fly from regional rather than hub airports because they are able to mix cruise and non-cruise customers on the same aircraft.

The product life cycle

When thinking about the product, it is important to consider its life cycle and this is done using the concept of the product life cycle, a fairly orthodox marketing idea and the more sophisticated 'dynamic product life progression' of Cartwright and Green (1997).

Products and services go through a life cycle from birth to decline and it is important for you to be aware of this life cycle in order to understand the behaviour of the market.

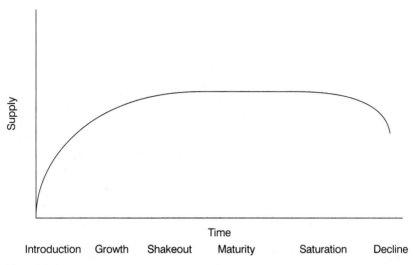

| | | | Time | | |
| Introduction | Growth | Shakeout | Maturity | Saturation | Decline |

Figure 3.2 The product life cycle (simplified)

Life cycles can be short as in the fashion industry or some of the more esoteric products that appear, for example hula hoops or products linked to other products such as Batman accessories, Power Rangers and the vast range of spin-offs from films and television series, or they may be very long – P&O's *Canberra* (1961–97), the Boeing 747 and Kit Kat chocolate bars being good examples.

The classic (and probably too simplistic) view of the product life cycle is shown in Figure 3.2. As we intend to build on this model, we will only give a brief description of each stage.

Introduction

In order to simplify this study, let us assume that there is a new product. At the moment it is not available but the organization believes that it will be successful.

At the point of introduction, they may be the only players in the market although others may be working on a similar product. Even if there are other players, there must be an excess of demand over supply. Airtours entered the UK cruise market in 1995 because there was very little provision for lower-cost cruising in the UK and they perceived a demand; they were right because within two years they had a fleet of three vessels in service. There are considerable advantages in being the first into the market but there are also some disadvantages.

A good example in the context of this book would be the Comet airliner because it was the arrival of the commercial jet transport that destroyed the ocean liner industry and the later huge availability of relatively cheap long-haul flights that has assisted the 1990s boom in cruising. The Comet was the first commercial jet airliner in service and in theory should have given its makers, De Havilland a considerable advantage. It was too small for viable, long-term commercial service and suffered from a hitherto unknown form of metal fatigue, which caused a series of accidents and these dented airline and public confidence. Boeing, who came into the market with the 707 at a later date, were able to learn from the teething problems of the Comet and delivered a product that, in the words of Eddy, Potter and Page (1976), 'could support itself both financially and aerodynamically'. In Boeing's case, being second proved to be an advantage, not a disadvantage. Their great rival, the Douglas Aircraft Corporation (now McDonnell Douglas) had as part of their philosophy a couplet from Pope: 'Never be the first by whom the new is tried, nor the last to cast the old aside' (quoted in Eddy, Potter and Page, 1976)

In the Western world Douglas was third into the market with the DC8 and never caught up with Boeing. Boeing built 917 civil 707s; Douglas only built 556 DC8s. Of the smaller jetliners that followed, the UK built 117 Tridents (introduced in 1962), Boeing a massive 1832 versions of the similar Boeing 727 (introduced in 1963) and Douglas 976 DC9s (introduced in 1965). Boeing seems to have done very well out of being second into the market. Their biggest gamble came with the introduction of the 'jumbo', the Boeing 747 in 1969 where they were the first into the market.

If, at introduction, our company can make sufficient impact, a long-lasting set of advantages can occur. If the product is of high quality then customer loyalty can be enhanced and subsequent purchases will be of the inventor's product. Repeat business is a very important market indicator and organizations need a range of products to offer both existing and new customers. Existing customers can be encouraged to trade up to new replacements. Of equal importance is making the product synonymous with your name. Many Britons 'Hoover' the floor, but the vacuum cleaner they use may have been made by any one of a number of manufacturers; the verb to 'Hoover' has entered the language and provides free advertising and reinforcement for the Hoover company each time it is used.

If you are another new company into the cruise market, e.g. Direct Cruises before they were acquired by Airtours, or Thomson, you will have assessed that there is room for another player within your chosen market segment and that your your particular product can attract sufficient customers to justify your entry into the market. Both assessments were right because even before Direct Cruises' first cruise was scheduled in 1998, they had to acquire a second vessel to fulfil the demand for bookings.

Growth

Our company has been successful and the product is in the marketplace and selling well.

As the success becomes apparent, others will enter the market. If a product or service is very successful it is often the case that demand will be greater than supply and this will allow others to enter the market with similar products, e.g. Airtours in the UK being followed by a cruise programme from Thompson offering a very similar product. Thus as the market grows, the number of supplying organizations increases and those organizations may well increase their capacity. Growth markets are often characterized by a large number of small organizations.

Shakeout

As growth begins to peak, the weaker organizations leave the market. Demand is reaching a plateau and the tendency is for the smaller organizations to merge or be taken over by one of the bigger existing players or a large organization using the shakeout to acquire an entry into, for them, a new market. P&O acquired Princess Cruises (see Chapter 2) at this point in the Princess product life cycle when P&O was having difficulty establishing its own identity in the USA's West Coast cruise market. Smaller organizations are vulnerable at this time to raids by cash rich predators.

New entrants may also discover that the market is not for them and may well sell out, as did Direct Holidays who sold their cruise operation to Airtours in 1998.

Larger organizations, it is claimed, can produce at lower cost and can benefit from economies of scale; what they have to be careful of is that they do not reduce quality and service along with costs. Service is a very important part of the product and there is evidence that customers will pay that little bit more for good service and higher quality, as we shall see when we look at market segmentation.

Maturity

As growth slows, the market becomes more mature and possibly dominated by fewer but larger suppliers. Entry is difficult as the existing suppliers will know the market well and will have developed customer loyalty. It requires true entrepreneurial skills and considerable resources to break into a mature market – Richard Branson and Virgin Atlantic is one of the rare examples, as are Airtours, Thompson and Direct Cruises in the UK cruise industry. Smaller companies that have tried to break into a mature market have found it very difficult, examples being American Family Cruises (1993–94) and Delfin Cruises (1989–90). Airtours and Thompson are part of much larger holiday and financial institutions and thus have the financial backing and customer base to succeed.

As the market place becomes saturated organizations need to be in a position to bring new products, or adaptations of existing products, to the marketplace.

In the car market, there are normally a number of versions of each vehicle introduced over time, with a completely new model being introduced every so often. In the cruise industry there are options of new vessels or new cruising areas, both of which will be considered later. There is also the option of changing the package by moving up market or by adding a new range of extra services. *Grand Princess*, 109 000 GRT was the first ship to offer a wedding chapel, a development of the on-board weddings that could be arranged prior to sailing on the first day of a cruise.

The product life cycle for a series of related products is shown in Figure 3.3.

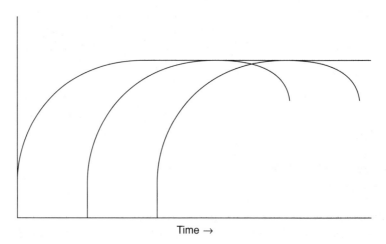

Time →

Figure 3.3 Product succession

Indeed in the cruise industry each new start could be the refit of an existing vessel. The *QE2* launched in 1969 became a 'new' product in 1977, 1982, 1984, 1986 and 1994 following major or minor refits, the aim being to keep the vessel in touch with contemporary thinking.

Another version of the product succession concept relates to the introduction of new vessels, i.e. always being able to give the customer the option of cruising on a relatively recent vessel. If the years from 1985 until 1999 are examined in respect of the Princess operation of P&O and Costa Cruises they demonstrate good examples of this with new vessels, each one introduced being more luxurious (and often bigger) than its predecessor (see Table 3.3).

Table 3.3   Introduction of new products by Princess and Costa

Year	Princess		Costa	
	Vessel	*Tons*	*Vessel*	*Tons*
1984	*Royal Princess*	44 348		
	Sky Princess	46 314		
1989	*Star Princess**	63 564		
1990	*Crown Princess*	70 000	*Costa Marina*	25 441
1991	*Regal Princess*	70 000		
1992			*Costa Allegra*	28 430
1993			*Costa Romantica*	53 049
1995	*Sun Princess*	77 000	*Costa Playa***	12 475
1996			*Costa Victoria*	74 000
1997	*Dawn Princess*	77 000	*Costa Olympia*	78 000
	Grand Princess	109 000		
1999	*Sea Princess*	77 000		

Notes: * to P&O Cruises UK 1997 as *Arcadia*; ** specifically for cruising Cuban/Dominican Republic areas.

To support this Princess also introduced a new concept, 'Grand Class Cruising' to take advantage of the facilities offered by the new vessels.

Without a succession of new products, customer loyalty can disappear very quickly because looking after the customer means anticipating their future needs as well as looking after their current ones.

Saturation and decline

When the market is saturated, supply exceeds demand, possibly because of changing tastes. As demand drops, so profits shrink and competition becomes even fiercer. As decline sets in, players leave the market or are forced out, or old products are removed from the product portfolio. If you are buying a car and you do not want the latest model, this can be a good time to buy as the manufacturers will cut prices to clear old stocks and free up production facilities. Prices on older ships may be discounted to encourage customers who may well otherwise want to travel on the latest product, which may be producing an imbalance of demand.

For a cruise liner the product life cycle is measured in years or even decades. The latest-fashion product life cycle may be measured in weeks but you need to know that it exists and that just because a product or service is in demand today does not mean that it will be required next year or even next week.

One of the most dramatic illustrations of the product life cycle is the facsimile machine (the fax). Virtually unknown at the beginning of the 1980s, there was hardly an office in the world that did not have fax facilities by the 1990s. Indeed, the market for straightforward commercial fax machines was probably saturated by 1995 but, as will be shown in the next section, clever marketing has produced a rejuvenation.

Although the cruise market has boomed in the 1990s, the market became saturated in the 1970s with famous companies such as Holland America laying up ships due to an excess of supply over demand in 1973. Happily the market picked up and the ships were returned to service.

Dynamic product life progression

Most models of the product life cycle lead from saturation into decline but in the following pages we want to present you with an alternative, and probably more realistic, model called the *dynamic product life progression*. Dynamic was developed by Cartwright and Green (1997) to provide for a series of alternatives and *progression* because there is life after apparent decline for many products.

This concept is slightly more complex than the simple product life cycle model and a slightly different graph with two decision points is used (see Figure 3.4).

When a product or service first enters the market, there always seem to be some people who must have the latest. Thus whilst initial take-up figures may

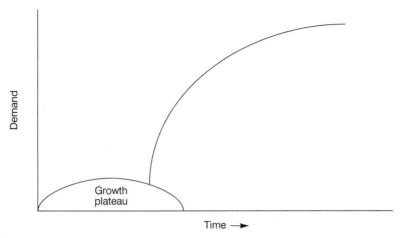

Figure 3.4 Dynamic product life progression – growth phase
Source: Taken from Cartwright and Green (1997) with permission.

be very encouraging, they may not point to a continuation of success. Demand may plateau whilst the bulk of the potential customer population makes up its mind. Some of the more esoteric products of the technological age (electric bicycles, the electric mini-mini car etc.) seem never to pass this point. If the product is acceptable to the mass of potential buyers, the growth phase is resumed, if not then the product will go into decline. The critical success factor for any new product or service is whether demand picks up after a short time at the growth plateau. A new ship or a new cruising area may show considerable initial promise but does not then fulfil that promise. American Family Cruises launched in 1993 with plans for the *American Pioneer* (ex *Costa Riviera*, 31 500 tons) and the *American Adventure* (ex *Eugenio Costa*, 30 567 tons) but lasted just over a year despite a product that offered much to the average US family. The *Eugenio Costa* was acquired by the new UK subsidiary of Direct Holidays, Direct Cruises, and renamed *Edinburgh Castle* to be home ported in north-west England and Scotland. As we have seen, this was a troubled acquisition and Direct Holidays sold the cruise operation to Airtours in 1998.

The next adaptation to the simple product life cycle model *can* occur at the shakeout phase. It is possible that one supplier or product gains such ascendancy as to *blastout* its competitors. Examples of this have happened in the videocassette market, VHS blasting out Betamax, Windows computer operating system gaining the major market share and, in the UK satellite television market, the dominance of BSkyB. In the cruise industry of the 1990s there are only a small number of major players who own many of the

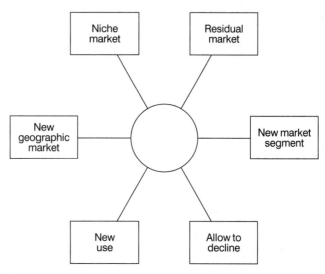

Figure 3.5 Dynamic product life progression – decline and alternatives
Source: Taken from Cartwright and Green (1997) with permission.

cruise companies. The *Berlitz Guide to Cruising and Cruise Ships* for 1997 (Ward, 1997) lists 213 vessels of between 2000 and 104 000 tons in service during that year or building and due to debut by the end of 1999, with a combined tonnage of 6 526 000 tons. Of this tonnage, 75 per cent was controlled by Carnival, RCI, P&O and NCL.

The final adaptation to the classic model occurs towards the end of saturation and the beginning of decline. As we shall see from the examples, not all fail.

There are six possibilities (Figure 3.5) and it is possible that decline *per se* can be avoided and a product or service can be rejuvenated.

Residual markets

In the 1960s, the British Leyland Mini was a revolutionary small car that carried with it considerable customer loyalty. Many UK citizens had a Mini as their first car. Its replacement, the Metro (later renamed Rover 100) was intended to serve the whole of the Mini market. There was, however, enough of a residual market for the Mini to justify Rover restarting the production line, albeit with reduced capacity and fewer models. Therefore, in the early 1990s both the Mini and the Rover 100 were available, catering for similar but slightly differing markets. Enough people wanted to buy the Mini to make it profitable for production to continue even after the Rover 100 was discontinued. Very few cruising markets have reached this stage in decline but even if the Western Mediterranean became so passé that it was no longer attracting vast numbers, there would probably still be enough of a residual market for at least one company to station a ship there.

Niche markets

Niche markets are small and specialized. The niche cruising market forms the subject of Chapter 8 of this book. Niche markets develop either by being set up especially to cater for that market or by a larger company selling off part of its product/service portfolio. Because niche markets are small, they often do not have the economies of scale that larger organizations require and may not fit into corporate plans. Selling an apparent loss-making product to somebody who is prepared to put in the hard work that a niche market requires can be a better alternative than the product leaving the market altogether.

World cruises are a niche market with the two major players being P&O and Cunard. Expedition cruises form another niche market where customers are prepared to pay for the privilege of travelling on smaller vessels to more inaccessible areas.

The MV *Americana* is one of the few freighters offering cruise accommodation, 108 passengers on a 19 000 ton hull and offers one- to two-month South American cruises for those with the time to spare.

Luxury cruises such as that offered by Silversea, Seabourne etc. also form a separate section of the market (covered in Chapter 4).

New geographic markets

The cruise companies have become adept at opening up new geographic markets and there is hardly a coast in the world that does not feature in the cruise brochures. As experienced customers search for somewhere new to go, the companies respond. In the 1960s, UK cruise companies, P&O, Shaw Saville and Albion, Royal Mail, Union Castle and Cunard concentrated on the Atlantic Islands and the Western Mediterranean. Then the Norwegian and Baltic areas were opened up, followed by the Caribbean as air travel became more freely available. Airtours started operating in the Eastern and Western Mediterranean with occasional cruises to the Caribbean; within two years the Caribbean was a regular feature.

A variation of the geographic market theme is where a cruise company seeks customers from a new geographic area, often by acquisitions; P&O

broke into the US market by its acquisition of Princess in 1974 – something we shall consider later in this chapter. (The geography of cruising is the subject of Chapter 5.)

New market segments

Earlier in this chapter we considered the facsimile machine and the fact that the commercial market was becoming saturated. The manufacturers and the telephone companies started marketing the fax machine as a domestic product in the middle of the 1990s. Thus demand has been re-stimulated. The television market was originally a one per household but now smaller models are available for the bedrooms, kitchen and even for boats! Homes used to have one telephone, now many have two or three, all stimulating demand and widening the market into a new segment.

When cruising first became popular in the years between the wars it was an older, upper/upper-middle class holiday. Now the market segment has expanded to include all kinds of people, cruises are affordable for more people, there are ships designed for families, and the age profile is dropping. What was a once in a lifetime experience is now a once a year experience for many.

New use

Products that were used for baking are now used for cleaning refrigerators! One way of stimulating demand for a declining product is to find a new use for it. Redundant British buses, no longer suitable for the rigours of the rush hour appear as sightseeing vehicles on the streets of New York. The early post-Second World War generation of cruise ships were ocean liners displaced by the commercial jet transport. Car ferries have been converted for cruise use. MV *Calypso* of Transocean Tours (8000 GRT) and *The Azur* (14 717 GRT) of Festival Cruises are examples, as is one of the most highly rated cruise ships in the world, the five-star (Berlitz rating to be considered later) *Hebridean Princess* (ex *Columba*, 2112 GRT) – a floating country house that takes fifty-five passengers around the Scottish Isles in considerable luxury.

Whilst no one has yet converted a warship to a cruise liner, although the sunning space on an obsolete aircraft carrier would be superb, there have been conversions of cargo and container vessels to quite sumptuous cruise liners. The *Costa Marina* (25 441 GRT) was once the container ship *Axel Johnson* and Leisure Cruises' MV *Switzerland* (ex *Daphne*, 9436 GRT) was once the cargo liner *Port Sydney*.

New entrants often acquire older tonnage to start their operations. Airtours started their operations in 1995 with the *Seawing* (ex *Southward* of NCL, 16 607 GRT) launched in 1971 and the *Carousel* (ex RCI's *Nordic Prince*, 23 200 GRT) also of 1971. Direct Cruises' first ship for the 1998 season, the *Edinburgh Castle* (32 753 GRT), was the veteran *Eugenio Costa* of 1966 but still in good condition.

Allow to decline

Some products and services have, of course, outlived their usefulness. New developments and customer expectations have changed the market. In these cases, a swift end is better than a long drawn out one; you do not want a declining product affecting your company's image. Older ships that cannot compete are sold for scrap and it was with much emotion that the famous P&O liner *Canberra* entered Southampton for the last time in September 1997, being later sailed to a scrap yard in Pakistan.

Branding

Branding, the name given to a product or group of products, is important because the brand serves as an identifier to particular groups of customers. When Carnival acquired HAL in 1988, they still kept the HAL identity and ship names. Carnival had gained a reputation for a fun-filled, family atmosphere on its ships; HAL catered for an older market. By keeping the HAL identity, Carnival was able to tap into a different market segment. Similarly P&O were not well known in the US prior to their acquisition of Princess in 1974; by keeping the Princess name they were able to expand into the fastest growing cruise market of all, a point we shall consider when we look at competition later in this chapter.

Brand names are very important as they often carry with them considerable customer loyalty perceptions. Even when a cruise company acquires another company, they will often keep the name and ambience of the acquired company in order to retain the company base. Thus the HAL, Seabourne, Cunard and Costa brands have been retained by Carnival, the Princess brand by P&O, the Celebrity brand by RCI and the Orient Lines brand by NCL. As has been shown in Chapter 2, acquisition has been a major method of growth for the major players in the cruise industry in recent years.

Even the name chosen for the product, be it the company or its ships, can carry important covert messages. Look at the list in Table 3.4 and consider how they put across messages of fun, quality, romance, tradition or exotic locations and wide oceans.

Table 3.4 Branding – ship names

Company name	Examples of ship names
P&O Cruises	*Oriana*; *Victoria*
Princess Cruises	*Grand Princess*; *Sun Princess*; *Regal Princess*
Carnival Cruises	*Sensation*; *Tropicale*; *Ecstasy*; *Holiday*
Royal Caribbean Cruises	*Majesty of the Seas*; *Rhapsody of the Seas*; *Splendour of the Seas*
Celebrity Cruises	*Galaxy*; *Horizon*
Airtours	*Seadream*; *Carousel*
Costa	*Costa Romantica*; *Costa Classica*

Another part of branding is making your product easily identifiable; shipowners have been doing that since the dawn of steam navigation through the colours painted on their funnels; cruise ship owners have carried on and refined the tradition.

The latest Carnival ships have distinctive red-winged funnels unlike any others afloat; Celebrity use the Chandris house flag cross as a bold display on their funnels coupled to a distinctive black and white hull. A red hull is distinctive of the Premier Cruise Line, and the famous 'Viking Lounge' situated part way up the funnel gives RCI ships a distinctive look as does the imposing 'rising sun' motif on the bow of every P&O Group cruise liner. These distinctive features form part of the brand image, a vital marketing tool. Cruise passengers see an unobstructed exterior view of their ship on only a few occasions. At major cruise terminals the view will be obstructed by buildings and cranes, but when tendering ashore dramatic views of the ship can be obtained. It is not only important that the customers feel they are part of that image but that they can also imagine how envious those who are holidaying ashore must feel of them. Every time a cruise ship anchors off a holiday resort it is a floating advertisement for the company. It is hard to sit on a beach at Playa del Rocha on the Algarve when the *Oriana* is anchored off shore and not wish you were sailing with her when, as dusk falls her lights come on, a spotlight illuminates her funnel and she slips gracefully away to the distant sound of gentle music. An extract from a P&O advertisement, no, but it could be because that is the image the companies wish to promote.

The product matrix

In the 1960s the Boston Consulting Group developed a model for examining the portfolio of products for a company. This model, known as the Boston Matrix, looks at the position of products against the two factors of *market share* and *market growth* (see Figure 3.6).

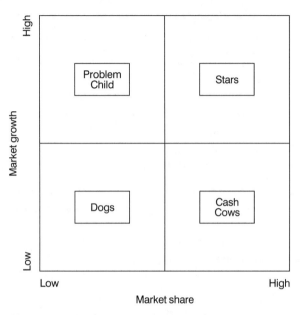

Figure 3.6 The Boston Matrix

To illustrate the matrix, let us imagine that a cruise company has just introduced a brand new ship. To be successful that ship will need to capture a certain percentage of market share, either by attracting customers from rival companies or new customers to the cruise market. Typically a vessel for the US market needs to attract 2 per cent of the share whilst one for the UK market needs a massive 10 per cent share for success (*Source*: *Oriana, From Dream to Reality*, a P&O video). Until bookings start, the vessel will have no market share at all. Assuming that the company has done its homework, they will be launching the vessel into a high-growth market. If growth is slow, then the introduction of a new vessel needs to coincide with the removal of an old one. That the UK market was expanding in the late 1990s was shown when P&O Cruises, who had been operating for many years with the *Victoria* (ex *Sea Princess*, 28 891 GRT) and the *Canberra* (44 807 GRT), introduced the

Oriana (69 153 GRT) in 1995 without withdrawing either the *Victoria* or the *Canberra*. When the *Canberra* left service at the end of the 1997 summer season, she was replaced with the *Arcadia* (63 564 GRT) which had been the *Star Princess* with P&O's US-based Princess operation. Thus P&O had increased their UK capacity by almost double as shown in Table 3.5.

Thus the introduction of the Oriana, increased P&O's capacity by 82 per cent in 1995 and the high bookings experienced must have been a major reason to shift to a three-ship operation. In 1998, P&O as will be shown in Chapter 7, ordered another *Oriana*-type vessel, the *Aurora*.

A new ship, a new company or a new cruising area may indeed be operating in an expanding market but on introduction the market share will be low. The combination of a low market share in a high-growth regime is known as a *problem child*: a problem because there are start-up costs to recruit, new customers to attract, perhaps large numbers of staff to train and an infrastructure to build; a child because with proper nurturing children grow to become adults earning their way in the world.

Even the best designed new ship or operation can have problems. Cunard refused delivery of the *QE2* in 1968, cancelling an advertised Christmas cruise, because the ship was not ready and the company did not take delivery until April 1969. A similar problem occurred in December 1994 when the ship was returned from Blohm and Voss in Hamburg in an unfinished state after a refit. This time passengers were embarked and the ship docked in New York amid much bad press comment and threats of legal action from passengers. The initial cruise of the first Carnival line vessel, the *Mardi Gras* in 1972 (ex *Empress of Canada*, 27 250 GRT) was marred by the ship running

Table 3.5   P&O capacity, 1994–8

Year	Ship	Berths	Total berths
1994	*Canberra*	1641	
	Victoria	743	2384
1995	*Canberra*	1641	
	Victoria	743	
	Oriana	1975	4359
1998	*Victoria*	743	
	Oriana	1975	
	Arcadia	1620	4338

aground. However, Ted Arison who had founded the company was not deterred and, with its new tonnage and acquisition of other companies such as HAL and Cunard, Carnival had 28 per cent of the world's cruise tonnage by 1999.

Some companies never make it past the problem child state; the initial start-up costs for a ship are high and if it is to progress beyond the growth plateau of the dynamic life progression model shown earlier there needs to be constant demand. American Family Cruises, Direct Cruises and Delfin Cruises had very short lives indeed.

In the early 1990s there were few cruises that featured the Amazon. By 1997 a number of operators were offering this as part of their programmes; the demand was there and the early trailblazers especially Princess Cruises had proved it could be done.

However, if the company or the ship or indeed the cruising area progresses past the point of low market share and begins to pick up new and repeat business at profitable load factors, there is the possibility of becoming a *star*. A star exists when the company, ship etc. has a high market share of a growing market, i.e. the best of both worlds.

In the UK market, ease of air transportation lifted the Caribbean cruising area into a star category during the later 1990s. Airtours tapped into the market, P&O Cruises stationed the *Victoria* there for substantial periods and Princess gained enough UK passengers for the *Dawn Princess*'s (77 000 GRT) one- to two-week cruises out of San Juan to justify a charter aircraft operation.

What will be the cruising stars of the early part of the twenty-first century? Bigger mega-ships of up to 200 000 tons and new cruising areas spring to mind. The Indian Ocean, Indo-China and even the Polar regions may see the next big expansion in cruising. We shall consider the implications of such expansion on the local environment in a later chapter.

Nothing can remain a star forever but provided that market share can be held, profits can still be maintained even when growth rates slow down. The whole operation is 'debugged' to become routine and then becomes a *cash cow*. It is cash cows that generate profits for shareholders and future expansion. The main cash cow for the US market is the Caribbean; for the UK it is the Western Mediterranean. Slightly older ships, whose teething problems have been ironed out, follow a series of itineraries that have proved to be successful. This is where the bulk of the mainstream market operates. Direct Cruises' one 1998 cruise to Greenland attracted those curious about a new area but the rest of the programme was traditional UK cruising to the Atlantic Islands or the Western Mediterranean. Cash cows will always represent the bulk of a mainstream cruise operator's programme.

Everything comes to an end and ships have a finite life. Sooner or later demand to travel on them declines. Some go for scrap, e.g. *Canberra* in 1997, others become somebody else's star and cash cow. Carnival Cruises started with redundant Canadian Pacific tonnage whilst Airtours purchased ships that no longer fitted into RCI's and NCL's operations and became very successful; one company's dog can, with a refit, become a new company's star.

Segmentation

Segmentation refers to those parts of the market at which a particular product is aimed. Within the cruising market there are a number of segments with products aimed at one or more of them. The main market segments will be covered in the next chapter but it is important to understand that within a market there are a number of segments and that much corporate strategy is concerned with ensuring that a company is in the correct segments of the market.

Examples of market segments within the cruise industry include:

> *Nationality*, the major market segments being:
> US/Canada – Princess, RCCL, NCL, HAL, Costa, Carnival, Celebrity
> UK – P&O Cruises, Direct Cruises, Airtours, Fred Olsen
> Japan – Mitsui OK, NYK
> Germany –Neckermann Seereisen, Hapag-Lloyd
> Italy – Starlauro, Costa
> *Customer profile*:
> Families – Disney, Carnival, Airtours
> Older and retired people – HAL, some Princess ships
> *Type of cruise*:
> Mainstream – Princess, RCCL, NCL, P&O, Cunard etc.
> Expedition – Noble Caledonia, Abercrombie and Kent
> Theme – Swan Hellenic (P&O)
> Private yacht – Hebridean Island Cruises, Seabourne

It is worth noting that companies such as Carnival, through their acquisition and tie-ups with HAL, Seabourne, Cunard, Costa and Airtours, are able to position themselves within a number of segments simultaneously – a concept that we shall be looking at in more detail later.

One of the extras added to the 4Ps (see earlier in this chapter) was *physical appearance*. In the case of a cruise ship this is very much part of the product. When Kotler (1980) introduced the term 'customer value' to replace 'product', he was reflecting that it is the total experience that the customer buys, and this has never been better shown than in the cruise industry. It is the combination of ship, destination, cuisine; entertainment etc. that makes the total package and that is what the customer puts a value on.

Price/cost

Price is a major determinant for the customer booking a cruise, even the cheapest seven-day cruise from UK will be dearer than many package holidays. Fuller details of prices, including the extras that customers may need to pay, will be covered in the next chapter but, as price/cost is such an important part of the marketing mix, an introduction to this aspect of the cruise industry is given here. For the cruise company there is a continuum of pricing. This continuum, which is a well known in marketing, ranges from *high volume/low margin* to *low volume/high margin*. It is common sense really; if you only sell a few units of your product, be it clothes, cars or cruises, you need to make as much as possible whereas if you sell large volumes you can afford to make a much smaller margin on each one. If you want to make £100 000 profit, you can either sell 1000 units with a margin of £100 each or 100 with a margin of £1000 each. Luckily one of the things people are prepared to pay for is exclusivity and space, and thus customers will pay more for a cruise on a 20 000 GRT ship carrying 600 passengers than one carrying 1000 passengers. That these differences exist is shown by Table 3.6 which is based on total

Table 3.6 Passenger space ratios for similar sized ships

Ship	Tonnage	Passengers		
		Full	2 per cabin	PSR
Carousel	23 200	1200	1062	20.50
Albatross	24 803	1100	940	24.40
Ocean Breeze	21 486	946	782	25.00
Marco Polo	20 502	915	848	23.25
Enchanted Isle	23 395	729	729	32.00
Pacific Princess	20 636	717	610	31.25
Astor	20 158	650	590	32.50

passenger capacities and those relating to only two persons per cabin (the norm on most vessels) of a series of vessels. The final figure is the all important average passenger space ratio (PSR) i.e. the space ratio for full capacity + that for 2 per cabin divided by 2.

What does this mean? Simply the higher the PSR the dearer the cruise because a supplementary product will be space and exclusivity. The private yacht type vessels, even those that are quite large, have very generous PSRs viz:

Hebridean Princess: 41.2
Seabourne Legend: 47.0
Sea Goddess 1: 36.7

Differentiation is the name given to this market positioning, normally in terms of the product that is offered and the price paid for it. It is not just a question of cost for the customer but one of value for money, and they are not the same thing. Whilst most customers do not want to pay a penny more than they have to, not only will they have a bottom line in monetary terms, they will also have one in terms of the quality they expect. Cartwright et al. (1996) produced the following model of excellence and quality for a series of case studies looking at, amongst others the Princess Cruise operation, and this work has been adapted for this volume as shown below.

Quality and value for money

A Rolls-Royce is possibly the best car in the world and in pure terms it is truly excellent. The most highly rated cruise ships in 1998 were Cunard's *Sea Goddess 1* and *Sea Goddess 2* (both 4260 GRT and carrying 115 cruisers) (Ward, 1998). However, how many people can actually own a Rolls-Royce? Even if the ships were full to capacity for fifty-two weeks of the year only a small minority of cruisers in the total market would be able to enjoy the experience, and no ship will be in operation for 365/6 days without time out for maintenance. Rolls-Royce and the Sea Goddess product are undeniably excellent. They are probably the best in the world but, for most of us, excellence is connected with things that we can actually do or experience.

Marks and Spencer and Tesco in the UK and Macy's in the USA may not be in the same league as very expensive stores but they offer an excellent service to a large number of customers. Ford Motors may not be perceived as in the same class as Rolls-Royce but they provide good, reliable transport for millions of people across the world. British Airways

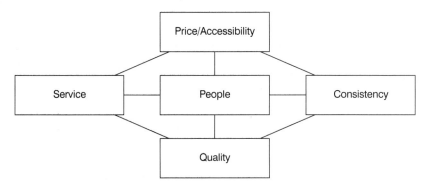

Figure 3.7 The excellence equilibrium
Source: Cartwright et al. (1998) reprinted with permission.

operate the largest route network in the world and at prices a large number of people can afford, and they do it to a consistently high level of service. Princess Cruises, Carnival, NCL etc. can carry vastly more cruisers in a year. To do that with a consistently high service and at prices that are described as moderate in the Berlitz guide is, for most people, a truer example of excellence.

Excellence as we would want to present it in this book is a balance between the best service or product for the price with the highest quality, delivered to a consistently high level. All this is done through people. Excellence is the equilibrium between the various components (Figure 3.7). If a conscious decision has been made to go for a small 'niche' market, then one cannot compare the products or services developed for this market with those that are aimed at a wider market. When considering excellence it is important that like is compared with like.

Service

Service is about staff taking responsibility and 'going the extra mile' for their customers. Customers make mistakes but the essence of good service is when staff take responsibility for the problem. We all have a fair idea of what is acceptable, excellence is when somebody does more than the customer might have expected. If the customer is angry or upset, staff may not receive any thanks but they and, more importantly, the customer, will know that they did all that they possibly could. Smiles and courtesy go a long way and the cruise companies pride themselves on this aspect of their operations.

Consistency

Everybody is entitled to consistency of service or product for the price they have paid. The days of two-class cruise ships are long gone. Whether the customer is in a 4-berth inside cabin or a luxury suite, as far as service and entertainment goes there must be an acceptable consistent minimum given to all. The suite may have enhanced service but all cruisers have the run of the public facilities of the ship and should not be treated differently based on their cabin grade and thus price paid.

Quality

Quality is never delivering second best. Whilst quality will vary according to cruise operators and prices charged, there will be an acceptable minimum below which the operation will start to lose customers. As we shall see later, the ratings customers provide at the end of their cruise are taken very seriously and people's jobs depend on high ratings.

Price/accessibility

Accessibility is linked to price. As we have stated, like must be compared with like. A lower priced product or service is likely to be more accessible. As mentioned earlier organizations often have two choices: low volume/high margin (Seabourne) or high volume/low margin (Airtours); each caters for very different markets and both may be considered excellent in their own way.

If there is an overriding factor, it is quality and as disposable incomes increase, so does the demand for quality.

However, quality is not solely about products or people, as Wille (1992) has pointed out:

> The total quality approach is about people and attitudes. It's not about techniques and procedures as such. It includes them, and it needs them. However, it's the people who actually use them, inspired with a simple idea that the purpose of work is to provide customers with something that will delight them and make them want to keep paying your salary, by buying the product or service that you provide.

Wille's book is worth reading in its entirety in order to understand how the concepts of quality have been brought about and to gain an insight into the thinking of the 'quality' gurus; Deming, Juran, Crosby etc.

The next chapter will look at price in some detail together with the difference between basic price and actual costs to the customer after additional travel, excursions, tips etc. have been taken into consideration.

Promotion/communications

It is no use having a good product at an acceptable price, if you don't let your potential customers know what is on offer. Whilst this aspect was originally known as *promotion, communication* is perhaps a better term, especially as some of the best advertising for cruise companies is done by satisfied customers telling their friends.

All promotional activities revolve around the acronym AIDA:

- Attention
- Interest
- Desire
- Action

Whilst as with any model the boundaries between these four are not discrete, it is possible to use the acronym to show how cruises are promoted.

Repeat business is always important because, if the previous experience was a good one, the first two, Attention and Interest, will be there together with, in all probability, the third, Desire. All that remains is for the customer to choose their ship, the cruising area and make a booking.

Attention

The mechanisms for letting potential and repeat customers know what is on offer in order to gain their attention are varied, major channels of communications used are:

1 *Newspaper/magazine advertisements.* In the UK, these are often within the colour magazines and travel sections of the weekend papers. As with all newspaper advertising it is carefully targeted, the more expensive cruises being advertised in the broadsheets with the cheaper end of the market appearing in the tabloids. Advertisements typically feature the romantic, exotic aspects of cruising.

2 *Television advertising.* A well-made television commercial can capture the magic of a cruise and has been used to great advantage by a number of companies. Increasing use is being made of television text services.

In March 1998, on page 228 of the UK Teletext service, the specialist cruising page had no less than seventy-five screens offering nearly 150 cruises. It may be that the potential customer will not scan these pages until interest has been generated by another means, thus showing how these models do not have discrete pigeon holing of their components. As mentioned earlier, in 1998 Celebrity Cruises had the ultimate in television coverage, a series of BBC documentaries about the MV *Galaxy* and her crew.

3 *Travel agents*. Not only do travel agents stock the cruise company brochures and advertise special offers; they may well carry posters. After the introduction of the *Oriana* in 1995, nearly every UK travel agent's window had a large cut-away poster of 'Britain's Newest Superliner'.

4 *Specialist cruise agents*. Some travel agents specialize in cruises and can offer very attractive discounts, as will be shown in the next chapter. They will mail their regular customers with offers. For example in March 1998, the Bolsover Cruise Club in Derbyshire (UK) were offering their cruise club members (those who had used them on a previous occasion) 47.5 per cent savings off the brochure price of a particular Cunard *Royal Viking Sun* cruise.

5 *Advertising hoardings*. Well-placed advertisements featuring the romance of cruising appear in major population centres where the bright colours often enliven a drab day.

All the above are designed to draw attention to cruising as a holiday and the companies hope that they will lead to the next step – interest/desire.

Interest/desire

Once attention has been gained, the next step for the company is to generate interest. Interest and attention are not one and the same. Attention is more passive, interest moves towards taking some form of action through the promotion of desire.

Brochures

The major format for interest and desire is the brochure. The cruise companies put a great deal of effort into their brochures, which are multicoloured and of high quality, although some are still very difficult to navigate. RCCL's 1998 UK brochure being an example whereby a great deal of information was presented in a form that was difficult to follow. Direct Cruises first brochure for the inaugural 1998 season was very easy to follow but made a graphic design error in placing the Red Ensign at the wrong end of the Edinburgh Castle – hardly confidence inspiring.

Most brochures follow a similar format in that they provide information on:

- what cruising is about
- the vessels operated
- the itineraries offered
- accommodation
- entertainment
- cuisine
- ports of call
- prices
- pre- and post-cruise hotel deals
- contractual conditions.

All of this information is normally presented in a glossy format designed to produce desire from interest.

Internet

Nearly all the major cruise companies and many travel agents now have World Wide Web 'home pages' which give details of products. These pages have become very sophisticated and potential customers with Internet access can derive a considerable amount of information from them. Searching for 'cruise holiday' in March 1999 produced 15 524 separate references.

On board

Given the importance of repeat business, it is not surprising that the companies keep a good stock of promotional materials on board their vessels; when better to sell somebody their next cruise than when they are enjoying the current one. A 1998 P&O Cruises advertisement featured a couple on board one of the company's vessels with the caption: 'It took us 10 years to book our first cruise and less than 10 days to book the second.'

The latest trend is to use computer technology to allow the customer to have a virtual reality tour of the organization's vessels and destinations.

Action

The final phase of the AIDA process is for the customer to make their booking, part of which we shall consider in the next section. It is no use having excellent promotional materials unless the product and price are such that the potential customer is prepared to part with money!

Place/convenience

Under the 4Ps model, *place* should be obvious, it is the cruise ship, but when one considers *convenience*, then complexities arrive. As seen earlier, prior to the arrival of affordable commercial air transport, cruisers in the UK were limited to leaving from Southampton, Tilbury and Liverpool. Now with the ease of transportation those who are willing to fly can choose from a vast number of departure points. RCI's 1998 brochure offers cruises departing from the following ports: Barcelona, Southampton, Harwich, Boston (MA) San Juan, Acapulco, Miami, Ensenada, Honolulu, Vancouver, San Diego, New York, Port Canaveral, Singapore, Hong Kong and Xingang. Distance from the required cruising area is no longer a problem.

One of the extra Ps is *process* and never has it been easier to book a cruise. Many customers may actually visit a travel agent; others can write or more often telephone the cruise company or an agent and make their booking. The easier the booking process, the more likelihood there is of desire being turned into action.

Later in this book there will be a consideration of another aspect of place – the linking of cruises to other forms of holiday thus widening the market.

Unique selling point

What every company wants, and cruise companies are no exception, is a unique selling point (USP) – that factor that sets it apart from its competitors. Examples of cruise companies' USPs are shown in Table 3.7.

Unique selling points may be more in the promotion than in reality but each company tries to make its product different to that of its direct competitors, which leads naturally to the next section of this chapter – competition.

Competition

Especially within the mainstream cruising sector, the industry is very competitive and provides a very clear illustration of the classic competition

Table 3.7 Unique selling points

Company	USP
Cunard	*QE2* name
Disney Cruise Line	Link with Disney
Direct Cruises (Airtours)	Sailings from NW England and Scotland, direct booking
RCI	Pre-paid 'Wine and Dine' programme
Airtours and Thompson	Value for money, links to other packages
P&O Cruises	Tradition and world cruises
Princess Cruises	*The Love Boat* connection

model of Michael Porter (1980; 1985) with additions by Cartwright and Green (1997) (see Figure 3.8).

Competition between existing suppliers

As would be expected, the greatest competition comes between the current players in a particular market. Even where prices are very much the same there is competition on levels of service, supplementary products and geographic provision. It is important, however, that even well-established organizations keep a careful eye on the various other options or threats that may occur from their traditional competitors as well as considering what the established competition may do to enhance their market share.

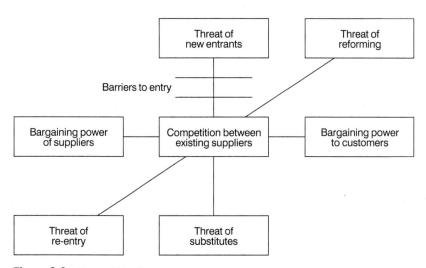

Figure 3.8 Competitive forces
Source: Adapted from M. E. Porter by Cartwright and Green (1997).

New entrants

The provision of some products and services has very high barriers to entry and this may make new entrants very few and far between. You need considerable cash resources to set up a transatlantic airline as Richard Branson has done with Virgin, and even if those barriers can be overcome you still have to establish your credibility in the workplace and may face intense pressure from existing suppliers. It is interesting that the recent new entrants to the UK cruise market, Airtours, Thompson and Direct Cruises, are practising vertical integration in that they were already established holiday suppliers and saw adding cruises to their portfolios as a natural progression. One travel agent actually described the Thompson and Airtours product to us as floating package holidays. They came into the market by using surplus, in some cases fairly old, tonnage; Direct Cruises' *Edinburgh Castle* had sailed since 1966 as the *Eugenio Costa*. Disney, on the other hand, another established holiday player, decided to build new tonnage, the 85 000 GRT ton *Disney Magic* making her debut in 1998, with her sister ship *Disney Wonder* due to enter the market later.

Reforming

This is an addition to the Porter model by Cartwright and Green (1997). If the organization is big enough and rich enough, it can enter a new market by buying an existing player. Whilst this strategy may seem attractive, the buying organization may not have the expertise, culture and knowledge to operate successfully in that particular market environment. Peters and Waterman, in their book *In Search of Excellence* (1982) talk about successful companies 'sticking to the knitting', i.e. staying close to what they do well. In the 1920s, automobile makers like Ford believed that it would be relatively easy for them to enter the aircraft making business. It wasn't. Ford only made one product, the Ford Trimotor, and then left the market to those who understood it; the skills required for plane making were, in fact, very different to those needed for the automobile industry.

P&O used reforming to re-enter the US cruise market by buying Princess Cruises in 1974 and thus acquired an existing infrastructure and vessels together with the reputation of the Princess operation. The initial P&O operation for the US market offered Mexican Cruises on the 17 370 GRT *Spirit of London* but it was not a success, the ship being renamed *Sun Princess* in 1974 after P&O acquired a 'US name', Princess Cruises.

Re-entry

Another Cartwright and Green (1997) addition to the Porter model. Organizations that were in the market and have left it but still possess expertise and a 'memory' by customers may pose a threat of re-entry. As demand ebbs and flows, British Airways re-enters markets; Virgin, having sold its original business, a record label, was talking in 1995 about a possible re-entry.

Re-entry is more likely where there are fewer problems about buying expensive plant or where the organization can use its cash resources to buy out one of the remaining suppliers or, as in the case of an airline, it already possesses all the necessary hardware. Union Castle (a very old name associated with the early days of the UK market, re-entered in 1999 by chartering P&O's *Victoria* for a millennium cruise, replacing the art work with stored Union Castle archives and even repainting the funnel.

Companies can also re-enter by re-branding themselves; Chandris by re-branding some of its products under the Celebrity brand was able to tap the Premium sector of the market (see next chapter).

Substitutes

After the Second World War, there was intense competition between the various US railroads operating transcontinental services just as the shipping companies introduced new and more luxurious tonnage on the lucrative North Atlantic routes between Northern Europe and the Mediterranean and the eastern seaboard of the USA. The UK, USA, The Netherlands, France, the Scandinavian countries and Italy introduced considerable new tonnage, and competition between Cunard, United States Lines, French Line, Holland America, Norwegian America and the Italian Line was intense. Yet when Boeing introduced the 707 jet airliner into commercial service with Pan Am on 26 October 1958, the writing was on the wall for the shipping companies. Whilst the British-built Comet introduced in 1952 was the world's first commercial jet aircraft, the 707 was the first successful model, carrying over 150 passengers compared with the Comet's initial forty-four (later stretched to ninety-four) in the Comet 4B. Cunard and the other shipping companies were no longer in the shipping business and the US railroads were no longer in the railroad business; they were in the mass transportation over a long distance business and the new jet airliners could do the job much faster. A classic example of substitution.

The shipping companies looked for new markets within the cruising market but ships designed for the 'liner' trade were not really suitable for the holiday market and many of the companies collapsed and their vessels were laid up, as was shown earlier. The railroads could not compete at all and eventually, in 1971, all long-distance passenger trains in the USA came under the AMTRAK banner and the route network was cut severely.

However, life appears to go around in circles and the railways in both Europe and the USA are now challenging the airlines. The flight from London (Heathrow) to Paris (Charles de Gaulle) takes a mere thirty-five minutes but the airports are a long way from the city centres and there is the time taken to check in. Eurostar trains using the Channel Tunnel complete the journey in three hours city centre to city centre. In a similar vein, by using newer equipment AMTRAK have gained 33 per cent of the market share between Washington, DC, and New York by offering a city centre to city centre in just over three hours service.

What will the substitutes to cruising be? A later chapter will look at the concept of land and air cruises. The cruise market is still buoyant and growing, but holiday patterns do change and it may be that alternatives will make a serious challenge to the cruise industry.

Bargaining power

In general, a supplier wants to supply the minimum acceptable quality at the highest possible price whilst the customer wants the highest possible quality at the lowest possible price.

If the supplier has a monopoly, they can demand a higher price. In a free market economy there is a point of quality below which a customer will not drop, regardless of the price. Indeed because customers often (wrongly in many instances) equate price with quality, too low a price may send the wrong messages.

The more suppliers of goods and services to an organization there are for a given product or service, the more it can force the price down and the quality up. The more competitors an organization has, the more likely it is that prices will need to come down whilst quality needs to be as high as possible.

In recent years, companies have sought closer relationships with their suppliers, offering them training and making them a full part of the manufacturing/service process. This has advantages for both sides in that the supplier has a greater guarantee of work but, conversely, they become tied to the fortune of the contracting organization.

This chapter has been designed to give you a basic understanding of the market concepts we shall be using throughout the book. The cruise industry is a very good case study for these concepts which make its operations more understandable.

Case study

Bolsover Cruise Club

In 1980, a small travel agency in Bolsover, Derbyshire (UK), decided to switch from being a general travel agency to a specialist cruise-booking agency. Derek and Michael Wilson run Bolsover Travel, a family business, which originated alongside an estate agency operation.

By concentrating solely on booking mainstream cruise holidays, Bolsover Cruise Club as it was renamed in the late 1990s, has built up a customer base of nearly 40 000 clients throughout the UK. The company has made a conscious decision to offer cruises from mainstream operators – NCL, RCI, Carnival Group, P&O/Princess, Silversea etc. – in the high end of Standard through Premium to Luxury categories (see Chapter 4). This is a good example of a successful company 'sticking to the knitting' (Peters and Waterman, 1982), i.e. remaining close to what they do well.

Derek Wilson of Bolsover Cruise Club sees the cruise industry as being a separate entity, and thus the company has decided to concentrate on cruising specifically and has left the general travel agency business.

By simplifying the booking system to one telephone call and a written confirmation, the company (one of several cruise-booking agencies in the UK) are able to provide a convenient service for their customers. Unlike US agencies, Bolsover do not block book cruise ship accommodation. The problems associated with this practice, especially when such accommodation remains unsold by the agency and is thus released back on to the market have been analysed by Dickinson and Vladimir (1997). The fact that UK cruisers are required to place a non-refundable deposit to secure a cruise unlike those in North America means that if a booking is taken from the UK, it is likely to be much firmer than a corresponding US or Canadian booking.

By selling literally thousands of cruises per annum, companies such as Bolsover are able to obtain extremely good discounts from the cruise companies and are thus able to offer lower prices than many high street outlets. Their knowledge of the industry also allows them to offer advice and, because they have a large percentage of repeat business, they know the client and are able to advise on the appropriateness of a particular product. The matching of product and customer helps ensure that the cruiser receives an experience that meets their expectations.

Bolsover Cruise Club rarely advertises, although they were one of the first UK companies to use the television Teletext service. Growth today is through personal recommendation. In 1999 the company were involved in national advertising of specific cruises in partnership with both RCI and Princess.

All those who book a cruise through Bolsover become members of the Bolsover Cruise Club and receive regular mailings regarding special offers, many of which carry very attractive discounts.

In 1998 the company moved to new purpose-built premises just off the M1 motorway in recognition of the fact that many customers liked to make a personal visit, although the customer base stretches throughout the UK making intensive use of the telephone necessary. Bolsover Cruise Club now employs thirteen staff, an indication of the level of business generated by the UK cruise market.

The development of booking agencies solely for the cruise industry indicates the degree of growth in this particular section of the holiday business. Bolsover does not deal in the 'package' type of cruise but in a more traditional product, an area that requires specialist knowledge if the customer is to have their expectations met. To that end, staff receive regular training and updating to ensure that they understand the nature.

4

Market segmentation and economics

This chapter includes:

- product cost positioning
- typology of cruisers
- cruise style inventory
- market segmentation
- passenger space ratio
- discounting
- differentiation
- integration and segmentation
- case study – Silversea.

In the previous chapter we introduced a series of marketing concepts. These concepts will be used in this and succeeding chapters to analyse the cruise industry.

Any typical day in a major cruising area will see a number of ships belonging to a variety of companies following very similar itineraries. What is it that differentiates these seemingly similar products?

What led to much of the research for this section is anecdotal, and yet completely true, and consisted of listening to two couples at different tables in a Mediterranean port of call describing the cruise they were on – the same cruise even down to similar cabin grades.

In fact, the only differences between their shipboard experience were a different cabin steward and a different waiter and bus boy at dinner, and those did not feature as factors in their satisfaction or dissatisfaction. What we could not help but investigate was that one couple believed that the cruise was superb and the other was very disappointed.

Douglas Ward, President of the Maritime Evaluation Group (MEG) has performed a great service to cruisers over the years with the ship evaluations and information published annually as the *Berlitz Guide to Cruising and Cruise Ships*. Unlike the Fodor cruising guides, the Berlitz product covers the whole market, not just that intended for North Americans, and thus some of the smaller European and Asian operators are evaluated.

Ward not only provides much information about the industry but also allocates individual ships scores and stars based on the MEG evaluations. The problem with these evaluations is that whilst the MEG is objective, individual cruisers are much more subjective and we have found cases where a ship rated as three stars by Ward has been perceived more favourably by certain cruisers as one rated four stars.

It is not our intention to devise another rating system. That is a task for experts such as Ward, but we have extended his work in order to provide a more detailed but simple description of the product so that those marketing and selling cruises can match cruiser and cruise company/itinerary more closely.

We believe that there are three basic factors in operation that differentiate one cruise product from another:

1 The customer requirements.
2 The ambience of the ship.
3 The product cost positioning.

What our two couples were showing was a combination of all three factors acting to bring about a different perception of the same product.

Typology of cruisers

As suggested in Chapter 1, the requirements of cruisers are derived from those generic to holidaymakers.

Using our sample of 100 cruisers (see Introduction) we were able, by a process of questioning, to develop what we have described as 'cruiser profiles', i.e. the tendency of any one person on a cruise to require certain ingredients to make that cruise a success. In developing these traits we used the developmental concepts of Belbin (1981) and Honey and Mumford (1986) who looked at team roles and learning styles respectively. Both authorities concluded that there were no absolutes in their chosen areas of study but rather tendencies. Thus a person's team role profile as described by Belbin was not a set of strict behaviours but a tendency to behave in a certain way dependent of the make-up of the profile.

Our discussions with our sample led us to the conclusion that there were seven aspects to cruising that made up an individual's 'cruise profile'. We did not come to this conclusion lightly. We spent time testing the ideas with the sample to ensure that we had not missed out any vital factors.

We found that the ideas could be expressed in the form of an acronym and one that was applicable to a maritime context: PRESSED. The press gang was the main means by which the Royal Navy acquired its men for the Napoleonic Wars – the 'press' roaming the taverns of seaports looking for likely recruits for the service. It was an early form of conscription and was both hated yet necessary.

We found that many of our 'cruisers' had originally been 'pressed'. It was their partner who was exceptionally keen on a cruise whilst they themselves were reluctant. That reluctance, for our sample, had in the vast majority of cases changed within a few days of embarking on their first cruise.

We commenced our study for this section by asking questions designed to prioritize what it was these people wanted from their cruise. We had already come to the opinion that what differentiated our two couples at the beginning of this chapter was related to dissonance. It was not that the cruise was good or bad but that it was more in tune with what one couple wanted and/or expected than what the other couple wanted and/or expected.

We discovered that a cruiser profile was made up of PRESSED – their propensity to:

- Party
- Relax
- Enthuse
- Stroll
- Seek
- Explore
- Dip.

We refer to the characteristics of these as being those of a:

- partygoer
- relaxer
- enthusiast
- stroller
- seeker
- explorer
- dipper.

First we shall explain each of the characteristics, set it into the context of recognized holiday typologies and then show how various cruise products match the characteristics.

In developing these characteristics we have taken account of the work of Fodness (1994), who examined the motivation of tourists especially in relationship to the tourist's wish to find out about the places visited rather than just have a personal experience. The questions we asked were based on ideas gleaned from Fodness.

We shall refer to each characteristic as though it existed in isolation. This is for the purpose of clarity and, as will be suggested, the characteristics do not exist in isolation but are acted on one with another. For many cruisers it was the cruise itself, i.e. the shipboard experience that was the major motivator, although all of sample agreed to some extent with McCannell (1973) in that they wanted some authenticity in the place they visited but perhaps not too much, especially if it involved confronting poverty. We believe that this could be a major problem in cruising in that the ease of returning to the cultural bubble of the ship is so great that the cruiser gains a very unrealistic view of the places visited – more unrealistic than that gained from a land-based stay, however well cosseted. As an experiment it was decided to see if it were possible for a couple to spend a reasonable day ashore in a port and never interact with a local inhabitant. The answer was, yes, it may be rare but it was possible to walk around a fairly sanitized area and not speak to anybody save other cruisers for over four hours and still feel that the day had not been wasted.

Partygoer

The partygoer is on a cruise for the activities and nightlife. They are likely to be happiest on a ship that has the latest in entertainment features, a lively casino and plenty of organized activities. For the partygoer, cruises which resemble the atmosphere of the traditional UK holiday, camp may well appeal.

By definition the partygoer is gregarious by nature and will therefore be less concerned at the higher density often associated with high-activity, intensive-destination oriented vessels.

Relaxer

The relaxer will not object to days spent at sea and may well only venture ashore briefly on port days. The relaxer is on the cruise to unwind and whilst he or she may well take in a degree of the action at night, the daytime is likely to find him or her lying on a sun lounger and devouring the ship's library.

Relaxation has associations with a degree of solitude and thus the relaxer is likely to be less comfortable with high-density vessels where private space may be at a premium.

Enthusiast

The enthusiast is addicted to cruising. The itinerary is not important, the ship may not be a major priority but a cruise is. Dickinson and Vladimir (1997) refer to people being addicted to cruising. Carole and Leonard Gosling from Bath in the UK agree that they fit into this category having between them taken fifty-four cruises (up to the end of 1998) mainly on P&O/Princess. They quote coming second in a Princess competition to somebody who had spent over 1200 days on P&O/Princess cruises. They themselves have won the 'most cruised' award on Princess no less than four times.

One distinction we noted between UK and North American cruisers who fit into this category is the higher degree of company loyalty amongst the former. Despite the fact that virtually all of the major cruise companies are accessible to both markets, UK cruisers interviewed were three times more likely to stick with one company for the majority of their cruises than their North American counterparts.

The enthusiasts we spoke to were very knowledgeable about the industry and the cruise companies. The companies use this enthusiasm through their various loyalty schemes to ensure that the cruisers feel a part of the family and thus cruising with somebody else becomes less a commercial decision and more an act of treachery!

Stroller

Strollers were those who originally 'strolled' the Boulevards of Paris in the late nineteenth century (Benjamin, 1973) both seeing and, as importantly, being seen.

Cruising is still one holiday where dressing up can be important. Whilst many of the newer entrants to the market stress the informality of their operation, we found that the opportunity to dress for dinner was welcomed by many cruisers. It gives the opportunity to escape from normality and to experience a perception of a glamorous yesteryear. Although we did not find anybody who only went on cruises in order to dress up, we did find a substantial number of both genders for whom a degree of formality was part of the attraction of cruising.

The cruise companies seem well aware of this as the following quotes show:

> After 6pm, the atmosphere becomes a little dressier; long trousers for men and smart – casual for women. On gala evenings, everyone dresses up: ladies change into party dresses (*sic*), while many gentlemen bring out a dinner jacket.

(Thomson 1998–9 Cruise Brochure, 1st edn)

> If you have not been on a Princess cruise before you may be reassured to hear that the days when starched collars were *de rigeur* every night are long gone. During the day, classic resort wear is now the norm, and stylish casuals are fine for most evenings too.
>
> In addition there are one or two semi-formal evenings (more on longer cruises) when everyone opts for something stylish with jacket and tie preferred for the men. And during every cruise there are two formal nights (up to four on longer cruises) when dressing up is half the fun, black tie or a dark suit adds an extra sense of occasion and glamorous outfits shimmer throughout the ship.

(Princess 1999 Caribbean Brochure)

We found that UK cruisers complained about too many semi-formal nights on some UK-market based cruises (on the grounds that the suggested dress for such nights was very similar to work clothes) and that some North Americans thought that dressing up was too 'classy'. However, in general it was seen as part of the atmosphere and something to be kept rather than done away with, especially as it did set cruise holidays apart from many land-based holidays.

Seeker

The seeker was not present to a great extent in our survey for the reason that most major cruise lines do not cater for this category. The seeker is concerned with finding out a great deal about the area he or she visits and will wish to imbibe and try to become a part of the culture. In general, cruises are more suited to those who sample cultures (our dippers to be covered later). Cruising does not provide the time in any one place as will be shown in the next chapter.

There are, however, a small number of cultural cruises of blue water as opposed to a river variety that may appeal to the seeker.

The specialist cruises offered by Swan Hellenic (P&O) on board the 12 000 GRT *Minerva* are characterized by itineraries that visit the more interesting places, often of antiquity, and the ship carries acknowledged experts in the fields related to the cruise destinations. Their lectures are delivered with considerable depth and knowledge and, interestingly, whilst the ship's library and lecture facilities are good, there is no casino or slot machines and only a maximum of 456 passengers.

A February 1999 cruise on the *Minerva* from Singapore to Columbo, with visits to Penang, Rangoon, Paradip and Madras, included the following notable guest speakers (Swan Hellenic Winter Cruise and Tour 1998–9 brochure):

Professor Richard Holmes CBE, TD, MA, PhD
(renowned UK military historian)

Sir Donald Hawley KCMG, MBE, MA, Dlitt, DCL
(former High Commissioner to Malaysia and Chair of the Royal Society for Asian Affairs)

Dr Dawn Rooney PhD, FRGS
(art historian)

The Right Reverend and Right Honourable Lord Runcie of Cuddesdon
(former Archbishop of Canterbury and sometime lecturer in Ancient History at Cambridge)

Mark Tully MA (Cantab)
(for twenty years BBC Correspondent in India).

It is only on low-density ships with itineraries very different to mainstream cruising that the seeker will truly be comfortable. However, more and more cruise companies are recognizing that there is a little of the seeker in many of their customers and are adding more interesting destinations and excursions to their traditional offerings.

Explorer

The explorer wishes to see those places few have seen before. The growth in expedition cruising (to be considered in Chapter 8) has made exploration even more easy. The explorer does not need shopping malls or West End shows. They are seeking different lifestyles (usually more primitive than their own) and the wildlife and scenery that exists in areas relatively untouched by man. As we shall see later in this book, the explorer does not need lavishly equipped tenders to take them ashore, a Zodiac inflatable boat landing in a small cove and depositing him or her on slippery rocks is what cruising is about for this type of person.

Dipper

The dipper takes in the vast majority of the 7.6 million cruisers in 1996. A little bit of culture, a small taste of a different lifestyle and then back to the welcoming cultural bubble of the ship. The dipper is truly the 'been there, seen that, experienced this and bought the T shirt' person. The dipper will be, in the main, satisfied with an explanatory leaflet, a briefing from the port lecturer and a tour of the highlights. We spoke to one US couple who on a two-week Mediterranean cruise managed to ride on a gondola plus visit the Doge's Palace in Venice, visit the ruins of Ephesus in Turkey, see the Parthenon and the Acropolis in Athens, have half a day in Pompeii, a day in Rome and another day in Florence, shop in Cannes and have a brief two-hour city tour of Barcelona – all the time dipping in and out of the cultures they were visiting. They enjoyed it, they had great memories but admitted that they learnt little, saw only what the tour guide wanted them to see and were desperately tired at the end of the cruise – hardly relaxing!

The above are our seven categories of cruisers. Dickinson and Vladimir (1997) have a different set more attuned to the US market. Their six categories (which they called segments) and their descriptions are:

1 *Restless baby boomers*. Newcomers to cruising who may still be inhibited by cost and with an average age of 44 and an average US income of $58 000 (£36 500 – a very high UK salary). They are relatively inexperienced travellers and the authors see them as trying out various holidays.
2 *Enthusiastic baby boomers*. With an average age of 49 and slightly less wealthy, with an average income of $55 000, they undertake (according to the authors) holidays for escape and relaxation although they enjoy activities and night life.

3 Consummate shoppers. These are people who shop around for the best value, which does not necessarily mean the cheapest. Average age 55 and average income $60 000.
4 *Luxury seekers.* Average age of 52 and a swaggering average income (to UK eyes) of $95 000, they can afford the best and demand it. They are also amongst the more culturally aware.
5 *Explorers.* Well travelled with an average age of 64 and an average income of $81 000, these explorers are not looking for rest or pampering but for experiences.
6 *Ship buffs.* We would equate these with the UK enthusiasts category. Dickinson and Vladimir found that ship buffs had an average age 68 and an average income of $78 000. We found that they were knowledgeable about ships, not because they were ship buffs *per se* but because they had cruised on so many.

Dickinson and Vladimir's segments are for the US market and whilst that is a huge market, as in our earlier comments on their work, it is not the only market. We believe that our PRESSED categories, which relate more to behaviour and less to age and income, are more useful in understanding the market segmentation that we will consider next.

Cruise style inventory

Whilst we do not suggest that those selling cruises give a questionnaire to prospective customers, we did devise and test an inventory of questions to allow us to evaluate our categories. Using ideas derived from the Belbin (1981) self-perception inventory to test for team role types, we devised a system that required a subject to allocate twenty points to seven questions. The use of twenty points was derived by trial and error. Subjects found that our initial choice of ten points was too restrictive. The inventory is shown in Figure 4.1.

The questions in Figure 4.1 are related to the categories as follows:

Question 1: Partygoer
Question 2: Relaxer
Question 3: Enthusiast
Question 4: Stroller
Question 5: Seeker
Question 6: Explorer
Question 7: Dipper

Thinking about the main things you want out of a cruise, allocate a total of 20 points amongst the 7 questions listed below:	
Question	Points
1 A lively ship with plenty of activities both day and night	
2 A chance to relax and watch the world and the ocean go by	
3 The opportunity to explore places few people have visited	
4 An opportunity to dress up for formal events and experience the finer things in life	
5 The chance to immerse myself in and learn about other cultures	
6 The total experience of a cruise package as often as I can afford it	
7 The chance to gain a quick overview of different places and people	

Figure 4.1 The Cartwright and Baird cruise style inventory

Testing the inventory we found certain patterns emerging as shown from results taken from a test group of twenty subjects (n = 20) of which six gave the highest score to Partygoing, eight to Relaxing, five to Enthusiast and one to Seeking/Exploring. Three typical results are shown in Table 4.1.

Most of the scores were of a similar pattern with Partygoing, Relaxing or Exploring/Seeking being the predominant score.

Table 4.1 Samples of the Cartwright and Baird cruise style inventory scores

Category	Subject A	Subject B	Subject C
Partygoer (P)	9	2	0
Relaxer (R)	3	8	4
Enthusiast (En)	2	3	0
Stroller (St)	1	2	0
Seeker (Se)	0	1	8
Explorer (Ex)	0	0	8
Dipper (D)	5	4	0
	20	20	20
Main categories	P/D/R	R/D/En	Ex/Se/R

This allowed us to group together certain of the categories to form three broad groups of cruiser:

1 *Resort cruisers: Partygoers/Dippers/Enthusiasts.* A 'resort' cruise ship or cruise line is an extension of the land-based holiday hotel/resort. There will be plenty of activity and the majority of cruises will be destination intensive. The cruise will tend towards informality and there will be considerable facilities and activities for children and families. The more modern ships will come complete with electronic games arcades and even miniature golf courses on the uppermost deck. The passenger density will tend to be on the high side (see PSR later in this chapter)

2 *Traditional cruisers: Relaxers/Dippers/Strollers/Enthusiasts.* The traditional ship or company will concentrate on the cruise experience itself. The ship feels like a ship and there will be adequate days at sea for relaxing with a number of formal nights. Cost wise (see later), the cruise will tend to be from the top end of Standard upwards. The passenger density will be lower than on a resort-style cruise.

3 *Niche cruisers: Explorers/Seekers.* Niche cruisers are seeking an experience very different from the traditional cruise or indeed the traditional package holiday. They require a cruise where experience may be more important than comfort and merit. They have Chapter 8 of this book to themselves as they are a growing market. Of the three categories, they are most likely to stray furthest from the comfort bubble of the ship but it is still required as a base from which to seek new experiences.

We offer the inventory to the industry not to replace traditional means of evaluating and describing cruises, cruise ships and cruise companies but to complement them. It is of utmost importance that the customer is matched to the correct type of cruise for their needs and this is what we have sought to do through the inventory.

Market segmentation in the cruise industry

To attract customers to your cruise line, you have to offer them something that your competitors do not. To survive, each cruise company needs what Porter (1985) has described as competitive advantage.

There are two basic ways to obtain competitive advantage:

1 Offer a similar product to your competitors but offer it cheaper – cost
2 Offer a different product – differentiation.

Cost

There is a problem with offering products in that this can affect quality and thus most cruise companies compete on the basis of value for money within a differentiated market. Within mainstream cruising the core product does not differ from one company to another but the supplementary product (see Chapter 3) is differentiated both in terms of added value and the target customer group.

Cost is an important component of the 4Cs (Chapter 3) and forms one of the most bewildering aspects of the cruise industry. Before considering the price paid by the cruiser we need to consider the costs incurred by the cruise company.

It is an axiom in management accounting that fixed costs must be met if any business is to be a success. Fixed costs as defined by Cartwright et al. (1998) are those costs you will incur even if you have no customers. To illustrate this let us look at a highly hypothetical worse case scenario.

A cruise company is running a cruise from Athens to Barcelona, then back to Athens and then to Barcelona again. The first cruise is 60 per cent booked, the second has *no* cruisers booked (we said this was a worst case scenario) and the third is booked at 75 per cent capacity. They have calculated that to break even they need 67 per cent occupancy. What do they do?

A simple answer might be to cancel the second cruise and remain in Barcelona. However, the crew will have to be paid, the leasing or other payments (see later) on the ship will have to be met on time and the ship will be in the wrong place for the third, profitable, cruise. Perhaps they should cancel cruises one and two. The crew payments etc. will need to be met as will increased berthing charges but at least the ship will be in the right place. Unfortunately the company will have also upset the cruisers booked on the first cruise and they may have rebooked with another company. As Cartwright and Green (1997) have pointed out, if you lose a customer to a competitor and that competitor meets the customer's needs, you may well have lost them forever.

It is unlikely that a cruise will attract zero cruisers but there may well be times when the company has to sail with an uneconomic number on board in order to keep their existing customers and to position their vessel for future, hopefully profitable, cruises.

No enterprise goes into profit until the overall income is at least equal to the overall fixed costs, a position known as breakeven. Provided the company has enough cash or credit to meet its recurring expenditure it can avoid a cash flow crisis and carry on trading.

Cruising carries high fixed costs. There is the cost of the vessel. As we have shown earlier modern cruise ships can cost upwards of £200 million. Even repaying that over a twenty-year life span is considerable and many ships are not actually owned by the company but by a financial institution and then leased back. Leasing is a common means of financial control in the transportation industry being used for railway rolling stock, airliners and cruise ships. Whilst the pomp and ceremony of naming ceremonies may be impressive it is the drafting and signing of complex financial instruments at the moment of handover that is the real rite of passage. Sabbach (1995) has detailed the financial methods used in the airline industry to ensure that airlines can acquire new aircraft and similar methods are to be found in the cruise industry.

Some ships may be owned outright but others are owned by banks and other financial institutions. Kludas (1992) lists some of the latter, UK examples: the *Pacific Princess* and *Island Princess* operated by Princess are owned by the Abbey National March Leasing, as was the *Canberra* which was operated by P&O. For tax reasons ships may be registered to a separate holding company as part of the main group, e.g. the *Jubilee* of Carnival is actually owned by Jubilee Cruises Inc., which is a Carnival subsidiary.

However the ship is owned, its construction has to be paid for either by leasing or by the repayment of interest and capital on loans, and that is a considerable portion of the fixed costs.

Wages, crew meals, marketing, maintenance, agents fees and berthing fees all have major fixed cost components irrespective of the number of cruisers embarked – costs that have to be met regardless of the income generated by a particular cruise. It makes ensuring that there is the right product with the right customer value available critical in the successful operation of a cruise company.

Variable costs associated with a cruise include excursions, cruisers' meals, costs of on-board sales, prizes for competitions etc. – not large sums. Dickinson and Vladimir (1997) estimate the cost of raw food for cruisers from $8 (£5) per person per day at the Standard end to $30 (£19) at the Luxury end of the market. As we shall, see this is not a large sum compared to the per diem price for most cruises.

A P&O video to accompany the book *Ballad of Oriana* states that a US market vessel needs to capture 2 per cent of the market to break even but a UK market vessel needs to capture a massive 10 per cent. On 1996 figures that means that *Oriana* needs 64 000 customers per annum, i.e. nearly 1300 on board at any one time allowing for changeovers and refits, to break even. That equates to an occupancy rate of 66 per cent of total berths on board as a minimum.

In their study of occupancy rates, Dickinson and Vladimir (1997) found that these had dropped from 90 per cent in 1970 to 79.6 per cent in 1995 and companies have taken drastic steps to halt the decline as we shall see when we consider discounting.

If *Oriana* sails with 75 per cent of her berths occupied, the profits for that cruise will come from the fares paid by the 9 per cent of cruisers over breakeven less the variable costs associated with them – not a huge margin for error.

A breakdown, or even bad weather, can have a dramatic effect on profits in what is a fairly marginal business depending on quite high occupancy rates.

It is therefore incumbent on the cruise companies to encourage as much repeat business and as much new business as possible.

In a major change to their evaluations, the Berlitz guide for 1998 (Ward, 1998) introduced a new method of classifying cruise ships, first by the size of ship as defined by the number of cruisers carried and, second, by the type of product namely; *Standard*, *Premium* or *Luxury*. We intend to use these categories but also add a fourth to accommodate those ships which undertake specialized cruising, either as freighters, sailing ships, estuarine or coastal cruises and expedition cruises. This category we have entitled *Niche* cruising. In the 1999 edition of the guide, Ward changed to a description based on 'Lifestyle' again using the Standard, Premium and Luxury descriptions. This has the advantage that it explains the dissonance created when a vessel categorized as Standard has a higher evaluation than one rated as Premium. In effect the categorization adopted by Ward (1999) has less to do with quality and more with ambience.

The Standard product covers a very wide range. Some Standard cruises are very basic indeed, whilst others border on the Premium category. This is illustrated by the fact that some Standard products have been awarded the same or even higher star ratings by Ward (1998) as some Premium products (see above for changes to Wards approach in 1999). Thus the 1998 rating for the *Carnival Destiny* (a Standard product) is four stars plus whilst that for the Victoria, a Premium, but older product is three stars plus. As will be shown later, it is the density of cruisers on board that is the main determinant of product category.

Vladimir and Dickinson (1997) use the categories, Budget, Contemporary, Premium, Speciality and Luxury for types of cruise companies. Whilst there is some merit in splitting Standard into two categories, Budget and Contemporary, we have decided to stay with the Standard category. This is a wide category but many of the 'Budget' operations approach the Contemporary classification as they add new tonnage.

Size is always problematic as a classification because it depends on whether one takes the GRT or the number of berths as the defining factor. To illustrate this, which of the following two is the smaller ship?

MS *Paul Gaugin*: 18 800 GRT; maximum occupancy 320
MVS *Seawing*; 16 607 GRT; maximum occupancy 976

Ward (1998) had the former as the smaller ship based on capacity but if the GRT is used as the measure she is larger than the *Seawing*.

In 1998 Ward classes smaller ships as those for up to 500 cruisers, medium ships as those for 501–1 000 and large for 1000 upwards. We would add mega-ships to this list for those able to carry over 2500 cruisers at any one time. Ward's 1999 guide reverts to listing ships in alphabetical order but gives them an S, M or L designation depending on size.

Our sample agrees with Ward that the number on board is a better indication of the atmosphere than actual size, especially where the sizes are comparable. Incidentally, it should come as no surprise that Ward allocates a Standard designation to the *Seawing* and a Luxury designation to the *Paul Gaugin*.

Passenger space ratio

A more useful measure used by the cruise industry is that of the PSR which is a measure of the tonnes available per passenger calculated by dividing the GRT by the number of available berths. Ward gives two readings for this which we have called PSR(m) for the maximum occupancy and PSR(2) for the calculation based on all cabins being occupied by only two persons.

As stated in the introduction, we have used maximum capacity as our standard measure in this book but the current downward trend in occupancy rates, mentioned earlier, means that both figures should be considered. However, PSR(m) is what the companies are aiming for, as they will want to fill every berth possible. In cases where this could lead to overcrowding, berths have been taken out of use and not sold. For instance, the *Costa Marina*

(25 558 GRT) has berths for 1025 cruisers but the 1999–2000 Costa brochure states that only 920 will be sold.

Using a sample of twenty Standard, twenty Premium and thirteen Luxury products as rated by Ward (1998) we found the relationship between product and PSR to be as shown in Table 4.2. (Out of the 210 ships evaluated by Ward for the 1998 guide and with the addition of our niche category, thirty small, forty-eight medium, thirty-one large and twelve mega-ships were in the Standard category. Five small, ten medium, nineteen large and five mega-ships came under the Premium category. Thirteen medium and five small ships were rated Luxury. thirty-two small ships fitted the Niche classification.)

Table 4.2   Passenger space ratios

Product	Best PSR(m)	Worst PSR(m)	Mean PSR(m)	Mean PSR(2)
Standard	29.8	15.1	22.1	26.8
Premium	47.5	24.1	35.7	40.1
Luxury	61.6	36.7	48.0	49.5

The reason behind the close correlation of mean PSR(m) and PSR(2) for the Luxury category is that most of the cabins are designed for a maximum of two people. The figures show that on average a cruiser on a Luxury cruise will have twice as much space available to them on the ship as those taking a Standard product, with Premium coming in midway between the two.

Using a similar sample it is possible to then consider the size of cabin (or stateroom as many US market companies call their accommodation) available in each category. To obtain a common standard we shall take a mid-range outside two-berth cabin, without a balcony, in each category for the comparison, together with the smallest and largest cabins in the category (see Table 4.3).

As will be shown in the next section, PSR and cabin size are the biggest determinants of price paid for a cruise of similar duration on any itinerary. Cruisers can make a choice: a huge suite on a high-density ship will be less than a similar suite on a ship with a higher PSR. Conversely they can pay more for a standard cabin on a Premium or Luxury ship compared with a much bigger cabin on a Standard vessel. It all depends on how much time they intend to spend in their cabin.

Table 4.3 Comparison of cabin sizes in sq. ft, 1998

	Average size of mid-range cabin	Average size of smallest cabin	Average size of largest cabin/suite
Standard	125	54	1059*
Premium	155	134	1515**
Luxury	210	138	1314

Notes: * RCI latest ships most expansive suites; ** Celebrity latest ships most expansive suites.

In this section we need to consider the price paid by the cruiser. We have elected to consider the price to a UK cruiser travelling from either London Heathrow or London Gatwick on a fly cruise, or from Southampton/Dover for a UK sailing. Prices are given in both sterling and dollars using a formula of £1 = $1.60. We have decided to concentrate on the UK price because the air component is included for UK cruisers booking in the UK (with the exception of some regional flights to and from London) and because the actual amounts are of less importance than the relative differences between products. The degree of difference does not change between markets.

The main determinates of price are:

- cruising area
- time of year
- category of product
- size of accommodation
- position of accommodation.

In general, one can say that for a given time of the season, Alaska will be dearer than the Caribbean; Standard products will have a lower start price and popular times for holidays (e.g. during school breaks or festive seasons such as Easter and Christmas) will be higher priced – a simple case of supply and demand.

As far as accommodation is concerned, large cabins will be dearer than smaller ones, cabins for more than two people will have a lower individual price and inside cabins will be cheaper than a correspondingly sized outside cabin. Cabins with balconies will command a premium and mini-suites and suites will be the highest priced accommodation on board. Because of the motion of the ship, cabins towards the centre will be more highly priced than those at either end and, perversely, although motion increases the higher up a ship a cabin is placed, such cabins command a higher price than those of

Table 4.4 *Oriana* cabin categories in order of price

Grade	I/O	Berths	Type	Location	Number	Price (£)
Z	I	4	Cabin with shower/WC	F (F&C) E(C) D(F)	20	1395
X	O	4	Cabin with shower/WC	F(C) E(F)	20	1495
V	I	3	Cabin with shower/WC	F(F) D(F)	10	1860
OC	I	2	Cabin with shower/WC	F(F&C) E(F)	37	1945
OB	I	2	Cabin with shower/WC	D(F) C(F&A)	78	1965
OA	I	2	Cabin with shower/WC	C(C) B(F&A)	50	1975
NB	I	2	Cabin with shower/WC	A(F&A)	40	1985
T	O	3	Cabin with shower/WC	E(C)	10	1995
NA	I	2	Cabin with shower/WC	A(C)	47	1995
LE	O	2	Cabin with shower/WC	F(F) E(F)	24	2195
LD	O	2	Cabin with shower/WC	F(F) E(F)	28	2295
LC	O	2	Cabin with shower/WC	F(F&C) E(C) includes 8 cabins for wheelchairs	50	2345
LB	O	2	Cabin with shower/WC	D(F) C(A) B(A)	50	2375
KC	O	2	Cabin with shower/WC	C(F)	22	2395
KB	O	2	Cabin with shower/WC	A(F&A)	48	2410
KA	O	2	Cabin with shower/WC	A(C)	56	2445
D	O	2	Stateroom with bath/ WC & sitting area	A(C)	66	2725
J	I	1	Cabin with shower/WC	D(F) C(C&A) B(C)	33	2775
H	O	1	Cabin with shower/WC	E(F) D(F) C(A)	44	3025
G	O	1	Cabin with shower/WC	C(F) A(F&C&A)	32	3095
CB	O	2	Stateroom with bath/ WC & sitting area & balcony	B(F&A)	60	3145
CA	O	2	Stateroom with bath/ WC & sitting area & balcony	B(C)	28	3395
B	O	2	Mini suite with bath/ WC & balcony	B(C)	16	4095
A	O	2	Suite with bath/WC & balcony	B(C)	8	4860
			Sofa bed where applicable in staterooms & suites			595

Notes: Cabin sizes: 2-berth approx. 150 sq. ft, staterooms approx. 220 sq. ft, suites approx. 414 sq. ft. I/O refers to inside or outside; for location F=forward, A=aft and C=central; Oriana decks are numbered with F deck being the lowest passenger deck on the ship; the Promenade deck is between decks E and D and has no passenger accommodation.

similar size lower down because of the view. Finally, cabins with portholes are cheaper than those with picture windows. It is rare to find cabins on board modern cruise ships that are without private facilities but baths are usually found only in more expensive cabins.

Examining a wide range of cabin accommodation, it is possible to list that accommodation in order of price. The examples given are for a twelve-night Southampton–Mediterranean–Southampton cruise in June 1999 on the *Oriana* (69 153 GRT) which has twenty-four cabin grades (Table 4.4) and is the subject of the case study at the end of Chapter 6. The record for the number of cabin grades appears to be held by the 109 000 GRT *Grand Princess* with no fewer than thirty-five distinct grades of accommodation.

Oriana's cabin grades clearly show the progression upwards (physically) and towards the centre of the vessel of prices charged. *Oriana* also shows a special feature of the traditional UK market in that there are a number of specially equipped single cabins, 109 in total. On the equivalent P&O Princess ships, the newer vessels have no single cabins but certain staterooms in defined grades can be occupied by only one cruiser at 160 per cent of the normally quoted price for one-half of a double occupancy.

A survey of prices across the cruise categories and companies in May 1999 revealed the price comparisons in Table 4.5 which are given as a per diem rate

Table 4.5 Comparative per diem prices, May 1999

Area	Company	Standard	Premium	Luxury
Caribbean & Eastern USA, Europe & Mediterranean	Thomson	£ 83–125		
	Costa	£119–190		
	Princess		£126–336	
	Cunard			
	Sea Goddess			£421–633
	Royal Viking Sun			£233–579
	QE2*		£160–351	£386–871
Europe & Mediterranean	Airtours	£ 88–153		
	NCL	£118–253		
	P&O		£150–363	
	Cunard			£212–666
	Silversea			£472–999
Alaska	NCL	£185–326		
	Celebrity		£285–627	
	Crystal			£250–796

rather than for an actual cruise as cruises ranged from seven to eighteen days. None of the prices have been discounted.

There is considerable overlap between the top end of the Standard category and the lower end of Premium. The products are likely to be very similar with the PSR becoming the differential factor.

One of the problems the cruise industry shares with airlines but less so with land-based hotels is that if a cabin is unsold at the start of a cruise, it remains unsold for the duration. An unsold hotel room is always available but once a ship has sailed with empty accommodation, there is no method of obtaining revenue from that accommodation until the start of the next cruise.

Discounting

There are times when the brochure fare seems to bear little relation to that actually paid by individual cruisers. As with airline fares those for cruises are very dependent on the time of booking. Discounts are usually available for early bookings, 33 per cent being not unusual in the UK for many Premium and Luxury products and for late bookings when the companies wish to sell unbooked accommodation. Dickinson and Vladimir (1997) comment that discounting has become almost endemic within the industry. In working out the economic profit per cruiser in 1994 they start from a brochure price of $2200 which is discounted down to $1540. Commission to travel agents, the air component of the package, transfers and credit card company charges reduces this to $987. Food and other costs bring the amount down to $850. To this must be added the profit from on-board sales of $150 giving a profit per cruiser of $1000 (Dickinson and Vladimir, 1997: 135, Table 5.3). Dickinson and Vladimir do not enter into a discussion of fixed costs, as considered earlier, but a considerable proportion of the $1000 will need to go on costs of the vessel, wages, agents fees etc. Thus it is imperative to fill as many berths as possible.

In the 1994 Berlitz guide, Ward (1994) comments that discounting had caused a certain slippage in standards but by the end of the 1990s discounting had become the norm. In January 1999 we surveyed a sample of actual fares compared with brochure fares across a range of categories and companies. The results of combining cruise line discounts and agents' discounts (see the Bolsover Cruise Club case study at the end of Chapter 3) gave rise to considerable savings, many of which were, it must be admitted, for long lead time advanced bookings or last minute deals to fill up unsold accommodation (Table 4.6). The figures in Table 4.6 relate to particular grades of accommodation.

Table 4.6 Discounting

Area	Nights	Category	Brochure price	Actual price	Saving %
Caribbean	13	Premium	£1595	£1248	22
Mediterranean	13	Premium	£3095	£2270	27
Atlantic Islands	12	Premium	£2130	£1534	28
Alaska	7	Premium	£2795	£1995	30
Caribbean	7	Standard	£ 829	£ 629	24
Atlantic Islands	13	Standard	£1300	£ 695	47
Mediterranean	7	Standard	£ 575	£ 399	31

It seems that discounts of up to 30 per cent are fairly easily obtained. Indeed many of the brochures offer early booking discounts, e.g. Princess Pricebreakers and Double Pricebreakers, so that the cruiser does not have to seek them out; they only need to see what extra discount their travel agent can give them.

Age of cruisers

The age of cruisers is coming down. What was once thought of as a holiday for the retired is rapidly becoming a family occasion. Rather than describe a ship as for a particular age group it is more useful to describe it in terms of its attractiveness to families or those without families.

Most Standard products have facilities for the whole family whilst many Premium products are targeted at the cruiser travelling without children or adolescents. Within one company, different ships may be aimed at different markets. The *Royal Princess* has no facilities for children, the *Grand Princess* has excellent ones; *Victoria* has some children's facilities, *Oriana* has plenty of activities for them. Within the Carnival group, Costa, Airtours and Carnival itself are family oriented; Holland America is less so. It perhaps goes without saying that Disney Cruises are very children friendly!

Differentiation

Within any cost grouping there are a number of ways a company can differentiate its products. Some relate to the provision of supplementary products, for example, theme cruises on antiques, jazz, motor vehicles, gardens etc. or private islands as considered in a later chapter. The availability of family activities has been mentioned earlier.

The cruise industry also differentiates by cultural/geographic market. Geographically the major customer groups that the cruise industry serves with the percentage of the market as defined by the 1996 MEG statistics quoted earlier are as shown in Table 4.7.

Table 4.7   The cruise market by country/region

Market	Cruisers 1996	Percentage of market	Percentage of Population
USA	4 656 000	64.2	1.8
UK	640 000	8.8	1.1
Asia (excl. Japan)	500 000	6.9	0.2
Germany	254 000	3.5	0.3
Canada	250 000	3.4	0.9
Italy	250 000	3.4	0.4
France	225 000	3.1	0.4
Japan	225 000	3.1	0.2
Australasia	150 000	2.1	0.7
Rest of Europe	100 000	1.3	0.01

There are two ways that these figures can be combined to make them more useful to our analysis.

There are three geographic markets, North America, Europe and the Far East with approximate market percentages of: North America 68 per cent; Europe 20 per cent and Far East 12 per cent.

Nearly all of the North American market consists of US citizens whilst Britons form nearly half of the European market. Interestingly cruisers from English-speaking countries account for 78.5 per cent of the world cruise market.

According to Thornton's Cruise World in the UK, the greatest growth in 1998 came from Scandinavia; the MEG figures have shown that whilst growth in the USA has been slowing, growth in the rest of the world is increasing. It is for this reason that we take issue with the fact that Dickinson and Vladimir ignored over 30 per cent of the world market in their book *Selling the Sea* (1997) and concentrated solely on the US and Canadian markets.

In 1999 RCI began a major advertising campaign on UK television showing that they recognized the importance of this market. Our research showed that Princess ships were regularly attracting up to 8 per cent of their customers from the UK for a product primarily designed for the US and Canadian markets – perhaps not too surprising given that the Princess parent company is the UK-based P&O.

For the purposes of this book we will concentrate on the North American and UK markets but we shall not be ignoring the impact of other markets.

The German market is well catered for by indigenous companies operating German-speaking ships and the French market gained a considerable boost with the announcement that the *Mistral* (47 900 GRT) was to debut in 1999 under the French flag for Festival Cruises.

The Mediterranean Shipping Company (MSC, originally Lauro Lines/ Starlauro and Royal Olympic) as well as Festival have been operating cruises for a generic European market for some time with considerable success despite the need to operate in several languages. Costa (now part of Carnival) have attracted a loyal Italian and US/Italian market with a decidedly Italian atmosphere on board their ships. We have considered the growth of the Asian and Japanese markets in Chapter 3.

There is no doubt that whilst there are considerable cultural and linguistic similarities between North America and the UK, there are also differences. Chapter 6 will indicate that UK cruisers prefer smaller but more public rooms than do North Americans and there are considerable differences in entertainment. As Chapter 6 points out, ships need to be designed to slightly different parameters to meet the different needs of the two groups. It is useful, therefore, for a cruise company if it can offer products that are generic enough to meet a whole series of markets or more specialized to meet individual needs. Carnival and P&O as corporations have chosen the latter step as will be shown later.

Integration and segmentation

Companies can grow in one of three ways (Porter, 1980) linked to the Porter model of competitiveness introduced in Chapter 3. They can vertically integrate by acquiring more in the chain of 'production' or horizontally integrate by acquiring additional market segments or finally by unconnected means. Taking each in turn we are able to find good examples in the cruise industry.

Vertical integration

In the UK, Airtours and Thomson were both well-known names in the package holiday market. Both sold holidays in hotels run by major hotel chains but both also owned their own charter airlines, Airtours and Britannia respectively, and chains of high street travel agencies. The move into cruise holidays, aided by established players in the market (NCL and Louis Cruise Lines) allowed them to offer a seamless web of cruise and stay holidays supported by flights on their own aircraft. The latest movement into the cruise sector has been by First Choice, again a package operator with their own airline, Air 2000. Both Thomson and First Choice also market other cruise products as part of their package portfolio including Premier and Star Cruises (Thomson) and Festival, Commodore, Royal Olympic and Carnival (First Choice). Since 1995 the three companies between them operate nine ships with a total tonnage of nearly 200 000 GRT plus the two ships gained when Airtours acquired Direct Cruises in 1998. All of the ships are fairly elderly and all operate high-density, destination-intensive cruises likely to appeal to the package holiday customer, more than likely a Partygoer, who form the core business of the companies.

Owning their own charter airlines primarily for the holiday trade also gives these companies good access to regional airports avoiding the use of hubs such as London Heathrow or London Gatwick.

Vertical integration is a good means of growth for established companies in a related industry or industry segment as they will already have a good customer base to build on. By buying in the expertise of other players (by means of marketing/operating arrangements) they are able to mollify some of the barriers to entry mentioned in Chapter 3.

A danger is that the company may assume that because they have expertise in the land-based holiday business, this will immediately transfer through to their cruise operations. This is not necessarily so as the cruise industry operates to its own, sometimes different, norms as Direct Holidays discovered when setting up Direct Cruises.

Horizontal integration

Two companies above all epitomize horizontal integration in the cruise industry – P&O and Carnival. Using the categories developed earlier it is possible to describe the product portfolios as in Table 4 8.

P&O operate a series of mini-cruises using scheduled ferries around the Orkneys and Shetland Islands. These really are mini-cruises, not just ferry

Table 4.8   Segmentation

	Standard	Premium	Luxury	Niche
P&O				
UK market	Mini cruises to Orkney/Shetland	P&O Cruises	Swan Hellenic River Cruises	
North American market		Princess		
European market				
Far East market	P&O Holidays, Spice Island Cruises	Spice Island Cruises		
Carnival				
UK market	Share in Airtours/ Direct Cruises	Cunard	Cunard	
North American market	Carnival, Costa	Holland America	Cunard, Seabourne	Windstar
European market	Costa			
Far East market	Plans with Hyundai abandoned 1998			

trips, as excursions are arranged and the standard of service is comparable with that on their more conventional cruises. The main UK cruising arm of P&O, P&O Cruises is a Premium product aimed at the UK market with (in 1999) two ships with excellent family facilities (*Oriana* and *Arcadia*) and one, *Victoria* for a slightly (but not exclusively) older market.

P&O have no presence in the luxury market or indeed in the UK/European or North American Standard market although there is a Far East operation, P&O Holidays, that provides a Standard product for the Australian market plus the small Spice Islands operation around Indonesia.

Within the Niche category, P&O, through Swan Hellenic, operate the 12 000 GRT *Minerva* which provides cruises with a high cultural and educational content plus river cruises (to be considered in Chapter 8).

For the North American market, Princess Cruises provide a Premium product that also attracts a fair number of UK cruisers. Princess have made a forte of their Alaskan cruises and hold 40 per cent of that market with a good series of pre- and post-cruise experiences in Alaskan and Canadian areas of outstanding natural beauty.

Carnival have a very wide product portfolio indeed covering the Standard market in almost its entirety and we would predict that they will make another attempt to enter the Asian market early in the twenty-first century. They also have a good spread of products with HAL offering Premium products and Cunard and Seabourne the Luxury end of the market. Carnival also has a stake in the Niche market through sailing cruises on Windstar vessels.

By acquiring Celebrity, RCI were able to expand their operation from the top end of the Standard market well into the Premium sector.

One wonders how many 1999 Cunard or HAL passengers realized that they were travelling on a Carnival ship. The aim of diversification is to provide linked products where possible, and a broad portfolio such as that for Carnival allows cruisers to trade up but to remain customers of the same corporate group.

What has been demonstrated is the importance of branding. Princess, HAL and Costa are brands as much as companies. It is brands that the customer identifies with rather than the actual company, a fact shown by the myriad of different brands of washing powder but made by only a handful of companies.

Appendix 2 lists the vessels owned by the major cruise groups during 1998–9.

Unconnected growth

Occasionally cruise lines become owned by companies with no other stakes in the industry or indeed in shipping. When Trafalgar House bought Cunard in 1971, it was just one of a diverse group of companies owned by them. When Cunard was sold in 1998 to Carnival, Cunard rejoined a shipping group and also brought to an end a long-running piece of history.

The United States of America finally gets Cunard

The US passenger shipping industry has always been small in terms of numbers of vessels but the influence of US commerce was immense in the early years of the twentieth century. The Morgan combine headed by J. P. Morgan provided the money behind the International Mercantile Marine Company that eventually owned Inman Lines, Red Star Line. Leyland Line and the prestigious White Star Line, owners of the *Titanic*. Senator Smith's 1912 hearing into the loss of the *Titanic* was quite anti-British in sentiment but although the ship was under the Red Ensign, registered in Liverpool, built in Belfast and crewed by Britons, she was controlled from New York. Morgan's ultimate target however was Cunard, founded by the Canadian Samuel Cunard (Davie, 1987). The UK government provided subsidies to Cunard to keep the company under British control and Morgan never succeeded in acquiring it.

Where Morgan failed at the beginning of the century, Arison succeeded. From his first venture with Kloster in 1966, including the near disastrous maiden voyage in 1972 of Carnival's first ship, the *Mardi Gras*, which ran aground off Miami, to 1998 Carnival had gained nearly 30 per cent of the total world cruise market. He had also acquired Cunard, and with it the Royal Viking operation and the prestigious *QE2* – all without a murmur of complaint from the UK!

In January 1999, John Prescott the British Deputy Prime Minister and an ex-merchant seaman requested that the recently announced £300 million Queen Mary be registered in the UK to maintain the Cunard tradition such was the perceived importance of the company to the UK merchant marine despite the foreign ownership.

Describing a cruise or ship

By using the marketing concepts in this chapter, it is possible to describe a cruise company or ship in a number of ways all of which should assist a customer in picking a cruise that will meet their holiday need.

A ship or company can be described in terms of the type of person it caters for as the following examples show:

- Partygoer – Carnival
- Relaxer – P&O Cruises
- Enthusiast – Fred Olsen
- Stroller – Cunard
- Seeker – Minerva (Swan Hellenic)
- Explorer – ib Yamal (Russian icebreaker)
- Dipper – Princess.

Or it can be described in terms of product related to cost and density of customers:

- Standard – Airtours
- Premium – Holland America
- Luxury – Silversea.

The ship or company can be further categorized into family oriented or not. Or the geographic market can be taken into account:

■ North American – NCL
■ UK – Thomson
■ Europe – MSC
■ Far East – Star Cruises.

One interesting point that we noticed when surveying cruisers was the position of Canadians. They form 3.4 per cent of the total market and are often 'lumped' in with citizens of the USA. Those we spoke to were often disparaging about this, especially on ships where there were both US cruisers and a sizeable minority of Britons. In these cases the Canadians felt totally ignored with little reference to their culture in entertainments etc.

We offer our method of description to the industry. It is not complex but when tested with our sample it proved useful in ensuring as close a match as possible between the cruiser and the product and that at the end of the day is what will generate repeat business.

Case study

Silversea Cruises

The case study for this chapter comes from the luxury end of the market and looks at the operations of award winning Silversea Cruises. The company has its origins in the Sitmar Line (Societa Italiana Transporti Marittimi) originally founded in 1954 in Genoa. The company originally operated a transatlantic service to North and South America and a Mediterranean–Australia service (Emmons, 1972), and then entered the cruise business in 1970 with the **Fairsea** (21 916 GRT, ex **Fairland** ex **Carinthia**) and her sister the **Fairwind** (ex **Sylvania**). The **Fairwind** was renamed the **Sitmar Fairwind** in 1988 just before the company was acquired by P&O who merged the Sitmar operation into their Princess business acquired in 1974. The **Fairstar** became the **Fair Princess**, the **Sitmar Fairwind** became the **Dawn Princess** and their latest vessel, the 38 876 GRT **Fairsky** became the **Sky Princess**. The 21 696 GRT **Fairstar** (ex **Oxfordshire**) was placed under the operation of P&O Holidays in Australia, being replaced by the **Fair Princess**, which was actually a year older, in 1997.

At the time Sitmar had considerable tonnage on order: **Sitmar Fairmajesty** (63 524 GRT) became the **Star Princess** and then P&O's **Arcadia**; two 69 845 GRT vessels which became **Crown** and **Regal Princess** respectively.

Princess and P&O acquired seven vessels, four of which were new or building and five of them were still in service in 1999; Sitmar Line with their distinctive V on the funnel were apparently no more.

However, some of those associated with Sitmar decided to enter a new market in the early 1990s, the luxury end of the cruise industry. There was at the time a gap in the market between small ships such as those operated by Cunard (**Sea Goddess 1** and **Sea Goddess 2**, 4260 GRT carrying 115 cruisers; **Seabourn Legend, Spirit** and **Pride**, 9975 GRT, 212 cruisers; Radisson's **Song of Flower** (ex **Explorer Starship**, ex **Begonia**, 8262 GRT) with accommodation for 200 passengers and the larger vessels such as the 37 845 GRT **Royal Viking Sun** with accommodation for up to 814.

The newly formed Silversea Cruises commissioned two sister ships, **Silver Cloud** and **Silver Wind**, each of 16 800 GRT with a capacity of 296, to enter service in 1994.

As a comparison Airtour's **Seawing**, 16 607 GRT carries up to 976 cruisers at any one time. Silversea cruisers have three times more room giving a PSR of 56.8 compared with **Seawing's** 17. The PSR for the **Sea Goddess** ships is 36.7 whilst the **Seabourn** vessels have a PSR of 48.8 (Ward, 1998).

The vessels were built by the Francesco Visentini Yard in Donada, Italy and fitted out by Mariotti in Genoa. The design team were Petter Yran and Bjorn Storbratten (see Chapter 6) and cost in excess of $300 million each. **Silver Wind** was delivered in 1994 with **Silver Cloud** following in 1995.

For those who wish for a traditional cruise experience with enough people to interact with, 300 fellow cruisers on a 16 800 GRT hull is a good combination and has proved very successful, posting operating profits in 1996 and 1997 and net profits since mid-1997.

In 1998 Silversea announced that they had ordered two new vessels for delivery in 2000 and 2001 (with options for two more for delivery in 2002 and 2003) from the same yard and designers as **Silver Wing** and **Silver Cloud**. The new ships will be bigger at 25 000 GRT.

Silversea's President and Chief Executive Officer is William L. Smith who joined the company in 1995 from Costa Cruises and is now based at the corporate headquarters in Fort Lauderdale, Florida.

That Silversea is successful can be gauged by the fact that their average occupancy is over 85 per cent (see earlier in the chapter) and despite the relatively high cost of a cruise, they have 45 per cent repeat business.

In addition to the luxury segment of the market, the cruises also provide a cultural experience with renowned guest lecturer's aboard and interesting itineraries. Under our early classification of cruisers, Silversea is able to appeal to Relaxers, Enthusiasts, Strollers, Seekers and Dippers, and have thus designed a product with a very broad market appeal.

All the accommodation is in outside suites the majority of which have balconies. Indeed, in design the ships show a marked resemblance, albeit much smaller, to the 48 621 GRT **Crystal Harmony** and the 50 202 GRT **Crystal Symphony** both with 1010 maximum capacity and operated by Crystal Cruises also as a luxury product. The smallest suite is 240 sq. ft (about the same size as an **Oriana** stateroom) whilst the veranda suites which form the bulk of the accommodation are 295 sq. ft. The full accommodation for **Silver Wind** and **Silver Cloud** is shown in Table 4.9.

In 1997, Silversea began a partnership with the National Geographic Traveler (sic) Series, and there were eight National Geographic cruises in 1998 and five in 1999, appealing very much to the Seeker market.

Table 4.9   Silversea accommodation

Type	Size (sq. ft)	Number
Vista suite (no balcony)	240	38
Veranda suite	295	74
Silver suites	541	3
Owners suite*	827	1
Royal suites*	1031	2
Grand suites*	1314	2

Note: * Can be configured as one or two bedrooms; there are two suites with disabled access.

As befits a luxury product, gratuities are included in the price of a cruise as are many drinks with the exception of the connoisseur wine list. An open dining policy has been adopted allowing cruisers to dine with whom they wish, a development that has been adopted by other companies and is now a regular feature of many Premium and Luxury cruises. Because of the size of vessel, Silversea are able to offer a full range of entertainment, the ships being equipped with a show-lounge for Broadway-type shows.

To illustrate the per diem charges of this type of luxury product, the examples in Table 4.10 are taken from the undiscounted eleven-day Adriatic Treasures cruise on the **Silver Wind**.

Table 4.10   Silversea prices

Type of suite	Price
Vista suite (no balcony)	£463
Veranda suite	£527
Silver suites	£872
Royal suites	£917
Grand suites	£972

A 10 per cent discount could be gained if a booking were made four months in advance and a further 10 per cent for six months in advance.

These are considerable sums, well over the average individual UK holiday spend (see Chapter 1) but it must be remembered that many of the costs of running a ship are the same no matter how many cruisers are carried. Earlier in this case study we compared the **Silver Wind** and **Silver Cloud** with the **Seawing** of similar size. Fuel costs, berthing, tugs etc. will be similar prices, as will staff costs. Despite carrying a third less passengers the Silversea ships have 210 crew to the **Seawing's** 320 (Ward, 1997), i.e. nearly two-thirds. It must also be remembered that gratuities, most drinks and some excursions are included as part of the Silversea experience, and these could add as much as £250 per person, per week to a cruise.

Nevertheless the price difference is considerable between the Luxury and the majority of Premium products. Why are people prepared to pay?

That they are prepared to pay is shown by the high occupancy rates and company profits.

The food is undoubtedly good as befits a Luxury product. The cruises have won a number of awards and the itineraries are interesting. We were fortunate that in addition to material supplied from Silversea we were able to talk with somebody who had actually cruised on one of the vessels and the report was very positive indeed. It was the space, the ambience and the 'culture' of fellow cruisers that was the main factor contributing to enjoyment. In the modern cruise industry, space on board has become a very important factor in choice for those trading up to a more expensive market.

There is no doubt that the Silversea ships are marvellous examples of the designer's art both from marine aspects and from the internal, holiday design perspective. The designs take the ideas from a private yacht and transport them into the world of larger ships. Naturally this is a great deal easier when the designer has so much space to play with and does not need to produce minimum-sized cabins.

The future for this particular sector of the market looks very secure. As other products move to more of a family orientation, there needs to be adequate provision made for the older age range of cruiser who are not only growing in number but have increasing disposable income — income they are prepared to spend on comfort.

We asked a number of our sample about Silversea. Our sample was used to paying an average per diem rate of £200. On examining what Silversea had to offer, there was agreement that the rates charged were high but not excessive. Whilst most of the sample would never be able to afford such rates on an annual basis, there might be a special occasion when they would be prepared to pay out that much given what they would get for it.

The luxury end of the market has one problem that we did perceive. Amongst our sample were a number of very regular cruisers who took four to five cruises per year, usually on the ships that were at the high end of Standard or in cheaper cabins on Premium ships. We calculated that they could swap their four to five cruises for one Silversea, but would they? Perhaps once, but they preferred to cruise regularly in moderate comfort to occasionally in complete luxury.

5

Cruising areas and the impact of cruising

This chapter includes:

- motivation
- cruising areas
- 4Cs related to cruising areas
- itinerary scores
- trends
- the impact of cruising
- case study: the Atlantic Islands.

Motivation

Where did the 7.2 million cruisers in the late 1990s go and how were the companies they cruise with positioned within the market?

Chapter 1 was concerned with why people cruise, this chapter explores the areas visited by the cruise industry – the where – and the companies they travel with – the who. The chapter is not intended to be a travelogue or a guide to cruise companies; there will be no descriptions of fabulous places but there will be an analysis of what it is that these places have to offer. We shall also be considering which are the major growth areas for the sector.

Two thirds of the earth's surface is covered by water and thus the cruise companies have, apparently, a huge choice of possible cruising areas. The actual dimensions of the world's oceans and seas are shown in Table 5.1.

However, a series of constraints act to restrict the choice considerably.

Table 5.1 The world's oceans and seas

Ocean/sea	Square miles
Pacific Ocean	63 986 000
Atlantic Ocean	31 744 000
Indian Ocean	23 350 000
Arctic Ocean	5 541 000
Caribbean Sea/Gulf of Mexico	1 450 000
Mediterranean Sea	1 145 000
South China Sea	895 000
Bering Sea	878 000
Hudson Bay	472 000
Sea of Japan	405 000
East China Sea	290 000
North Sea	221 000
Red Sea	178 000
Black Sea	168 000
Yellow Sea	161 000
Baltic	158 000

Source: Reader's Digest Great World Atlas

Mill (1990) states that there are four major dimensions to tourism – attractions, facilities, transportation and hospitality. The latter two dimensions are well catered for by the cruise industry, hospitality is 'guaranteed' and transportation is at least arranged from the embarkation port. Deals with air carriers, as we shall see in a later chapter, have ensured that there is a complete package available from the cruisers home country so that the choice of destination is likely to be influenced by attractions and facilities.

As Mill goes on to point out, attractions come in a number of guises – natural resources, culture, ethnicity and entertainment. To these must also be added climate. We are now only too aware of the harmful effects of the sun's rays on the human body but for much of the latter part of the twentieth century, holidays, for the vast bulk of Western Europeans and North

Americans, meant some time in the sun. The arrival of mass air transportation transformed secluded Mediterranean beaches into forests of sun umbrellas with bodies packed so densely that movement to and from the beach resembled an obstacle course.

The search for the sun is still a major feature of the cruise industry with no less than 77 per cent of the world's cruise capacity (see later figures) operating within areas renowned for their long, hot, sunny days. As can be seen from Chapter 1 where climate was the third priority for the younger age range, it is still a major feature for many cruisers. It may not always be given as the reason for taking a cruise over another type of holiday, but climate is a factor in where holidays are taken.

When we questioned cruisers about their choice of cruising area and itineraries we were surprised to find that the area to be cruised was less of a factor than we had imagined. As a rule of thumb the responses indicated that whilst the choice of a first or second cruise might be heavily influenced by the cruising area, experienced cruisers were more influenced by the cruise company or the ship *per se*, the actual itinerary being of less importance. By talking to a large number of cruisers of varying experience we concluded that itinerary formed 75 per cent of the choice of first cruise but only 25 per cent of the choice of the tenth or more cruise. By that stage, cruisers have a good knowledge of the ships and companies and have probably cruised a number of areas before. What was important, however, was that the area was safe, a factor we shall return to.

In order to refine those figures we examined the product from the major cruise companies, factoring in the maximum capacity of a ship and the number of voyages made in each area. This allowed us to compute the ratio between the various cruising areas. In doing so we made some general assumptions:

■ Cruises through the Panama Canal which commenced or terminated in the Caribbean or the West Coast of the USA or Mexico were classified as Transcanal not Caribbean or West Coast cruises as the major marketing emphasis on these cruises is the passage through the Panama Canal.
■ Cruises up or down the coast of South America that commenced or terminated in the Caribbean were classified as South American not Caribbean cruises.

On a general worldwide basis the averaged figures work out as shown in Table 5.2.

It is interesting to break these figures down even further by considering the markets cruises are offered to. Much of the Carnival group tonnage is in the

Table 5.2 1998/99 cruising areas by percentage berths offered

Area	Percentage
Caribbean	51
Mediterranean	21
Alaska	10
Asia	4
Eastern US Seaboard and Bermuda	3
Transcanal	2
US West Coast	2
Eastern Atlantic Islands	1
Baltic	1
Transatlantic	1
Norway etc.	1
Hawaii	0.4
South America	0.3
Black Sea	0.3
British Isles/Channel	0.3
Africa	0.2

Caribbean offering cruises to a predominately North American market and, whilst this leads to the Caribbean accommodating over half of the world's cruisers, non-US market operators need to consider the needs of their particular marketplace.

Comparative figures calculated from the major UK players, P&O, Airtours, Thomson, Fred Olsen etc., give a different set of preferences for the UK based sector (see Table 5.3).

The UK Caribbean sector began to grow considerably in 1998 when Thomson and Airtours began to run a major operation in the region. Prior to

Table 5.3 UK-based sector top three cruising areas

Area	Percentage
Mediterranean	42
Caribbean	28
Atlantic Islands	21

that many UK cruisers availed themselves, as they still do, of the major US players, especially Princess, for Caribbean cruises.

First, we shall conduct a survey of the cruising areas and then consider the infrastructure necessary to attract cruise passengers and the cruise companies. In Chapter 3 we introduced Kotler's (1980) '4Cs' of marketing and the Boston matrix and these will be related to the cruising areas in order to provide an analytical framework.

Cruising areas

The general areas given earlier break down into subsections, some of which are what we will term traditional cruising areas and others which have grown in popularity during the 1990s.

Caribbean

The Caribbean comprises three main subareas, Eastern, Western and Southern Caribbean. We shall examine each group in turn and then look at the area as a whole for population statistics that are important when examining the impact of cruising on an area.

Eastern Caribbean

This was the first of the Caribbean areas to be developed for cruising given its proximity to Miami and the growth of cruising from that port by Kloster etc. (see Chapter 2). The major visit ports for the Eastern Caribbean are those in the Virgin Islands (mainly St Thomas (see later), St Croix, Tortola) Puerto Pico, The Windward Islands (mainly Grenada, Barbados, St Lucia and Martinique) and the Leeward Islands (mainly Dominica, Guadeloupe, Antigua, St Kitts St Maarten/Martin). As will be shown later, these islands are all fairly close to each other and have the advantage of being developed by different Western nations thus providing contrasts in style. The islands offer French, US/Danish, British and Dutch influence. The French and Dutch islands still have major links with the 'mother country', the French Islands being classed as an integral part of France and use the French franc as their currency, whilst the Dutch islands form part of the Netherlands Antilles using the Netherlands Antilles guilder and include the Southern Caribbean ABC Islands (see later). Unites States' possessions are integrated into the USA and use the US dollar as their currency. Many of the formerly British islands have formed a currency union using the Eastern Caribbean dollar, whilst Barbados has its own dollar currency.

Also a traditional area but situated a little further north in the Atlantic are the Bahamas which frequently feature as three to four-day cruises from Miami.

To summarize:

- French islands: Martinique, Guadeloupe, St Martin part of the joint St Maarten/Martin)
- British influenced islands: Barbados, Grenada, St Lucia, Dominica, St Kitts, Tortola
- Dutch islands: St Maarten part of joint St Martin/St Maarten
- United States islands: Puerto Rico, St Thomas, St Croix.

During the wars between Britain, France, Spain and Holland in the seventeenth to early nineteenth centuries the islands changed hands many times due to their strategic position and, thus, influences from a number of European countries can be found within any one island. The US Virgin Islands were originally Danish and were purchased by the USA during the First World War for strategic reasons.

Western Caribbean

The Western Caribbean provides another route for the cruise companies and was developed following the success of the Eastern Caribbean. The main visit ports are Jamaica, Grand Cayman, Cozumel and Playa del Carmel (Mexico), and Ochos Rios, For political reasons Cuba has not been a cruise destination due to the embargo on US citizens visiting the island, although Costa did base a ship there during the mid-1990s. A change in relationships between the USA and Cuba could see the island featuring as a major destination. The Dominican Republic became a major cruise destination in the late 1990s when UK companies, especially Thomson, used it as a base for their Caribbean cruise and stay holidays.

Southern Caribbean

The last of the Caribbean areas to develop as a major cruise market, the Southern Caribbean contains destinations set on the route into the Atlantic from the Panama Canal. The development of Puerto Rico as a base port has enabled cruise operators to reach the Southern Caribbean in less time, thus improving the economics of visiting the area.

The main visit ports are La Guaira (Venezuela, for Caracas), the Dutch ABC Islands of Aruba, Bonaire and Curaçao, The San Blas Islands, Cartagena

(Columbia), Limon for a short excursion into part of the Panama Canal but not a full transit, and Trinidad. Many of these visit ports feature in Transcanal itineraries.

The Caribbean, with its three distinct itineraries provides a good market for the cruise companies; being relatively near to continental USA and with English as the predominant language and the US dollar accepted nearly everywhere. The region, as shown above, provides 51 per cent of the world market for cruising which equates to nearly 4 million cruisers per annum to the region in 1996.

Seasonal aspects

The Caribbean is not always a year round area due to the hurricane season. Whilst companies have extended their seasons in the Caribbean, the hurricane season between June and November can restrict operations. This does not present too much of a problem; the summer months are the best for cruising in Alaska and ships, with the exception of the latest superliners, are able to use the Panama Canal to move from the Caribbean to Alaska or can cross the Atlantic to the Mediterranean. For 1999 and 2000, Princess operated in the Caribbean from January to May, recommencing operations in October. Thomson operated a full-year service in 1998 but this was disrupted and at least one cruise had to be curtailed as reported on the BBC television programme *Watchdog* because of the danger of running into a hurricane. NCL were another company offering a year-round operation, whereas Costa followed the Princess pattern although their parent company, Carnival, ran a year-round operation.

Panama Canal

Transcanal cruises from east to west (Pacific to Atlantic) or west to east (Atlantic to Pacific) – you may like to check a map but the canal is cut in such a way that the normal west–east, Pacific to Atlantic, is reversed because of the shape of the Isthmus of Panama – form 2 per cent of the world market, approximately 150 000 cruisers in 1996.

As the canal transit is only part of the cruise, albeit an important highlight, Transcanal cruises form part of the North American West Coast or South American and Caribbean sectors.

In addition to the regular cruises that the companies offer through the Panama Canal, it is also important for positioning cruises (see later) especially when transferring ships between the Caribbean and Alaska.

Mediterranean/Black Sea/Red Sea

As far as the European market is concerned the Mediterranean forms the original traditional cruising area. Like the Caribbean, the Mediterranean is divided into a number of discrete but overlapping sections, Eastern and Western Mediterranean, and to these must be linked the Black and Red Seas.

Eastern Mediterranean

The Eastern Mediterranean cruise area was for many years linked to the Greek Islands. Based mainly out of Piraeus, a large number of Greek companies operated a series of cruises to the islands of the Aegean region. Zenfell (1995) claims that there were thirty cruise companies operating in the Greek Islands in that year. These included the major players, RCI, Princess, P&O, NCL etc., but also Royal Olympic and a number of smaller concerns operating combined cruise/ferry operations. The traditional visit ports of the Eastern Mediterranean in addition to Piraeus (for Athens and a major base port) include Corfu, Katakolon, Rhodes, Crete, Zakynthos, Santorni, Venice (as a base port), Cephalonia and Dubrovnik (Dalmatia). For much of the late 1990s, the Dalmatian coast including Dubrovnik was left out of cruise itineraries due to the conflict in the former Yugoslavia but by 1998 the port was reappearing in the brochures.

The introduction of *Oriana* by P&O Cruises in 1995 allowed Southampton to become a base port for Eastern Mediterranean cruises offered by the company, her speed allowing her to cruise from Southampton to Haifa in Israel during a seventeen-night cruise.

An extension to the traditional Eastern Mediterranean cruise that was offered from the mid-1990s onwards was to the Holy Land and the Egyptian coast. Airtours began to offer regular three/four- or seven-day cruises out of Cyprus and most of the major companies now have such an itinerary, normally taking in Haifa, Ashdod, Port Said and Alexandria, allowing cruisers to visit both Jerusalem and Cairo. These particular itineraries are, naturally, dependent upon the security situation in the area and in 1998, Costa revised their schedule for the *Costa Riviera* by cancelling their 'Eastern Delights' programme to the area due to the political situation.

An extension of this itinerary is to cruise the Suez Canal and visit Jordan's Red Sea ports (especially those close to Petra) or to include Beirut, a city recovering after years of warfare.

The political events in the former Soviet Union has opened up the Black Sea as a cruise destination. Normally linked to visits to Turkish ports – Istanbul, Izmir, Kusadasi – and often based out of Piraeus, Odessa (Ukraine), Constanza (Romania) and Yalta (Crimea) are becoming popular destinations.

Western Mediterranean

This sector of the Mediterranean has largely seen political stability since the Second World War and has ports and resorts well able to accommodate cruise passengers. Civitavecchia (Rome), Livorno (Florence), Naples and the surrounding area, Portofino, Malta, Sicily, the French Riviera, Barcelona, Cadiz and Gibraltar have retained their popularity with cruisers. The US market is well represented in this area, in part due to the large numbers of US citizens who have ancestors in the region, especially Italy. The area is also easily reached from Northern European ports.

Thomson and Airtours, as major UK package holiday providers have used their position in the Western Mediterranean land-holiday market as the springboard for their expansion into cruises. Both use Majorca as one of their major base ports, the island being very popular with UK holiday-makers and thus being ideal for cruise and stay packages.

The Mediterranean, long the preserve of the UK and the European market, is rapidly being discovered by North American cruisers. Thus in the same port one can find ships on almost the same itineraries but with a British, North American or general European ambience on board, e.g. P&O Cruises, Princess and MSC.

Whilst the Mediterranean and Black Sea only account for just over 21 per cent of the worldwide cruise market, they are the favoured destinations for 43 per cent of the UK market, reflecting the ease of reaching the area in the same way that the Caribbean attracts the most North Americans.

There is no specific season for the Mediterranean although, for the US market, the summer months are preferred and this fits in well with the Caribbean hurricane season. Over 1.6 million cruisers were visiting the Mediterranean by 1996.

Alaska

After the Mediterranean, Norway and the Caribbean, the next major cruising development was Alaska. The grandeur of the scenery, the wildlife and the suprisingly mild summer climate has given Alaska 10 per cent of the market, i.e. nearly 760 000 cruisers in 1996.

The major base port for Alaskan cruises is Vancouver with itineraries being of seven to ten days duration and taking in Glacier Bay, Scagway, the Inside Passage, Juneau, Seward, Sitka and Ketchican. Those we interviewed who had been on an Alaskan cruise rated it as one of the most interesting and dramatic holidays they had experienced. The cruise companies also offer extension packages to see the Alaskan and Canadian hinterlands and these appear very popular with European cruisers for whom the journey to Vancouver is relatively long and who require a longer holiday experience.

Given the nature of Alaska and the sensitivity about shipping following the *Exxon Valdez* oil spillage, environmental concerns are uppermost in the state authority's mind and representations have been made to limit the number of large cruise ships visiting the area at any one time.

The Alaskan season is relatively short lasting, from May to September, and given the growing popularity of the area this is leading to increased pressure on the facilities at visit ports. Cruising in Alaskan waters is set to grow in popularity but that growth will be constrained by the ability of the infrastructure to cope. People go on an Alaskan cruise to experience the wilderness nature of the area and there is considerable danger that in taming the wilderness to accommodate cruise growth, the very thing cruisers want will be lost.

Eastern Atlantic Islands

The Eastern Atlantic Islands were one of the earliest cruise areas, Madeira being especially popular with the British. The cruising area comprises two sectors: the Canary Islands (Tenerife, Las Palmas and Lanzarote) and the Moroccan ports of Agadir and Casablanca for seven-day cruises normally based from the Canaries; and for the traditional eleven- to fourteen-day cruises from the UK, the Canary Islands plus visits to a selection of ports on the Iberian Peninsula. The most popular visit ports for the latter are La Coruna, Vigo (Spain) and Lisbon and the Algarve (Portugal). The visit to Northern Spain allows cruisers to visit the famous pilgrimage shrine of Santiago de Compostela.

All of the visit ports are either mature holiday destinations in their own right or major cities, and thus the cruise industry is a welcome but marginal addition to the tourist industry in these places. The Canaries are especially popular for cruise and stay holidays.

The area developed very early for cruising because it lay close to the traditional P&O routes (the company having been originally formed to serve the Iberian Peninsula). The climate is such as to allow year-round cruising; Madeira having long been a popular winter destination for financially well-off British since the early years of the twentieth century.

Although the area accounts for only 1 per cent of the world market – 76 000 cruisers in 1996 – it attracts 21 per cent of the UK market. With Thomson and Airtours operating fairly intensive seven-day cruises based on the Canaries and regular cruises from Direct Cruises, P&O, Fred Olsen etc. out of the UK, plus operations by Costa and MSC out of the Mediterranean, the area looks set to grow considerably and has the tourist infrastructure to cope with this growth.

The above areas are the 'cash cows' for the cruise companies. They know the areas well, there is good repeat business and the facilities to handle cruise ships are in place. (See the case study at the end of this chapter.)

Asia

Although Asia as an area attracted only 4 per cent of the world market in 1997, it was the fastest growing cruise destination area in two respects. First, more and more Western cruisers were visiting the area and, second, the indigenous Asian market was growing rapidly.

The Japanese indigenous market has developed into a self-standing entity with ships dedicated to the Japanese cruiser and fitted out with the type of facilities required by that market. Examples of such ships include the 28 717 GRT *Asuka* of NYK Cruises launched in 1991 and the 23 340 GRT *Fuji Maru* of Mitsui OSK launched in 1989.

There was tremendous growth between 1994 and 1998 in cruises around the Thailand/Singapore area with considerable take up by both North American and UK cruisers. By 1998, Thomson were including Star cruises out of Phuket (Thailand) as part of their brochure and Star cruises themselves plus Sun Vista Line were expanding their fleets. The young Indonesian market was set to be tapped by Awani Cruises who acquired the 11 724 GRT *Awanai Dream* (ex *World Renaissance*) and the 17 593 GRT *Awani Dream 2* (ex *Cunard Countess*) to operate for their home market.

Awani Cruises never got off the ground, having been hit by the 1998 collapse in the Asian economy and the political instability in Indonesia that led to the fall of the government in late 1998 when the whole of the indigenous market in Asia became depressed. However, the strength of Western currencies against the depressed Asian ones has made the costs of cruising in Asian waters relatively attractive, at least in the short term, and the market looks set to attract more and more Western cruisers as it offers an affordable taste of the Orient but with Western food etc. when required. Princess operated a full service using the *Sky Princess* (45~000 GRT) in the Asian areas of the Pacific, their year 2000 itineraries including China, Japan, Vietnam, Thailand, Australia and New Zealand.

Carnival Cruises (Asia) was due to commence operations in 1998 as a joint venture with the Korean Industrial giant Hyundai but this deal was terminated and the *Tropicale* returned to full Carnival control (Ward, 1998)

The Australian market has relied heavily on the major companies offering cruises out of Australian waters as part of their product portfolio but P&O Holidays have had a ship operating high-density cruises out of Australia for a number of years. Originally using the *Fairstar* (23 764 GRT) the former Bibby Line troop carrier *Oxfordshire* of 1957 was replaced by the (one year older!) *Fair Princess* (ex *Fairsea/Fairland/Carinthia*, 24 724 GRT) in 1997.

In 1992, 95 000 Asians including 20 000 Japanese cruised. By 1996 this had increased to 725 000 (225 000 Japanese) (Ward, 1995; 1998) showing the tremendous increase in the Asian market, a market that the downturn in economies may slow only temporarily.

Eastern United States Seaboard and Bermuda

Bermuda has always been popular for short cruises from the Eastern Seaboard of the USA, being a popular destination for the 'booze cruises' of the Depression (see Chapter 2). The area has retained its popularity for short cruises out of New York, Miami and Boston (MA) but there has been an increasing growth in the 1990s in cruises from Quebec, down the St Lawrence to the ports of the North Eastern USA, Boston (MA) and New York. Normally operated in the autumn, the climate is mild and cruisers are able to sample the French atmosphere of Quebec, the scenery of the St Lawrence Seaway, the foliage of New England in the 'Fall' and one of the metropolitan centres of the North Eastern USA. Led by NCL and Princess, a growing number of sailings are being offered for this growth region which, like the Atlantic Islands and the Mediterranean, has a good infrastructure to support that growth. Although the cruise industry is welcome, the areas visited are not dependent upon it.

United States West Coast

The US West Coast cruises are normally based out of the Los Angeles area and take in the Pacific Coast ports of Mexico between Los Angeles (USA) and

Acapulco. The area does not attract the same numbers of cruisers as the Caribbean – only 150 000 cruisers in 1996 (2 per cent of the world market). There is really only one country to visit on a short cruise although some of the Transcanal cruises operate up to Los Angeles or even San Francisco.

Northern Europe: Norway/the Baltic/the British Isles

Norway has been a firm favourite with European cruisers since the earliest days of cruising and is now firmly established as a traditional itinerary usually operating from Dover or Southampton. The scenery is magnificent although, like Alaska, it is definitely a summer cruising area. Typical cruises take in a number of fjords plus Oslo or Bergen and often another Northern European city – Copenhagen, Amsterdam etc. The area has grown both by extending cruises northwards towards Spitzbergen – a move made possible by the easing of tensions with the former Soviet Union as this was an area of major strategic significance for both the North Atlantic Treaty Organization (NATO) and the Warsaw Pact – and by including Greenland and Iceland as part of the itineraries with cruises entitled 'Land of Fire and Water' (Direct Cruises).

Norway received approximately 76 000 cruisers in 1996 but the UK market for the area is increasing and it features regularly in P&O Cruises, Fred Olsen, Cunard, Direct Cruises and Page and Moy brochures. The area is also receiving increased attention from the North American market; the area being so close to the Baltic as to allow for the alternation of cruises based on Dover or Southampton.

The Eastern end of the Baltic was for many years a closed area due to the tensions between the Warsaw Pact and NATO. St Petersburg (formerly Leningrad) was one of the first USSR ports to welcome cruise ship passengers by relaxing visa requirements (a group visa was acceptable for all those travelling on organized excursions). Following independence for Latvia and Estonia and the opening up of Poland the ports of Tallinn (Estonia), Gdansk (Poland) and Riga (Latvia) have also welcomed the cruise industry, together with Helsinki and Stockholm.

Easily reached from the UK Channel ports, the Baltic offers a chance to visit what was part of the Soviet Union and towns that have not changed as much as their Western counterparts. More and more UK and North American operators are including Baltic itineraries as part of their portfolio.

The British Isles began to attract the North American market in the late 1990s. United Kingdom ports have long been associated as base ports for the UK market but there has been little indigenous British Isles cruising. British

Rail offered such a cruise with the converted ferry *Avalon* in the 1960s and a series of mini-cruises to Orkney and Shetland are operated by P&O out of Aberdeen as part of their normal ferry operation.

The excellent *Hebridean Princess* began operations in the middle 1990s (to be covered under niche cruising) but by 1998/9 the major cruise companies were offering cruises that circumnavigated the British Isles with calls at a variety of ports including Guernsey, Falmouth, Cork, Dublin, Holyhead, Glasgow, Orkney, Invergordon and Edinburgh. Princess offering eight such cruises in 1999 with NCL also offering an around Britain experience. To the British it may seem strange that the second largest provider of cruisers should have become a cruise destination in its own right.

Many of the areas being developed for the North American market are also those where many North Americans have their roots – the UK, Ireland, the Baltic States, the Balkans, Italy, Greece etc. – and many of the North American cruisers we spoke to in these areas were 'seeking' some form of family history.

Hawaii

The Hawaiian Islands may seem like an ideal area for cruising, given their climate, romantic connotations and proximity to each other. In fact they account for only 0.4 per cent of the world market (just over 300 000 cruisers in 1996). This is owing to their isolated nature, miles away from the US mainland, the lack of other visit ports in the region and the fact that US shipping laws forbid foreign-flag ships from operating a service between US ports – Hawaii is a State of the Union. This forces the cruise companies to add another destination if undertaking an inter-island cruise or commencing/terminating the cruise in another country, usually Vancouver in Canada.

Hawaiian Island cruises which operated two US-flag vessels for a number of years has been unable to compete with the newer tonnage operated by the main companies. The *Independence* and the *Constitution* (each 20 221 GRT) were built in 1951 and lack many of the facilities of newer ships, including stabilizers. The former was withdrawn from service in 1997 and the future of the latter looked doubtful in 1998.

Despite the problems the main cruise companies do offer a number of Hawaiian cruises as part of their portfolio; NCL offered three in 1998 and Princess offered such cruises as well. A typical itinerary, showing the distance problems, especially for a UK cruiser, is shown in Table 5.4.

Table 5.4 Typical NCL 1998 Hawaiian itinerary from the UK

Sat. 4 April:	Fly London–San Diego
Sun. 5 April:	Drive San Diego–Ensenada and join *Norwegian Dynasty*
Mon–Fri 6–10 April:	Cruising in the Pacific
Sat. 11 April:	Hilo, Hawaii 1200–2000
Sun. 12 April:	Kona, Hawaii 0800–1800
Mon. 13 April:	Lahaina, Naui 0800–1800
Tues. 14 April:	Nawaiiwili. Kauai 0800–1800
Wed. 15 April:	Honolulu, Oahu, disembark and spend day and night
Thur. 16 April:	Fly to continental USA for transfer to flight to UK
Fri. 17 April:	Arrive London

South America

In Boston matrix terms (Chapter 3), this is a 'star' area. In the early 1990s the Amazon from Manaus to the sea and thence to the Caribbean began to be offered by a growing number of cruise companies.

The Amazon offered a unique experience including native villages and a very warm but humid climate running as it does along the equator for much of its length. In 1992 the crew of the *Pacific Princess* had to proceed ashore before the passengers at one location in order to construct a temporary landing stage, so remote was the area.

Since then, South America has begun to feature more and more with cruises taking in both the West and East coasts of the continent, and the Falkland Islands – of especial interest to UK cruisers following the 1982 conflict with Argentina. Cape Horn, so feared by the sailing ships of earlier years, now features as a cruise attraction, albeit a seasonal one due to the very severe Southern Hemisphere winter in that region.

Africa

The other 'star' is Africa. Political instability has long made Africa, with the exception of Tunisia and Morocco in the north and Kenya/Tanzania for safaris, a problematic holiday destination.

South Africa and Kenya began to feature as cruise destinations in the late 1990s both for the main cruise companies and for smaller operators such as the Swiss-based African Safari Club. The latter uses the 5360 GRT *Royal Star* (ex *Ocean Islander*) operating out of Mombasa and, like the main companies, offers a safari experience in addition to the cruise. (See Chapters 4 and 8.)

139

In 1998 there were a number of attacks on tourists in Kenya and thus the area became something of a 'problem child' but the authorities promised urgent action.

Transatlantic

Chapter 2 on the history of cruising pointed out that today's cruising had its roots in the transatlantic passenger trade. By the 1980s there was only one ship making regular passenger crossings of the North Atlantic – the *QE2*.

Nevertheless it is still possible to make an Atlantic crossing on other liners, usually by the longer southern route with its better weather. Such cruises are offered because the companies need to position ships between the Caribbean and the Mediterranean and thus there are usually a series of such cruises eastward in spring and westward in autumn.

World cruises

The dream of many lottery winners is a world or partial world cruise. Lasting for up to three months, a world cruise circumnavigates the globe and for that period the ship really does become the cruiser's home.

Ward (1998) lists eighteen world or partial world cruises (normally a half-navigation of the globe) offered by fourteen companies. For those unable to spend so long away from home, the companies usually offer a series of sector cruises on a fly out/back, sail out/fly back or fly out/sail back basis.

To illustrate the wide variety of experiences a world cruise offers, the itinerary for the 1999 *Oriana* world cruise, which commenced on 4 January is given in Figure 5.1.

Southampton - at sea - at sea - at sea - Tenerife - at sea - at sea - at sea - at sea - at sea - at sea - Rio de Janeiro - at sea - at sea - at sea - at sea - at sea - at sea - Cape Town - at sea - at sea - at sea - at sea - at sea - Reunion - Mauritius - at sea - at sea - at sea - at sea - at sea - at sea - at sea - Penang - Singapore - at sea - at sea - Bali - at sea - at sea - at sea - Perth (Australia) - at sea - at sea - at sea - Hobart (Tasmania) - at sea - Sydney - at sea - at sea - at sea - Christchurch (New Zealand) - at sea - Auckland (New Zealand) - at sea - at sea - Pago Pago - at sea - at sea - at sea - at sea - Honolulu - at sea - at sea - at sea - at sea - at sea - Vancouver (Canada) - at sea - at sea - San Francisco - at sea - at sea - at sea - Acapulco - at sea - at sea - at sea - transit Panama Canal - at sea - Aruba (Netherlands Antilles) - at sea - Grenada - Barbados - at sea - at sea - at sea - at sea - Madeira - at sea - at sea - Southampton

---

Figure 5.1   The 1999 *Oriana* world cruise

The 4Cs related to cruising areas

Customer value

Despite itineraries being less a deciding factor for regular cruisers, once embarked upon their cruise most people (not all) want to spend some time ashore, and the ports of call need to offer something for them to see and do and to spend their money on. St Thomas in the US Virgin Islands is an almost mandatory port of call for North American sector vessels in the Caribbean because of its duty free prices; Civitavecchi (for Rome) and Livorno (for Florence) offer culture, Amazon villages offer an insight into a unique way of life. Alaska offers spectacular scenery and the possibility of seeing a whale, whilst the Panama Canal allows cruisers to marvel at the engineering skills needed to connect the Atlantic and the Pacific.

Cruising is not a means of immersing oneself in a culture. The 1999 approximately two-week itineraries in Table 5.5, Cruise A from the Caribbean and Cruise B from the Mediterranean, show just how little time is spent in port. From the arrival and departure times must be subtracted at least two, and probably three, hours to allow for port clearance, breakfast and ensuring that passengers are back on board before the ship sails. Passengers who 'miss the boat' can be a major problem! Cruise A is a typical 'back-to-back' Caribbean cruise made up of two seven-day cruises.

We have discounted embarkation and disembarkation days as these are effectively lost to the customer through jet lag, waiting for luggage, being hampered by hand luggage etc.

Thus we can see that a cruise gives very little time to immerse oneself in a place. How much can you see and do in eight to ten hours, especially when many of the places are very similar?

The Caribbean cruise (Cruise A in Table 5.5), being a back-to-back package gives the cruiser two opportunities to shop in St Thomas. The American Virgin Islands were acquired from Denmark during the First World War as a means of the USA establishing a presence to guard the Atlantic end of the Panama Canal. Even today the Danish influence is still strong with names like Charlotte Amarlie (the capital of St Thomas) and the Royal Danish Mall and the fact that the Virgin Islands are the only part of the USA to drive on the left as Denmark did at the time of transfer. St Thomas is not only famous for its shops, of which there are many but also for its beaches, St Megan's Bay being one of the world's most beautiful beaches, and attractions such as Coral World. It is a matter of conjecture as to whether St Thomas really is a place

141

Table 5.5　Times in port

Date	Port	Arrive	Depart	Time in port	Effective time in port

Cruise A: Caribbean, MV *Dawn Princess*, Princess Cruises, Tropical cocktail cruise

Date	Port	Arrive	Depart	Time in port	Effective time in port
Sat. 16/1	San Juan		2300	Embarkation	0
Sun. 17/1	At sea			0	0
Mon. 18/1	Aruba	0700	1800	11	9
Tues. 19/1	La Guaira	0800	1800	10	8
Wed. 20/1	Grenada	1200	1800	6	4
Thur. 21/1	Dominica	0700	1700	10	8
Fri. 22/1	St Thomas	0800	1800	10	8
Sat. 23/1	San Juan	0600	2300	17	15
Sun. 24/1	At sea			0	0
Mon. 25/1	Barbados	0700	1800	11	9
Tues. 26/1	St Lucia	0700	1700	10	8
Wed. 27/1	St Maarten	0800	1800	10	8
Thur. 28/1	St Kitts	0800	1800	10	8
Fri. 29/1	St Thomas	0700	1800	11	9
Sat. 30/1	San Juan			Disembarkation, day at leisure	
Total				116	94

Cruise B: Mediterranean, MV *Pacific Princess*, Princess Cruises Eastern classical cruise

Date	Port	Arrive	Depart	Time in port	Effective time in port
Sun. 9/5	Istanbul			Embarkation 7	3
Mon. 10/5	Istanbul		1300	13	3
Tues. 11/5	Ephesus	1200	2000	8	6
Wed. 12/5	Mykanos	0800	1800	10	8
Thur. 13/5	Crete	0800	1800	10	8
Fri. 14/5	Athens	0800	1800	10	8
Sat. 15/5	At sea			0	0
Sun. 16/5	Malta	0800	1500	7	5
Mon. 17/5	At sea			0	0
Tues. 18/5	Barcelona	0800	1700	9	7
Wed. 19/5	St Tropez	0900	1800	9	7
Thur. 20/5	Portofino	0800	1500	7	6
Fri. 21/5	Civitavecchia	0800	1800	10	8
Fri. 29/1	St Thomas	0700	1800	11	9
Sat. 30/1	San Juan			Disembarkation	
Total				121	78

for bargains, US citizens seem to think so, but it does attract the cruise ships. We counted no fewer than three large ships alongside plus one medium-sized ship and another large ship at anchor on one spring morning in 1997. That gave a possible maximum of 10 400 passengers and crew to add to the 12 500 population (1992) of Charlotte Amarlie, and that was not the busiest day of the season. Despite being devastated by hurricanes in the late 1990s, St Thomas remains a major attraction for the US cruise sector. St Thomas is far different to the sleepy atmosphere to be found on the neighbouring British Virgin Islands (BVI).

Every port of call needs at least one attraction, in a way its own unique selling point (USP). The main categories of attractions are:

- scenery and wildlife
- lifestyle
- shopping
- culture and history
- activities.

Note: these are not exclusive. a port may have two or three attractions but, even if it has all of them, it would be difficult to experience so many in the short time the ship will be there.

In order to quantify the attraction of an area, we asked our 100 cruisers to allocate ten points between the various attractions of an area (if they had visited it, why, or why they *might* visit it). After averaging out the responses we were able to allocate scores to the attractions of various cruising areas with a score of ten being the highest and one the lowest.

Scenery and wildlife

Alaska and Norway offer towering cliffs and icebergs and the possibility of seeing whales. The Falkland Islands provide a glimpse of almost total isolation whilst the Amazon provides an opportunity to see the world's largest rain forest in a degree of luxury, and islands such as Trinidad are able to offer package excursions to see humming birds at close quarters. Nearly every Caribbean port of call offers the opportunity to snorkel or view the underwater world from the comfort of a semi- or full submersible. More cruises are beginning to offer spectacular scenery and wildlife as part of the package and the growing success of cruises to the north of Europe, the very tip of South America and Alaska is testimony to this trend amongst cruisers. Princess Cruises have become experts in the packaging of Alaska with a series of

Alaskan and Canadian add-on packages (to be considered in more detail in a later chapter) in order to enhance the customer value. Given that the majority of passengers will have travelled a considerable distance, it makes commercial sense to offer the opportunity to see more of the area.

In the search for grander and wilder scenery recent trends have seen Iceland and Greenland added to some Northern European itineraries, and Antarctica beckons. There are some niche cruises that take in the Antarctic (as we shall see later) but the area is protected under a number of international agreements, the climate is not especially hospitable and there is little to do other than to marvel at the wilderness. There are certainly no shopping malls or quayside folkloric demonstrations.

The scores for wildlife and scenery for the various cruising areas are shown in Table 5.6.

The prime reason for people choosing Alaskan and Norwegian itineraries was the scenery and the possibility of seeing endangered species, especially aquatic mammals and bears, on the Alaskan inland packages. African cruises are frequently linked with safaris especially those offered by Princess and the smaller *Royal Star* (GRT 5360) operated in conjunction with the Swiss-based African Safari Club. The Eastern Seaboard of the USA which includes St Lawrence River itineraries normally as part of a Montreal–Boston/

Table 5.6   Scenery/wildlife scores

Area	Score
Caribbean	2
Mediterranean	1
Alaska	8
Asia	1
Eastern US Seaboard and Bermuda	2
Panama Canal	4
US West Coast	0
Eastern Atlantic Isles	2
Baltic	0
Norway	9
Hawaii	3
South America	4
Black Sea	0
British Isles	2
Africa	6

New York cruise was found to be popular for the St Lawrence scenery and the Fall foliage in New England, most of the cruises being timed to coincide with the autumnal colours.

Areas of special scientific interest such as the Galapagos Islands have cruise ship visits heavily regulated and, in the example given, are not easy to visit due to distance. Cruises to such areas, known, as expedition cruises, will be examined in more detail in Chapter 8.

Lifestyle

Amazon villages, quaint cobbled streets and even a deserted beach: they may be the cruisers' for only a few hours but they do provide an opportunity to 'get away from the day-to-day existence' and savour some atmosphere.

One of the advantages of cruising over air travel is in the manner of arrival and departure from a port. The days of spectacular send-offs as seen in the film *Titanic* or on newsreels of celebrities embarking and arriving on the great Atlantic liners may be a thing of the past, but for those who can rise early enough there is still romance in seeing your destination emerge over the horizon and the whole experience of docking, often quite near the centre of a town – an experience sadly lacking in air travel where all international airports seem the same and the only smell is that of jet fuel. As the ship nears the quay, the senses can be assailed with sights, sounds and even smells (pleasant spices and some of the more unpleasant odours that can hang around port areas). Certain areas are famous for their 'entries'. New York with the Verazanno Narrows Bridge, the Statue of Liberty, Ellis Island and the Manhattan skyline, Istanbul with the minarets of the mosques emerging out of the haze and Venice with a passage past the Doge's Palace are prime examples.

Passengers leaving Southampton on a P&O Cruises operation are treated to a military band to play them out of port and many communities now provide bands etc. to welcome and say goodbye to cruise ships.

Within the Caribbean, the islands themselves and their descriptions within the cruise company brochures make considerable play on lifestyle USPs. Barbados emphasizes its British influence, Martinique and Guadeloupe and St Martin (the French part of St Maarten) are distinctly French in ambience (and currency); the ABC Islands, Aruba, Bonaire and Curaçao are distinctively Dutch, as is the Dutch part of St Maarten. For US cruisers, these islands have the added bonus of a European ambience giving added customer value.

Recent Caribbean trends have included places such as the San Blas Islands with their 'unspoilt' Indian lifestyle, although for how long an area can remain unspoilt once a succession of cruise ships begin to call is debatable.

Many of the companies even have their own Caribbean islands where cruise passengers can be castaways for a day, albeit with a bar and buffet not too far away. Princess Cays (Princess Cruises), Castaway Cay (Disney) and Great Stirrup Cay (NCL) are examples of these private islands. Having the vessel stop at them has decided advantages for the company as they are in control of spending and thus do not have to share any income with shore-based traders. For the cruiser they provide a safe, if somewhat artificial, environment.

Experiencing lifestyles whilst on a cruise is a very safe experience. Just as a group of tourists we spoke to in a Tunisian hotel rarely ventured away from the air-conditioned interior and the beautifully laid out grounds, so cruise ship passengers can experience a different lifestyle but always within a short distance from their cultural bubble, i.e. their cruise ship. It is debatable just how much of the flavour of a place one can obtain in such a short period of time but nevertheless, the stops do seem to meet the need for experiencing something different, albeit superficially. See Table 5.7 for lifestyle scores.

The highest lifestyle scores are for those areas that are least like the cruisers' home areas. Asia, the former Soviet Union and the Holy Land figure

Table 5.7   Lifestyle scores

Area	Score
Caribbean	3
Mediterranean	3
Alaska	2
Asia	5
Eastern US Seaboard and Bermuda	3
Panama Canal	1
US West Coast	4
Eastern Atlantic Isles	5
Baltic	4
Norway	1
Hawaii	3
South America	4
Black Sea	5
British Isles	4
Africa	3

highly. Perhaps surprisingly so do the US West Coast and the British Isles. Round-UK cruises for the US market are a rapidly growing feature of the cruise lines' itineraries and the case study at the end of this chapter is concerned with the effects of the cruise industry in Scotland.

Shopping

As the scores in Table 5.8 indicate, shopping *per se* is not a major reason for choosing an itinerary but, as mentioned earlier, most Caribbean cruises for the US market include at least one day in St Thomas.

Table 5.8 Shopping scores

Area	Score
Caribbean	2
Mediterranean	1
Alaska	0
Asia	2
Eastern US Seaboard and Bermuda	1
Panama Canal	1
US West Coast	0
Eastern Atlantic Isles	0
Baltic	0
Norway	0
Hawaii	0
South America	0
Black Sea	0
British Isles	0
Africa	0

One of the major developments of the late 1990s in the Caribbean was the building of quayside shopping malls. Barbados, St Lucia, Willemstad (Curaçao) and St Thomas itself have all invested in such facilities. In the main they are populated with the well-known Caribbean shopping names, H. Stern, Colombian Emeralds etc. The close proximity to the ship makes it even easier not to leave the environmental bubble. Other Caribbean Islands may have market stalls near the quay and in many other areas local traders will set up temporary stalls to sell the obligatory T-shirts. Port Said in Egypt still presents a dazzling picture to the cruiser with traders hanging on to pontoons, and even the ship's gangway, in order to offer their wares. The development of quayside malls raises the concern that the cruiser may spend even less that directly benefits the local economy as most of the stores that are accommodated in these facilities are international in nature and thus their profits will eventually find their way back to their home base.

The ships themselves also run their own retail outlets on board. International regulations ban the use of shipboard facilities such as shops, casinos and passenger radio messages whilst in port, and thus there is no direct competition with shore-side retailers but the shops on board stock not only essentials but also clothes and souvenirs. The on-board shops are described as 'duty free' and this is true; they do not charge duty on goods but they are not profit free and savings may not always be as great (or as actual) as is claimed. A $350 'duty free' piece of jewellery on sale on a Caribbean cruise vessel was available for only $280 in a well-known New York department store during the same week!

It is also important to remember that customs allowances differ between nationalities. European Union citizens on a Mediterranean cruise that only includes EU countries have virtually no limit on what they can buy. If they are on a cruise in any other area strict limits apply, as they do to US citizens re-entering the US after a cruise. Custom's allowances and the amount that can be physically carried especially on to an aircraft can limit the amount bought. In some areas, especially Turkey, items such as rugs can be sent direct to the cruiser's home address, giving a little more scope for shopping.

Our research showed that the amounts spent on shopping were not great, averaging about $30 (£20) per person per day in port excluding excursions. Our figure was slightly higher than the 'paltry' $20 per day quoted by Hamlyn (1998) as the average spend per day per cruise ship passenger in the Caribbean.

As the Asian cruise market grows, Hong Kong and Singapore are likely to attract more cruise ships but, because of their already dominant positions within the Asian retail market, this will provide only a marginal increase in total trade. For St Thomas the cruise ships passengers provide the bulk of retail income.

Culture and history

Mayan, Greek and Roman ruins plus cities such as Rome, Venice, Istanbul, Beijing, Jerusalem and St Petersburg enable the cruise passenger to imbibe a little culture.

Closely linked to lifestyle preferences (see earlier), certain areas – notably the Mediterranean, the Black Sea and the Baltic – enable the cruise passenger to visit some of the cultural Mecca's of the world. Given the length of stay, these visits will be very brief and the cruise passenger is likely to rely on arranged excursions to enable them to see the main attractions. The stays are certainly not long enough to visit major art galleries such as the Uffizi in Florence or the Hermitage in St Petersburg and will normally allow time for a visit to only one major attraction. Some cultural sites, e.g. Florence or Lisbon, are small enough for the passenger to walk around but the large cities such as Rome can only be tasted.

Swan Hellenic (part of P&O) cruises on the 12 000 GRT *Minerva* are directly targeted at those who wish a cultural experience and carry academic authorities to aid passengers in their understanding. *Minerva* will be considered further in Chapter 8. See Table 5.9 for culture scores.

Table 5.9   Culture scores

Area	Score
Caribbean	2
Mediterranean	5
Alaska	0
Asia	2
Eastern US Seaboard and Bermuda	3
Panama Canal	3
US West Coast	4
Eastern Atlantic Isles	3
Baltic	6
Norway	0
Hawaii	2
South America	2
Black Sea	5
British Isles	4
Africa	2

Activities

Most of the off-ship activities on offer by the cruise lines relate to water. Snorkelling, paragliding and barbecue trips abound in the Caribbean. Our research showed that these virtually never formed the reason for choosing an itinerary and as far as the Caribbean is concerned (where most of these

Table 5.10 Activity scores

Area	Score
Caribbean	1
Mediterranean	0
Alaska	0
Asia	0
Eastern US Seaboard and Bermuda	1
Panama Canal	1
US West Coast	2
Eastern Atlantic Isles	0
Baltic	0
Norway	0
Hawaii	1
South America	0
Black Sea	0
British Isles	0
Africa	0

activities take place) each port of call offers very much the same. Our sample was virtually unanimous that if it were activities that they wanted, they would book a hotel holiday. Nevertheless, the offer of such activities does provide an opportunity for people to try something in a safe environment. The activity scores can be seen in Table 5.10.

Port lecturers

The cruise companies provide port lecturers on board to advise passengers on the facilities available at each port of call in addition to the leaflets that are normally provided for passengers. The quality of these lecturers is extremely variable. Some are very knowledgeable about local customs and history, others appear to work for the shore-side retail outlets and provide a mere list of suitable places to shop.

Cost

For many years Dover in Kent has been the major UK departure port for cross-Channel ferries to France and Belgium. The introduction of services through the Channel Tunnel in the early 1990s led to a degree of decline for the cross-Channel car ferry trade with the resultant redundancy of some of Dover's port facilities. The Dover Harbour Board has been very successful in attracting the cruise industry into using Dover as a base port for cruises, especially to the Baltic and Norway. Because they already had a fully equipped harbour with passenger-handling facilities including customs, immigration etc., this was not too difficult a move and, indeed, forms a good example of the concept of a new use for an old product as described in Chapter 3. It is far harder for a place to become a cruise venue without the supporting infrastructure already in place.

Whilst there are perceived economic benefits in attracting the cruise trade, but not, as we shall show later, always as great as might be imagined, there will be costs associated with attracting and servicing the trade. These costs also form part of the *convenience* factor of the 4Cs.

There are certain basics that an area must possess to become a port of call:

■ adequate berthing or anchorage facilities
■ a landing stage that can be made safe for the whole range of cruisers, young, old, those with disabilities etc.
■ onshore facilities
■ onshore attractions
■ security.

In order to attract and deal with ever-increasing sizes of cruise ships, it is necessary to have the 'shipping' infrastructure in place. Whilst some areas still require ships to anchor off shore and to take their cruisers ashore in ships' boats or local tenders, this is not a preferred option. Cruisers need to wait for a tender and there are always safety implications in the operation of small boats; indeed bad weather may make landing impossibly dangerous. Tendering also further reduces the time that cruisers can spend in the port of call and there is a need, in hot climates, for the cruise company to set up a watering station and to staff the landing stage. Wheelchair access may also be difficult, reducing the customer value to those with disabilities. More of the smaller ports of call are thus building quays and jetties to accommodate all but the largest cruise ships. St Kitts, Dominica and Bonaire in the Caribbean are examples of places that have been improving their facilities by building new jetties. Cruise lines also find advantages in tying up at a jetty as it means that any stores can be brought on board and gash (rubbish) etc. can be offloaded into containers.

Port areas and anchorages may need dredging and will certainly need navigational aids. There may also be a need to provide new or additional tug facilities to aid berthing and extra pilots are likely to be required generating associated training costs. The building of a jetty also allows for the provision of shops and retail outlets that cruisers can access easily without the need for a boat ride.

Deeper draft ships such as the *Norway* may well need to anchor at most of their ports of call, especially in the Caribbean, and that ship carries her own landing-craft type tenders in addition to the ship's boats. A glance along the side of any modern cruise ship will show that in addition to the conventional lifeboats there are a number of covered boats. These are both lifeboats and tenders, and in a tender port of call they carry out a continuous shuttle service between the ship and the landing stage.

On-shore attractions were covered in an earlier section but if a place wishes to attract cruise ship custom, then both the attractions and the supporting infrastructure will need to be of sufficient quality to provide a worthwhile experience.

Finally, over 2000 cruisers arriving in a place provide a security issue. They may be targets of crime or they may not understand local customs and cause offence. The local law enforcement agencies and medical authorities may need to be expanded to cope with a large influx of very temporary visitors.

All of the above will involve both start-up and recurrent costs. The better the facilities, the more the port of call can charge in berthing fees etc. but, again, the higher the fees the greater the expectation from the cruise companies.

Communications

Because cruises are rarely purchased based on a single port of call in the itinerary, the tourist authorities do not need to advertise directly to the cruise customer. They do, however, need to ensure that the cruise companies are aware of changes in facilities especially where these affect the operation of the cruise. Ports of call have also realized that it is important to allow those on board cruise ships a convenient method of communication home. On-board telephone calls are expensive and at increasing numbers of ports of call a feature of the areas close to where the cruise ships berth is banks of telephones, telephone call sales kiosks and an associated line of cruisers and crew waiting to make contact with home.

The development of proper quayside facilities, as described earlier, has also provided local tourism authorities with a venue from which to offer information about local attractions, and many ports of call are now able to provide a much better information service to cruisers. Our discussions with those manning these facilities in the Caribbean suggest that most activities and excursions are booked on board ship and that whilst they may well perform a welcoming function, they do not have much of a commercial impact in generating business.

Convenience

For a visit port to be successful, it needs to be convenient in two ways. First, it needs to be accessible and have the necessary facilities as mentioned above. Second, it needs to be on a convenient route to other visit ports. An example is Ponta Delgada in the Azores. An interesting place, it receives relatively few visits except for transatlantic cruises because of its distance from the UK or Mediterranean–Madeira–Canary Island–North Africa cruise route.

Most of the Caribbean visit ports e.g. the Virgin Islands of St Thomas and St Croix (US) and Tortola (BVI), The Leeward Islands of St Kitts, Antigua, Guadeloupe (France, St Maarten/St Martin (Netherlands and France), Dominica and the Windward Islands of Martinique, Barbados, St Lucia and Grenada, are very close to each other. They are easily reached during a seven-day cruise from Puerto Rico or Miami to the extent that a series of 'bus routes' exist for cruise ships within the Eastern Caribbean as the examples of seven-day cruises for the years 1999 or 2000 in Table 5.11 show.

As Table 5.12 shows, Transcanal cruises are much more like the ocean voyages of yore with much more time spent at sea and thus they are attract the more traditional cruisers.

Table 5.11 Eastern Caribbean itineraries

Carnival	Princess	RCI	NCL	Thomson
Miami*	San Juan*	San Juan*	Miami*	Dominican Republic*
At sea	At sea	St Thomas	At sea	At sea
San Juan	Trinidad	Martinique	At sea	Guadeloupe
St Thomas	Barbados	Barbados	St Maarten	Barbados
St Croix	Antigua	Antigua	St Thomas	St Kitts
At sea	Martinique	St Maarten	At sea	Tortola
At sea	St Thomas	At sea	Bahamas	San Juan
Miami*	San Juan*	San Juan*	Miami*	Dominican Republic*

Note: * Base port

Table 5.12 Typical transcanal cruises

Pricess Day	Port	NCL Port	Celebrity Port
1	San Juan*	San Juan*	New York*
2	St Thomas	At sea	At sea
3	Martinique	Aruba	Cape Canaveral
4	Grenada	At sea	Ft Lauderdale
5	La Guaira	San Blas Island	At sea
6	Curacae	Panama Canal Transit	Cozumel
7	At sea	At sea	At sea
8	Panama Canal transit	Puerto Caldera	At sea
9	At sea	At sea	Panama Canal Transit
10	At sea	Puerto Quetzel	At sea
11	Acapulo*	At sea	Puerto Caldera
		Acapulco	At sea
			Huatulco
			Acapulco*

Note: * Base port

Visit ports fall into three categories:

1 Visit ports that are also base ports.
2 Ports whose main trade is cruise ships.
3 Ports that are also fully operational commercial ports in their own right with the majority of their trade being freight or ferry operations.

The first category include Dover, San Juan, Barbados, Acapulco and Athens (Piraeus). They are fully equipped to handle cruise ships of almost any size and also fall into the third category.

The second category includes many of the traditional visit ports in the Mediterranean and Caribbean and can be distinguished by their lack of cranes etc.

The third category are traditional ports that are conveniently near to main attractions and thus have found a ready market in the cruise ship business. They include Curaçao (beyond the cruise ship berths at Willemstad is a huge lagoon containing ship repair yards, an oil terminal and freight berth reflective of the island's position off oil rich Venezuela), Civitavecchia (for Rome), Livorno (for Florence), Amsterdam, Hamburg, Istanbul and Barcelona.

Because of their facilities they are also able to act as base ports for cruisers joining or leaving a ship.

Base ports

There are special requirements for a base port. Base ports must not only be able to accommodate a large number of tourists for a day but also need the infrastructure to process cruisers as they join or leave their ship.

Given the importance and frequency of flying to join a cruise ship, base ports need to be within reasonable distance of an international airport. Southampton and Dover (London Heathrow and London Gatwick), New York (JFK and Newark), Boston (Logan), San Juan, Acapulco, Venice, Miami and Fort Lauderdale, Vancouver, Singapore, Sydney and Hong Kong are all base ports with excellent international airports within an easy coach drive of the port. The cruise companies need to be assured that there are sufficient coaches for the passengers and that the airports can handle the direct transfer of luggage to the ship. Major airports also have the necessary customs and immigration facilities. Base ports have invested in departure and arrival terminals with airport-style facilities to process cruisers speedily and efficiently.

In the late 1990s the major base ports for the main cruising areas were as shown in Table 5.13.

Table 5.13 The world's major cruise base ports

Area	Ports
Caribbean	Miami, Fort Lauderdale, San Juan, Dominican Republic (Thomson), Houston, Jamaica
Western Mediterranean	Palma (Majorca), Southampton, Venice, Genoa
Eastern Mediterranean	Venice, Cyprus, Athens, Cyprus
Atlantic Islands	Southampton, Dover, Genoa, Canaries
Transcanal	Los Angeles, Acapulco, San Juan, Miami
Alaska	Vancouver
Norway/Baltic	Dover, Southampton
Black Sea	Venice, Athens
South America	Santiago, Manaus
North American East Coast	Montreal, Boston, New York
North American West Coast	Los Angeles, San Diego, Acapulco
Asia	Singapore, Tokyo, Phuket (Thailand)
Africa	Mombasa

The list in Table 5.13 is by no means exhaustive but those are the ports that process the vast bulk of the world's cruisers and which have the necessary infrastructure to do so. Other ports are vying to join their ranks. For example, a state-of-the-art cruise terminal is planned for the early years of the twenty-first century at Leith (the port for Edinburgh) and this will provide an alternative to ports in the South of England for cruises to and from Northern Europe as well as the growing market in round British Isles cruises (see later).

Trends

What can we predict as trends for the cruising industry?

Like all forms of tourism, cruising is affected by the economic situation of those cruising and the political/security position of the areas visited. The collapse of many Asian economies in 1998 caused considerable distortion to the market. The strength of the dollar and sterling against many Asian currencies made the area an attractive economic proposition for Western cruisers whilst having an adverse effect on the indigenous market. Against that needs to be set political unrest in Indonesia and UK Foreign Office advice warning travellers to avoid certain Asian areas.

The Middle East, especially the Holy Land is something of a 'problem child' for the cruise companies. It is an interesting area but politically volatile. Dubai and other Gulf States may well make useful base ports but the 1990s contained a number of instances of military action by the West against Iraq and terrorist attacks on tourists in Egypt and Yemen. We would predict that given a more stable security situation there would be growth in the Levant area of the Eastern Mediterranean and that the Asian market will continue to grow after the downturn of the late 1990s.

The Caribbean and Mediterranean will retain their pre-eminent positions given their current popularity and infrastructure for tourism in general and cruising in particular.

In Northern Europe, cruises will be extended to offer visits further north with Iceland becoming a more routine visit. South America will attract more cruise ships and, provided the USA changes its shipping law, Hawaii will boom as a cruise destination.

Having surveyed the areas cruised; the impact in social and economic terms for the base and visit ports used by the cruise industry is now considered.

The impact of cruising

It has already been shown how the population of Charlotte Amarlie, the capital of the US Virgin Island of St Thomas could nearly double during a busy day at the height of the Caribbean cruise season.

The arrival of a large number of cruise passengers can have a dramatic impact on a visit port. It is not just on small islands that there can be a major impact. Dover (UK) has already been mentioned as an example of the dynamic life-cycle progression in that a new use as a cruise terminal was found for an old product, excess ferry capacity, and Edinburgh, Scotland, is investing in a cruise terminal as part of the regeneration of the Port of Leith. The aim of this section of the chapter is to explore the impact cruising may have both on a place and its population.

Part of any strategic analysis carried out by organizations is the conduct of a PEST analysis, the acronym standing for *political, economic, social* and *technological*. To this it is intended to follow recent trends and an extra category – *environmental* – thus making it a STEEP analysis.

This analysis is normally used to identify the factors that an organization needs to consider when producing its strategic plans; we intend to use it as an analytical tool for discussing the impact of cruising by considering that impact in terms of its social, technological economic, environmental and political effects.

First, we must consider a major difference between land-based and cruise holidays. Land-based holidays bring in tourists to a fixed infrastructure which includes accommodation as well as airports, roads etc. Within that infrastructure tourists are a captive market for the duration of their holiday, or holiday segment in the case of multi-centre holidays. With the cruise industry the accommodation moves and the tourists may well spend a relatively short period of time in the place (see the previous chapter).

As most cruise companies operate fairly fixed routes, especially in the Caribbean, there is time for the cruise ships and their operators to impact on the place but little time for the place to impact on the cruiser.

There are also differences in employment; land-based holidays are more likely to provide employment to local staff in hotels, whereas cruise ships can pick their staff from around the world, lessening the economic benefits to the ports of call. A similar situation may occur in enclave resorts in developing countries where staff may be shipped in and thus the economic benefit to the indigenous community is reduced.

Social impact

The social impact of the cruise industry can be considerable. Cruise destinations can be divided into two general categories: those which had developed industries, tourist or otherwise, before the growth of cruising and those which have developed as a result of the cruise industry itself.

For major commercial centres such as the areas around Rome and Athens, cruising and indeed tourism is a marginal activity. Whilst any income that the tourist industry may bring is welcome, those areas are major commercial centres in their own right. Other areas, for example the Canaries, the Balearics and the more developed Caribbean destinations, have a tradition of land-based tourism. UK holiday-makers have been visiting Majorca, Minorca, Ibiza, Cyprus and Crete etc. on package holidays in large numbers for decades. There is a good tourist infrastructure and again the impact of cruising is marginal. The social effects of the tourist industry in these regions have evolved over time. In the 1990s there were problems with alcohol and drug abuse in many of the popular Mediterranean resorts but these are not exacerbated by the growth of the cruise industry. Holiday-makers at the top end of any tourism market segment are likely to be law abiding and the fact that they need to be back on board ship for the evening lessens the problems associated with nightlife.

The tourist industries in these areas are a mature product and many of the local population are employed within the industry. Hotels, bars nightclubs, local tour operators and the suppliers of consumables and maintenance provide a major source of income to the area. The cruise industry does not provide much employment save that associated with the berthing of ships. Even if the area becomes a base port, as Majorca has, there will still be very little extra employment associated with the arrival of cruising.

If the area is also one suitable for cruise and stay packages, with a sufficiently developed infrastructure to support the hotel part of the holiday, then the industry may attract extra employment. Some additional temporary employment may be gained, as facilities for the cruise trade are improved and major building works undertaken.

The biggest potential social impact of cruising is in those areas where there is little tradition of major tourism and an initially inadequate infrastructure to support a massive boost in visitors. Because, as mentioned above, cruise ships rarely berth overnight, some of the disadvantages of becoming a tourist haven – drunkenness, drug abuse and prostitution – will be mitigated against. The disadvantage is that there will be very little gain financially (see later in this chapter) and socially. We had the opportunity to talk to local people in a number of Caribbean and South American visit ports about the effect that the arrival of cruise ships had had on their lives. Unless they were directly involved either through working at the port, selling souvenirs or being involved in excursions, the answer was that there was very little impact save putting them on show. Older people expressed the view that apparently rich tourists coming ashore and wandering through the streets of what are relatively small towns could have a negative effect on the self-image of younger people and could lead to an increase in petty street crime and drug abuse. The disruptive role of tourism in encouraging unrealistic expectations amongst host communities has been noted by Bryden (1973), although he states the dangers of oversimplifying what is a complex relationship. Such an effect has been reported by Caribbean Islands and superficially appears to have a correlation to the increase in number of cruise ship visits.

Acculturation (Nuñez, 1989), the process whereby groups borrow aspects of culture from each other, is a very one-sided process in respect of the cruise industry due to the short time an individual cruiser spends in a single place. Thus an individual American or Briton may spend only a few hours on a Caribbean island but the inhabitants of the island will be exposed to thousands of Americans and Britons during the course of the season. Aspects of US and British culture, especially linguistic aspects, will be incorporated into the day-to-day life of the destination. The constant exposure as more cruise ships arrive may lead to what Mathieson and Wall (1982), quoting Collins, have termed 'cultural drift', changing the nature of the destination by increasing and persistent contact with those having a different culture. Such drift is likely to result in acculturation. They have suggested that cultural drift is affected by three main factors:

1 The type of tourist.
2 The spatial, temporal and communicative context in which contacts take place.
3 The role of the cultural broker (e.g. the local guide). Times of rapid growth are often exploited by those who have been at the margins of organized economic activity but who can see the potential for guided tours, souvenirs (even drugs and sex). Nuñez (1989) refers to such people as 'marginal man'.

Begging (panhandling in US parlance) is on the increase in a number of cruise visit ports. Indeed, the fall of the Soviet Union has seen a major increase in the practice (Nelson and Kuzes, 1995) and this is a geographic region that is becoming increasingly popular as a cruise destination especially the Baltic and Black Sea areas. In more commercially oriented areas ships dock in defined port areas with main gate security, and begging is thus dispersed throughout the main tourist attractions of a town. However, in less developed regions berths are often directly accessible and whilst the main problem is still an overproliferation of souvenir sellers, the opportunity for cruisers to be assailed by beggars is growing. One can hardly blame the poor for being attracted to the apparent wealth of extremely transient visitors.

For all the apparent wealth, the arrival of a cruise ship does not have much social impact on the individual inhabitant of a visit port, nor, according to our sample has it much impact on the cruiser. The transient nature of the visit allows little time to soak in any atmosphere or to experience the living conditions of the local population. We surveyed a group of cruisers in the Caribbean on an island where the route from the berth to the main town traversed a very poor area. Out of 40 people, only four had (perhaps unwisely) walked into town (they reported no problems) and of the remainder who had travelled by motor coach, they reported that the area seemed 'run down' but the visit had made little impact. This is not a phenomenon exclusive to the cruise industry. Many holiday-makers to North Africa report that they rarely leave the confines of the resort hotel to sample local life except as part of an organized excursion to a site of interest. Modern air-conditioned motor vehicles, especially coaches, do not allow the outside atmosphere to seep in. Only vision is available; smell, touch sound, and even taste are often excluded.

If there is one city which has grown as a result of the cruise industry, it is Miami. Although known as a resort for wealthy Americans, it was the 1970s boom in US market cruising that led to a major expansion of the port facilities. Miami was fortunate that the climate and infrastructure permitted it to become the centre of a Florida tourist trade that was independent of the cruise industry, and with major investments by the large hotel groups and the development of theme parks the city, whilst still base port to many ships, does not depend on the industry for its security.

Infrastructure improvements such as roads benefit the whole community and can improve the commercial prospects of an area. However, as Doxey (1975) has pointed out, the euphoria of becoming a tourist destination can soon change to increasing irritation as the natural and cultural attractions which first enticed tourists are actually destroyed by them.

Given the short length of stays in port, the cruiser can only, at best, gain an impression of the culture and true nature of a destination. Arranged cultural events and 'folkloric' shows can only accurately be described as staged authenticity (MacCannell, 1973).

Technological impact

The technological impact of the cruise industry on its visit and base ports has been much greater than the social impact. The relatively lesser draft of modern cruise ships has opened up areas to cruising that were previously difficult to access. Cruisers and cruise companies, for reasons of convenience and safety, prefer ports where the ship can be secured alongside a berth. Whilst there are still many tender ports where larger ships need to anchor (the *Norway*, ex *France*, 76 049 GRT with a draft of 34.4 ft [10.8 m] docks in very few ports especially in the Caribbean and has specially constructed landing-craft type tenders), increasing numbers visit ports and are investing in shore-side facilities. These bring not only employment during construction but often contain retail outlets that provide a small degree of seasonal work, increased navigational aids and a facility for more freight traffic.

As a visit port grows in popularity, so it requires investment in the infrastructure around it in order to accommodate excursions etc. New roads may be built and local industries are able to diversify into tourist attractions, breathing new life into occasionally moribund industries.

Economic impact

One would expect that the arrival of cruise ships carrying up to 3000 passengers into a small port in the Caribbean, or any other part of the world, would have a major economic impact.

As quoted earlier, Hamlyn (1998) gives the average spend per cruise ship passenger in any one Caribbean port as just a few dollars and De la Viña and Ford (1998) have found a similar pattern in their analysis of the economic impact of proposed cruise ship business. They point out that previous research tended to concentrate on the impact on port development *per se* rather than on the more general effects. Only Archer (1995) actually considered this issue and then in a very general way relating to tourist-related economic developments on one particular destination, Bermuda. This destination is in itself atypical, as Bermuda is primarily a destination for very short – three- to four-day – cruises out of the USA. De la Viña and Ford were primarily concerned with developments in Corpus Christi (Texas) which is one of the newer base ports on continental USA. Given the port's position on the Gulf of Mexico, it is not surprising that it has been growing in demand, not only as a base port but also as a pre- and post-cruise destination, and in the late 1990s this area began to appear more frequently as an offering to the UK market through companies diversifying their North American market destinations.

NCL were offering cruises based on Houston, P&O Cruises were commencing certain MV *Victoria* cruises from New Orleans and De la Viña and Ford (1998) reported operations by Celebrity's 76 522 GRT *Mercury* and Dolphin Cruise Lines' 21 486 GRT *Ocean Breeze*, a real veteran having been built in 1955 as Shaw Saville and Albion's *Southern Cross*, for the UK–Australia run.

Using figures from Archer (1995) and a study by Price Waterhouse (1996), the economic impact on Corpus Christie was found to be in the region of $610 (£380) per passenger. That for visit ports where, as stated earlier, there is rarely an overnight stay ranged from $107 (£67) at Key West (in Florida) and $118 (£74) in Barbados (which also has a thriving hotel-based tourist industry) up to $467 (£290) for the shopping mecca of St Thomas which is reported to have received over 1.2 million cruise ship visitors in 1995. It must be stressed that these are total impact figures and are not necessarily reflective of direct passenger spend. They include port charges, servicing arrangements, berthing, excursions etc., in addition to direct individual spend.

Barbados, which as a base and a visit port has a higher spend per cruise ship individual – $95 (£60) – but this is very small when compared to the average spend of $1100 (£687) per land-based visitor (including accommodation costs) as quoted by Dann and Potter (1997). The same authors show figures indicating that the number of cruise ship visitors increased from 156 500 in 1981 to nearly 400 000 in 1992, indicating the increasing popularity of Barbados.

The figures do indicate the increasing reliance of visit ports like St Thomas on the cruise ship business as opposed to Barbados, which although receiving an increasing number of ships is also a major land-based tourist destination.

Islands, especially the smaller ones, can become very dependent on single sources of income. The reluctance of the EU to comply with a World Trade Organization (WTO) ruling on banana imports in 1999 and the threat of a trade war between the EU and the USA was based in part on the fragile dependence on the banana crop of many of the Caribbean islands. Thus tourism can provide a welcome extension of economic activity. As Hall (1992) has commented, it would be beneficial to the Cuban economy if the country could become a visit area for cruise ships. Some European cruise lines began visiting Cuba in the 1990s but major expansion could not occur due to US government embargoes on trade with Cuba. The net beneficiary of the growth of cruise tourism in that part of the Caribbean was the Dominican Republic, which became a base port area in the late 1990s.

Wilkinson has written of the perceived economic importance of the cruise industry to Jamaica, an island that saw its number of cruise visitors increase from 133 400 to 649 517 between 1981 and 1992 (Wilkinson, 1997).

Environmental impact

Not so long ago the traditional method for removing rubbish from ships was to dump it overboard. Such practices are now, quite rightly, outlawed and cruise ship companies have become very environmentally aware. There are large fines applied to any shipping company found guilty of pollution.

A modern cruise ship is designed to retain as much rubbish as possible for safe disposal at designated sites. *Oriana* contains four sewage plants so that if there is a need to discharge into the sea, it is clean, safe effluent (P&O, 1995) and there is a worldwide ban on the discharge of fuel oil into the oceans. A cruise liner, like a small town, generates a vast amount of rubbish and today this will be offloaded into containers at ports where facilities exist to process it.

However, it is not just pollution that is a concern. Large numbers of visitors may have an adverse effect on flora and fauna, especially as many excursions are to sites of natural interest. In some respects the cruise industry has helped conservation by the development of special attractions, e.g. the Coral World operations on many Caribbean islands, but the development of the supporting infrastructure can have a detrimental effect on wildlife.

During the research for this book, we also began to notice what we have described as visual pollution. Taking a break from interviewing cruisers, one of us happened to be on a hillside overlooking the port of Castries, the capital of the Caribbean island of St Lucia. The only major ship in the harbour was the P&O Cruise's *Victoria* (ex *Sea Princess*, ex *Klungsholm*, 28 670 GRT) a classic design of ship that looked quite at home in the port, almost an extension of the scenery. This contrasted with a view a few years earlier of Charlotte Amarlie in St Thomas with six huge ships either tied up alongside or at anchor, and with the comment of a non-cruiser on a Caribbean holiday about the 'huge monstrosity that anchored off his hotel and blotted out the view'.

Primary (elementary) school teachers have long known that there is a perceived image of an ocean liner that appears at an early age. Ask any young child to draw a passenger ship and it will often have a black hull and two funnels. It can be no coincidence that the new Disney ships, whilst being futuristic in many ways, conform to this traditional design and present a non-dissonant image to the eye.

Modern ship designs are dramatic but they beg the question as to whether they should be at one with their environment and to what extent a large number of ships in a small port – the new facilities in Castries can handle up to six ships – actually detract from the charm of a place, especially for those who are either residents or are on a non-cruise holiday. Perhaps it is a sign of age but many of our sample believed, and we agree with them, that a ship should complement a small port, not dominate it.

Political impact

The major omission of a port from the North American Caribbean market is that of Havana. That so few cruise ships call at Cuba is nothing to do with the attractions or facilities; it is because for many years it has been illegal in US Federal law to trade with Castro's Cuba, even to extent of smoking Cuban cigars! No such restrictions apply to UK and European citizens, and first Costa (with a short-lived operation based on the 12 475 *Costa Playa*) and then Thomson began to include Cuba as a destination.

Political factors can affect the operations of cruise companies but usually not as an outright ban as in the case of the US and Cuba but more of a reluctance of cruisers to travel to areas where they feel politically and physically insecure.

The Eastern Mediterranean and the Holy Land are 'problem children' (see Chapter 3) of the cruise industry. They are desirable destinations but they are somewhat unstable politically and in terms of security. They have been increasing in popularity, especially with the European market, but the security situation needs to be kept in mind at all times, hence Costa cancelled a series of cruises in the area in 1998 because of a fear for their passengers' safety.

It is worth noting, as with all aspects of tourism, that impact is a two-way process. The arrival of a cruise ship full of apparently wealthy tourists may well have considerable impact on the population of a less wealthy area. The experience of being in such an area will also impact on the cruiser. However, owing to the short time spent in an area and the method by which organized excursions cocoon the cruiser from actual realities, the impact may be less than expected.

The effects of the cruise industry on destinations and cruisers appear complex and it is to be hoped that this is an area that will receive greater study in the future.

Case study

The Atlantic Islands

As shown earlier in this chapter, the Atlantic Islands (also known and marketed as the Fortunate Isles) cruising region, an area which includes Madeira, the Canaries, the Moroccan Coast, and often takes in parts of Portugal and Spain, is very popular with European, and especially UK, cruisers. A sample twelve-night Atlantic Islands cruise on the **Oriana** (69 153 GRT) for August 1999 is shown in Table 5.14.

Table 5.14 Atlantic Islands cruise from UK, August 1999

Day 1	Depart Southampton
Day 2	Cruising
Day 3	Cruising
Day 4	Madeira
Day 5	Tenerife, Canary Islands
Day 6	La Palma, Canary Islands
Day 7	Lanzarote, Canary Islands
Day 8	Cruising
Day 9	Praia da Rocha, Portugal (Algarve)
Day 10	Lisbon, Portugal
Day 11	Vigo, Spain
Day 12	Cruising
Day 13	Arrive Southampton

As the Caribbean draws a strategic advantage for cruising from its proximity to continental USA, so the ease with which the Atlantic Islands can be reached from Europe has led to their popularity both as a land-based and a cruising holiday area.

Some of the earliest European cruises used Madeira as a port of call and by 1952 the island was featuring on P&O cruise advertisement posters ('The P&O Art Catalogue').

The Atlantic Islands serve three cruising markets:

1 Sailings from the UK.
2 Sailings from Southern Europe.
3 Ships based in the Canaries.

Madeira is approximately two days sailing from Southampton and the trip gives the cruise companies an opportunity to include a visit to Northern Spain, normally Vigo or La Coruna. Cruises then progressing on to the Canary Islands with a visit to a Moroccan port (see, for example, Table 5.15).

Table 5.15   Thomson 'Fortunate Islands' package, 1998–9

Day 1	Depart Tenerife, Canary Islands
Day 2	Gran Canaria, Canary Islands
Day 3	Madeira
Day 4	Cruising
Day 5	Casablanca, Morocco
Day 6	Agadir, Morocco
Day 7	Lanzarote, Canary Islands
Day 8	Arrive Tenerife and fly to UK or transfer to hotel for seven nights

The islands are not noted for their historic or cultural aspects and thus there is little to satisfy the Seeker or the Explorer, but the climate is mild to hot throughout the year and there is an excellent tourist infrastructure.

Madeira has a small sister island, Porto Santo and in the late 1990s it began to appear in the cruising itineraries as 'a new to place to visit', as did the small Canary Island of La Gomera. In much the same way the San Blas Islands have been added to many Transcanal and Caribbean cruises.

The other islands in the warmer areas of the Atlantic are the Azores, lying well out to the west of Madeira, and the Cap Verde Islands west of Senegal., both Portuguese.

Ponta Delgada in the Azores was a regular port of call for the **Reina del Mar** in the 1960s (see Chapter 2) but now is normally only visited as part of a transatlantic repositioning voyage. The Cap Verde Islands have not been featured on cruise itineraries but are well known to those crossing the Atlantic in yachts and small boats as they form one of the waypoints for the southbound small boat crossing of the Atlantic.

The temperature in Madeira ranges from a minimum of 15°C in February to a maximum of 22°C in August/September (thus it is comfortable all year round) and the island has an average annual total rainfall of 21.5 inches which is similar to that of London.

With a series of visit ports within easy distance and the ability to visit North Africa, it is little surprise that the Atlantic Islands are so popular with European cruisers, especially those who dislike flying but still wish to find some sunshine.

Many of the visit ports are connected with the EU through their parent countries (the Canary Islands are outside the EU but owned and administered by Spain) and the area is safe – an important consideration to most mainstream cruisers.

6

Design philosophies

This chapter includes:

- basic principles
- propulsion
- length and draft
- topweight
- interior design
- builders
- environmental considerations
- case study: Oriana – P&O Cruises

Customers boarding a cruise ship probably pay little attention to the vast design process that has gone to making their experience what it is. This is not a chapter about ship design but to understand where and why particular design themes have become so prevalent. It is necessary to examine the evolutionary process that has been followed.

Basic principles

As soon as humanity ventured on to the seas in specially constructed craft, certain physical constraints quickly became apparent, constraints that still act on designers today and which dictate certain shapes for ships.

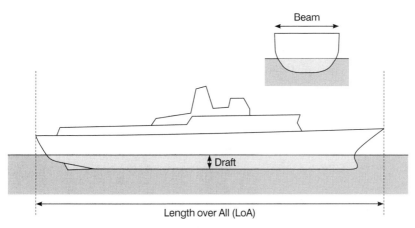

Figure 6.1 The principal dimensions of a vessel

There are four major physical dimensions to any ship (see Figure 6.1):

- length
- breadth
- height below the water line
- height above the water line.

At the widest part of a ship the breadth is known as the *beam*, the deepest part of the ship below the water line is known as the *draft*. The length is normally measured at the maximum which is found by drawing perpendiculars at the foremost part (which may in a modern ship be the bulbous protuberance under water at the front, *bow*, and the back, *stern*. These dimensions are not just esoteric facts; they will be vital to the effective functioning and seaworthiness of the vessel. The height above the water line is rarely quoted but is extremely important from a stability point of view.

As soon as vessels moved past the stage of being either bare logs or logs lashed together as rafts, shipbuilders, just as builders on land, realized that there was a critical relationship between length, beam and draft, and that this relationship affected two critical factors – stability and speed.

Water is a difficult medium for which to build. A hull moving through water is subjected to a number of stresses as shown in Figure 6.2.

The movement of a ship about its longitudinal axis is known as pitching and whilst it can be very spectacular when the bow dips into the water and a ship moves into the direction of the waves, it is perfectly safe. Of far more danger

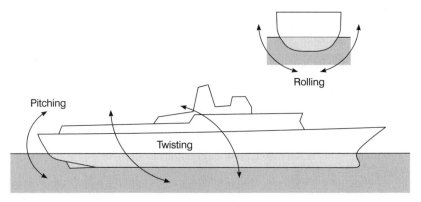

Figure 6.2 The main strains on a hull

is when the sea breaks over the stern. The bow is designed to 'confront' the waves; sterns are not so designed and a large wave breaking against the stern can cause considerable structural damage. Good captains ensure that this does not happen.

Rolling, the movement of a ship on its horizontal axis is also normally perfectly safe. As we shall see later, ships have built-in righting movements and a ship rolling from one side to another is perfectly safe, if rather uncomfortable. Should the waves be so large as to put the ship at risk when rolling, the perceived wisdom is to put the bows of the ship into the waves so that the stresses can be absorbed by the those parts of the ship best designed for them.

Because water is a fluid medium, ships are also subject to the shearing motion produced by a combination of pitch and roll, and designers need to take into account the likely stresses that a ship will meet.

Up to the Second World War the normal method of building a steel ship was to construct a skeleton of frames from the very bottom of the ship (the keel) upwards to form the hull. Steel plates would be riveted to these frames and then the superstructure would be added above the frames. The area enclosed by the plated frames was known as the hull of the ship. To combat all the stresses likely to be encountered by the hull and to minimize the size of plates required, the frames had to be fairly closely spaced (about 2 feet in the case of the Olympic Class ships of 1912). Many millions of rivets were required.

Indeed, up to 1914 many liners were stronger than they needed to be for commercial purposes as they were also designed with strengthened decks in order to be armed as AMCs (armed merchant cruisers) in the event of war. The famous Cunard liners, *Mauretania* and *Lusitania* (40 000 GRT) of 1906 were among seven built with British government subsidies for this very purpose although they were never armed. The later *Aquitania* (45 700 GRT) of 1914 did serve briefly as an AMC between 1914 and 1915.

Since the Second World War the trend has been towards the welding of ships and they are now constructed, out of pre-assembled sections. Modern welding techniques produce very strong joins; well able to handle the stresses they will encounter during service. Such techniques also make it possible to add extra sections throughout the life of the ship and many of the older vessels from the 1970s and early 1980s have been lengthened to accommodate the growing numbers of passengers.

Propulsion

Up to the growth of the cruise industry one of the major selling points about any passenger ship was speed. Sea travel was merely a means to an end and passengers sought out the fastest ships. The fastest were always on the North Atlantic routes between Europe and the USA, and the major shipping companies competed for the coveted 'Blue Riband' for the fastest crossings. Until the early 1900s speed was limited by the physical capacities of the steam reciprocating engine, in the same way that aircraft speeds before the Second World War were limited by propellers. (The behaviour of a propeller in air actually puts a finite limit on the speed that can be achieved by an aircraft and it was only the invention of the various forms of jet engine that allowed speeds to be increased.) When Parson's introduced the steam turbine for marine use in 1897 it allowed for a significant increase in the speeds that ships could travel, as shown in Table 6.1.

The Blue Riband has never been regained by a passenger liner, but various 'publicity' crossings of the Atlantic have been attempted by purpose-built craft, especially in the 1980s and 1990s.

Part of the appeal of cruising is its leisurely pace and thus speed has become less important save for the voyage from the home port to the cruising areas. As we shall see in the case study on *Oriana* at the end of this chapter, this is of some importance in the UK market where there are still sailings from UK ports for Mediterranean cruises and thus there is a need to reach the sunshine speedily. Nevertheless the speed of today's ships is considerably less than their predecessors, comfort and facilities being of more importance.

Table 6.1 Blue Riband holders 1909–52

Year	Ship	Line	Average speed (knots)
1909	*Mauretania*	Cunard	26.06
1924	*Mauretania*	Cunard	26.16
1929	*Bremen*	Nordeutsche Lloyd	27.83
1930	*Europa*	Nordeutsche Lloyd	27.91
1933	*Bremen*	Nordeutsche Lloyd	28.51
1933	*Rex*	Italian Line	29.92
1935	*Normandie*	French Line	29.98
1936	*Queen Mary*	Cunard	30.63
1937	*Normandie*	French Line	31.30
1938	*Queen Mary*	Cunard	31.69
1952	*United States*	United States Lines	35.59

The declining importance of speed has led to the introduction of engines that, whilst providing less speed, are more efficient. Very few modern cruise ships are powered by other than diesels and, indeed, many have been re-engined. The *Sky Princess* was the last steam vessel built, and the *QE2* and the *Norway* (ex *France*) were both re-engined with diesels.

Oil-fired ships began to appear in the early years of the twentieth century, first as warships, and by the 1930s all newly built passenger ships used oil instead of coal. Oil is, paradoxically, less flammable than coal and takes up less space. Ships built for coal-firing needed huge bunkers and a vast army of stokers, trimmers etc. to service the boilers. Refuelling coal ships (coaling) was an immense undertaking with dirt and grime getting everywhere. Oil-fired ships brought about better crew conditions, less crew and a cleaner environment, plus more spaces for passenger accommodation.

From a marketing point of view, customers in the 1890s and early 1900s appear to have equated speed with the number of funnels. Nordeutsche Lloyd (NDL) made great advertising play on the four funnels of their ships whilst the aftermost funnels of many vessels were actually dummies, being there for aesthetic reasons.

When the *Disney Magic* was introduced in 1998 she was the first two-funnelled vessel since the *France* (now *Norway*). Even her aftermost funnel was non-functional and, indeed, included public rooms.

Funnels have always been an important design component of passenger ships. Originally there to take away the smoke caused by coal-burning boilers, they have survived into the present day with a slightly changed role. Many ships still use the funnel to carry away the diesel exhaust from the ship and the height of the funnel means that fumes are carried well away from passengers. However, funnels are things we equate with ships (as a child's drawing often shows) and thus, even when separate exhausts are provided as in the *Enchanted Isle*, there is still a mid-ships funnel.

From the very early days of steam, as soon as heat resistant paints (black was the best colour originally) were developed, ship owners have painted their ship's funnels in a distinctive house style. Red and black was often used – Cunard, French Line, United States Lines, Union Castle – whilst P&O funnels were always yellow. Nowadays funnels provide an ideal platform on which to place a company logo (Princess, Costa, NCL) and, in a 1970s development, a lounge. The Viking lounges of NCL were distinctive trademarks as well as providing a unique viewing point for passengers. When ships were sold, the lounges were removed.

Length and draft

The length of a ship is also governed by physical rules. Water, being a fluid medium provides less support than a solid. Thus a very long ship may be subject to considerable bending stresses if it is too long in relation to its width. Imagine a metal rod. The greater the ratio of length to width, the easier it will be to bend and then, eventually, snap. If the hull became balanced between two large waves, one at the bow and one at the stern there would be the very dangerous possibility of 'hogging', where the hull sags between the two supporting waves. Therefore increases in length need to be accompanied by corresponding increases in width (beam). This brings about two problems. First, the larger a ship, the more space alongside a dock it takes and the harder it is to manoeuvre into and out of a dock and, second, vessels with a beam of over 33 metres cannot use the Panama Canal. Prior to the launching of the *Carnival Destiny* in 1996 all passenger vessels were built bearing the PANMAX standard in mind. The Panama Canal, opened in 1914 allows companies to switch ships between Pacific/Alaska and Caribbean/European operations with the maximum speed and avoid the heavy seas around Cape Horn at the tip of South America. In addition the Panama Canal has become an integral ingredient in a number of cruise holidays. However, major companies have decided to forgo the flexibility offered by the canal in favour of larger vessels, i.e. a larger beam than 33 metres.

The standard relationship between beam and length is approx. 1 metre of beam for every 7.6 metres of length, 1:7.7 (based on a survey of fifty cruise ships in operation in 1998) compared to 1:8.9 for those built in the early years of the twentieth century. Thus on average ships are becoming wider in relation to their length.

Of equal importance is the draft of a ship. Ships need a certain proportion of the hull, and a certain proportion of their weight below the water line. Paradoxically, deep draft ships with a V-shaped hull section have proved to be not only more stable but also faster. For the modern cruise operator speed is less important than accessibility. Cruise operators would prefer their ships to tie up alongside in the ports they visit. Not only does this aid re-provisioning but also there are always risks associated with taking passengers ashore in small boats (tendering). However, many of the most popular ports for cruise passengers require deep draft vessels to anchor offshore and tender their passengers in.

The question of weight distribution comes into play here. Coal-burning and oil-fired ships had considerable weight situated low down in the vessel. Not only was there the weight of the fuel but there were massive boilers and steam engines to be accommodated. This weight was exactly where it was needed. Even so, ships had massive extra keels fitted to the outside of the hull below the water line known as bilge keels, to increase the weight below the water line.

The weightiest parts of the accommodation with their large number of internal partitions were also accommodated in the hull, and perhaps the first deck of the superstructure, again adding to weight being placed low down – exactly where the centre of gravity needs to be for maximum stability. However, the modern trend towards diesel engines and cabins with sea views has led to the centre of gravity being raised. Not only has the hull become lighter, the superstructure has become heavier.

Topweight

The accumulation of 'topweight', i.e. weight high up on the ship is a problem for all designers and, indeed, is a problem throughout the transport industry. Designers of all forms of transport wish for as low a centre of gravity as possible. As early as 1847 the UK railway locomotive designer Francis Trevithick slung the boiler of a locomotive below the frames in an attempt to achieve this. The dangers of too high a centre of gravity at sea were tragically shown by the loss of HMS *Captain* in 1870. Designed by Captain Coles, HMS

Captain was a revolutionary design of battleship with a low freeboard, i.e. her main deck was quite close to the water line with her guns in massive turrets. Not only had she steam propulsion but she also had a full rig of sails and masts. There was just too much weight high up on the ship and on her maiden cruise in 1870 she capsized in the English Cannel with the loss of 475 lives, including the designer.

Even as late as 1982, there were comments that the Royal Navy had placed so many new radar receivers etc. on the masts of their ships that guns had been sacrificed to reduce topweight and that this caused major problems during the Falklands War (Hastings and Jenkins, 1983).

Balcony cabins need to be high up on the ship and the need for lavish entertainment features have presented designers with a dilemma. As draft has decreased, height and weight high up on the ship have tended to increase. Whilst modern design techniques are unlikely to lead to an unstable design, they could lead to one that is tender, i.e. has a propensity to roll and then to recover slowly. In his study of the sinking of the Italian liner *Andrea Doria* in the North Atlantic following a collision with the *Stockholm* on 25 July 1956, Hoffer (1980) comments that the ship was nearly at the end of her journey to New York and that with her fuel and water stocks depleted, there was less weight low down in the ship and therefore she could have become slightly more unstable. He also postulates that the placing of all the passengers' luggage on the same side as the collision may have induced a slight list that was enough to aggravate the damage done by the *Stockholm*'s bow. The rescue of the vast majority of the *Andrea Doria*'s passengers and crew was a miraculous feat, and the fact that the ship stayed afloat for so long after the collision was a credit to her designers.

There is another problem associated with height and that is the wind. High, slab-sided ships can act as gigantic sails and this effect is magnified by a shallow draft. Modern propulsion systems can counteract the effect of the wind but it is still a factor that the master of a ship must take into consideration, especially when approaching a berth at slow speed.

It is interesting to make a comparison between Cunard's *QE2* of 1969 (70 327 GRT), a traditional type of vessel, 293.5 metres long and a draft of 9.87 metres, and the *Dawn Princess* of 1997 (77 000 GRT), a modern design with a length of 261.5 metres and a draft of 7.95 metres. The *Dawn Princess*, in common with modern designs has a much 'squarer' stern which has allowed her designers to place cabins right into the stern of the ship, in part accounting for the maximum capacity of 2250 berths compared with 1531 for the *QE2*.

Table 6.2   Comparison of dimensions between the *Norway* and the *Grand Princess*

Ship	Year	Tonnage	Length (m)	Beam (m)	Draft (m)
Norway	1962	76 049	1035.1	33.5	10.8
Grand Princess	1998	109 000	935.0	36.0	8.0

The more box-like design of modern cruise ships is of considerable economic importance to cruise ship operators. A 2 per cent increase in accommodation on a 1400-berth ship is said to lead to $1–1.5 million increase in income, a not inconsiderable sum (Ward, 1998). On average older ships tend to have a draft of over 8.5 metres whilst the newer builds are likely to be shallower at 7–8 metres.

The tendency, therefore, has been for wider, higher ships with less draft as shown by a comparison between the *Grand Princess* and the *Norway* in Table 6.2.

Interior design

Whilst modern cruise ships may look somewhat different to their liner predecessors from the outside, higher sides, shorter forecastles, square sterns etc., it is inside that a passenger from the earlier years would notice the most difference.

In the days of the liner trade prior to the expansion of the cruise industry in the 1960s, designers had to cope for up to three classes of passengers. Even in the early days of the twentieth century, third class accommodation (known as steerage) had improved considerably. The companies on the North Atlantic run were aware that those who emigrated to the USA and Canada might well want to visit their old homes. If they had been given a good experience on the way out to the USA, they might well use the same company when visiting the Old World, and if they had been successful in their new country they could well be travelling second or even first class. First class accommodation, both public and private was, in the main very grand indeed with palatial public rooms fitted out in the latest style.

Cruise operators soon found that class distinction was not acceptable. Some of the earliest 'modern' cruise ships for the UK market, e.g. P&O's *Orsova*, retained a two-class system with first class passengers having approximately two-thirds of the ship for their use. In the US market, the only acceptable distinctions were based on cabin grades and thus the divisions between classes was removed, leading to complications in interior layout. Perhaps the nearest to class-based cruising that still exists is on the *QE2* where restaurant facilities are allocated based on cabin grade, although the ship's facilities are open to all passengers.

The development of specialist cruise ships led by NCL and RCCL (later RCI) freed designers from the necessity of duplicating facilities for different classes of passengers at a time when those cruising were demanding more than just accommodation, food and drink and a selection of interesting ports, but also entertainment. The concept of the Las Vegas style of review entertainment was just beginning to become the norm on cruises and, thus, specialist show lounges were required. Prior to the 1960s, cruisers made much of their own entertainment through fancy dress competitions and much dancing; the shipping company providing a small number of musicians with some members of the ship's company tasked to help. Even in the 1990s, some low-budget cruises for the UK market, especially those operated by former Soviet Union companies still featured a crew show as the main entertainment.

By the 1970s, the main ingredients for a cruise ship interior were in place. Newly built or adapted vessels normally had one or two decks; fairly high up in the superstructure dedicated to public access facilities and entertainment.

Our survey of 150 main stream cruise ships in 1998 carrying over 400 passengers shows the facilities that have become accepted as being part of a cruise vacation:

- a range of passenger accommodation ranging from basic to deluxe, 100 per cent
- a reception area, 100 per cent
- at least one shop, 100 per cent
- beauty facilities, 100 per cent
- outdoor swimming pool(s), 99 per cent
- a show lounge, 100 per cent
- an observation area (often used as a bar or disco), 95 per cent
- an intimate bar, 100 per cent
- a casino, 93 per cent
- slot machines, 91 per cent
- library facilities, 89 per cent
- a cinema, 66 per cent
- gymnasium/fitness centre, 95 per cent.

Note: Ships used in the German market are less likely to have casino/slot machine facilities on board; all ships operating for the mainstream US market have these facilities.

Other facilities to be found on board in increasing number of ships include:

- self-service launderettes, 45 per cent
- children's facilities (many ships have a children's pool) but, increasingly, play areas are included where appropriate), 63 per cent
- indoor swimming pool, 20 per cent.

The lack of children's facilities on 55 per cent of ships surveyed reflects the market that the ship operates in; if the ship is designed for the older age range, the lack of facilities for children may be an incentive to the target customers.

Freed from the restrictions of needing to provide separate facilities for different classes, designers have been able to concentrate public facilities within the ship. Traditionally, the early designs of cruise ships placed inside public facilities fairly high up within the ship with a single deck of premier accommodation above them as the following list of the *Pacific Princess* (ex *Sea Venture*) of 1970 shows.

Pacific Princess's passenger decks, working upwards from the water line are as follows:

Coral:	5 outside cabins, restaurant, medical centre
Fiesta:	100 outside, 28 inside cabins, reception
Aloha:	100 outside, 39 inside cabins, beauty salon, photo shop, shore excursion office
Rivera:	Shop, show lounges, bars, disco, cinema, casino, outside pool
Promenade:	4 suites, 9 mini-suites, 16 outside deluxe cabins, 4 deluxe inside cabins, library, quiet area
Sun:	Observation lounge, lido area, pool.

Contrast this with the layout of the *Royal Princess* of 1984, all of whose cabins are outside:

Main:	medical centre
Plaza:	38 cabins, restaurant, reception, beauty salon (1)
Rivera:	all lounges, cinema, library, shop, casino

Dolphin:	Outside promenade, 136 cabins, pool, self-service laundry
Caribe:	140 cabins
Baja:	134 cabins
Aloha:	84 balcony cabins, 28 mini-suites
Lido:	2 penthouse suites, 12 suites, 24 mini-suites, lido café, pool
Sun:	aft observation lounge/disco, pools, beauty salon (2), gymnasium.

In placing the majority of the passenger accommodation above public rooms, *Royal Princess* set a trend that was followed by a succession of new vessels, a trend that allowed the cruise companies to offer more cabins with private balconies. The *Dawn Princess* of 1997 and her sister ships offer nearly 70 per cent of outside accommodation with such facilities.

Cabins on modern cruise ships are smaller than comparative hotel rooms but modern use of materials and designs can make them appear quite spacious. On vessels for the US market all ordinary cabins are often referred to as staterooms whilst for the UK market, P&O Cruises differentiate between cabins and more expensive staterooms. We shall refer to all accommodation that is not included under the description 'suite' as a cabin.

Accommodation can vary in size from 70 square metres on First Choice's *Ausonia* through to the huge 1314 square metre suites on the *Silver Wind*. Average standard cabin size normally varies between 140 and 190 square metres and will comprise twin beds, en-suite facilities (normally a shower, wash basin and toilet) plus wardrobe space and a dressing table.

Cabin design is a branch all of its own and designers such as Yran have excelled themselves. The use of fire resistant laminates has meant that designers can replicate the wooden fittings of the early years of the twentieth century without the attendant fire risks. The fittings may be smaller than on land, but careful use of curves and the use of picture windows instead of portholes wherever possible increases the perceived size of cabins. Televisions (with satellite news) and personal safes are now a regular feature of even the most basic cabins. Premier cabins often also include sitting areas and, as mentioned earlier, balconies.

Designers

Certain designers have become well known in the cruise industry, either working alone or, frequently, as a consortium. Tillberg, Farcus, Yran, Storbraaten, Katzourratkis, McNeece and Najal Eide are prime examples of designers who have been involved (Tillberg for many years) in designing ships that are customer friendly and intended for particular market segments. To illustrate their prodigious output, Table 6.3 details just some of their work in recent years on either brand new ships or the reconstruction of older vessels.

As Table 6.3 shows, certain designers work predominantly but not exclusively with particular companies. Thus Farcus is very closely tied to Carnival Cruises. Joe Farcus has proved to be an innovative designer whose

Table 6.3   Principal designers

Designers	Ships
Tillberg	*Caledonian Star, Ausaka, Crystal Harmony/Symphony, Island/ Pacific Princess, Saga Rose* (with Platou Design), *Victoria, Costa Victoria* (with Gregotti Associates), *Disney Magic/Wonder* (with Yran and Storbraaten), *Norwegian Sea, Oriana* (with Yran and McNeece), *Star Aquarius/Pisces* (with PM Design), *Superstar Leo, Westerdam* (with VFD Interiors)
Farcus	*Olympic, Carnival Destiny, Celebration, Ecstasy, Elation, Fantasy, Fascination, Holiday, Imagination, Inspiration, Island Breeze, Jubilee, Maasdam/Ryndam/Statendam/Veendam* (with VFD Interiors), *Paradise, Sensation, Tropicale*
Yran and Storbraaten	*Clecia II* (with Bertelotti), *Renaissance 5–8* (with Bertelotti), *Sea Goddess 1/2, Seabourne Legend/Pride/Spirit, Silver Wind/Cloud, Song of Flower, Leeward* (with Heikkinen), *Norwegian Dynasty, Superstar Gemini, Disney Magic/Wonder* (with Tillberg), *Norwegian Dream/Wind, Oriana* (Yran, McNeece and Tillberg), *Viking Serenade* (Yran, Eide and Snoweiss)
Katzourratkis (A. or M., or both)	*Costa Playa, Royal Star, Salamis Glory, Sapphire, Switzerland, Aegean Dolphin, Bolero* (with Wandborg), *Calypso, Flamenco, Marco Polo, Melody, Norwegian Star, Ocean Breeze, Princesa Victoria, Sea Breeze I, The Azur, Century/Galaxy/Horizon/Mercury/ Zenith* (with McNeece), *Norwegian Crown* (with Terzoglou), *Norwegian Majesty, Starship Oceanic*
McNeece	*R1, Rhapsody, Century/Galaxy/Horizon/Mercury/Zenith* (with Katzourakis), *Oriana* (with Tillberg and Yran)
Najal Eide	*Black Watch, Royal Viking Sun, Sun Viking, Superstar Capricorn, Carousel, Dawn/Sun/Ocean Princess* (with Mortola), *Enchantment/ Grandeur/Rhapsody/Vision of the Seas* (with Snoweiss, Hoydahl, Iwdal, Grabonski and SMC Design), *Legend/Majesty/Monarch/ Sovereign/Splendour of the Seas, Nordic Empress, Royal Princess, Song of America, Sundream, Viking Serenade* (with Yran and Snoweiss)

ships are very contemporary with much use of chrome and neon lighting, whilst Tillberg tends to be more traditional. Carnival ships are aimed at a younger market than those designed by Tillberg and this illustrates the importance of design relating to function and markets.

Trends

If the trend of the late 1980s and early 1990s was towards more balconies, the trend since then tends towards enhanced public facilities. Where ships once had golf driving nets, now they have miniature courses laid out on the lido deck (complete with palm trees!) plus business centres and, increasingly, conference facilities. *Oriana* (see case study later in this chapter) was the first major ship to be equipped with a West End/Broadway-type theatre instead of a 'Las Vegas'-style show lounge. The traditional type of show lounge had been bedevilled by the need to place supporting pillars to hold up the roof of such a large space within a ship and such pillars would have been unacceptable in a theatre. However, the designers of the *Oriana* were able to build such a structure by strengthening the surrounding areas, and theatres look set to become the norm on large ships.

Another trend has been towards the provision of a central atrium within the ship, three decks on the *Arcadia* (ex *Star Princess*) and no less than six decks high on the Farcus-designed Ecstasy series for Carnival, such developments mirroring those in contemporary hotels. The *Grand Princess* also has a wedding chapel, thus being equipped for weddings at sea – a new niche market!

An important trend in the late 1990s was for the addition of alternative dining venues. Many ships still have just one or two dining rooms operated on a two-sitting, fixed-table basis. The more expensive products have begun to operate moves away from this traditional arrangement, first, by removing the fixed seating basis and allowing passengers to dine with whomever they wish and, second, by providing other dining venues on board. Thus the *Grand Princess* offers no less than nine alternative venues for a snack or light meal in addition to the three main dining rooms.

Builders

It was a great pity that no UK yard was able to bid for the *Oriana* or *Aurora* contracts from P&O Cruises. The Tyne, the Clyde and the Mersey were once the centres of world passenger-ship building, but no more. Building a large passenger vessel is a specialist task requiring massive

Table 6.4   Ocean-going passenger-ship building in the UK since 1960

Year	GRTage built
1953	22 979
1954	43 354
1955	62 355
1956	68 091
1957–8	0
1959	79 555
1960	46 667
1961	32 697
1962–6	0
1967	65 863
1968–71	0
1972	24 292
1973–99	0

capital investment and the major centres are now in Germany (Meyer Weft), Italy, France, Finland and Japan.

The decline of ocean-going passenger shipbuilding in the UK has been dramatic as shown in Table 6.4.

The last ocean-going passenger ship from a British builder was the 24 292 ton *Vistafjord* for Norwegian American (later Cunard) launched by Swan Hunter on the Tyne in 1972.

The massive building programme of the late 1980s and 1990s was carried out in just a few locations as shown in Table 6.5.

Table 6.5   Major building by country

Country	Percentage of total build
Finland	24.8
France	15.8
Germany	15.9
Italy	37.9
Japan	4.0
Other	1.8

Plans have been made for cruise ships of over 200 000 GRT and if these come to fruition they will resemble floating towns rather than ships, or even floating resorts. The effect of such ships carrying over 5000 passengers on some of the traditional cruise destinations will be a matter of some concern.

Conversions and additions

The massive growth in the industry has led to a situation (see Gwyn Hughes comments later) that has resulted in yards having full order books for new building and thus leading to the conversion of other types of ships, normally freighters or car ferries into cruise liners. Such conversions usually involve massive reconstruction so that only the hull remains as originally built, but it is a slightly quicker (and cheaper) method of bringing a new vessel into service.

Examples of this trend include: the excellent *Hebridean Princess* (2112 tons) of Hebridean Island Cruises, converted from the ferry *Columba* for short cruises around the Scottish Islands in a country-house style; the *Minerva*, 12 000 GRT built on the hull of a former Soviet spy ship of Swan Hellenic (P&O); the *Orpheus* (5092 tons) of Royal Olympic converted from an Irish Sea steamer and *The* (*sic*) *Azur* (14 717 tons) of Festival Cruises that was originally the cross-channel car ferry *Eagle*. The 25 000 ton *Leeward* of NCL still retains the car deck ramps installed when she was built as the *Sally Albatross/Viking Saga* and could still be used for a Miami–Cuba service if US/Cuban relations improve.

Costa Cruises converted the container ships *Annie Johnson* and *Axel Johnson* into the *Costa Allegra* (28 432 tons) and *Costa Marina* (25 441 tons) respectively in 1990 and 1992 to produce two very spectacular liners with glass walls at the sterns. The *Switzerland* (15 739 tons, ex *Therisos Express*, ex *Daphne*) was launched as the *Port Sydney*, a cargo-passenger ship for Port Line designed for the UK–Australia–New Zealand run. The *Monterey* (21 051 tons) of Mediterranean Shipping Cruises started life in 1952 as a C4 cargo vessel of the US Maritime Commission before major reconstructions in 1955 and 1987. No major company has yet converted a warship to a cruise liner, although there were plans to so convert the Australian destroyer depot ship, *Stalwart* in the early 1990s but these did not come to fruition. A number of former Soviet Navy icebreakers have been used for specialist cruises in the Arctic and the Antarctic, and these have been heavily refitted to provide suitable passenger accommodation.

The design of cruise liners has come a long way from the early days when unconverted liners were first used. Today's ships are customer friendly and reflect the change from the liner trade to the sea-going holiday market, changes that are seen in the accommodation, public facilities and the internal layout of the vessels.

Safety

Films such as the *Poseidon Adventure* and the many made about the *Titanic* do not provide a true picture of the passenger shipping industry. A large cruise ship is at very little risk of sinking through collision with other ships or natural features such as reefs, icebergs etc. The last ocean-going passenger ship to sink through collision was the *Andrea Doria* (29 082 GRT) in 1956 after her collision with the *Stockholm*. Owing to her modern construction she took hours to sink and there were only fifty-one fatalities from a combined total of nearly 2500 passengers and crew (Hoffer, 1980). Compare this with the loss of 1012 lives out of the 1477 on board the Canadian Pacific liner, *Empress of Ireland* (14 000 GRT). She was rammed by the Norwegian collier *Storstad* on a foggy May night in 1914 during her passage down the St Lawrence en route for the UK, and sank in just fourteen minutes (Croall, 1978).

The loss of the *Titanic* in 1912 has been well chronicled, including comments about the lack of lifeboats. At the time of her launch, Board of Trade regulations did not require a lifeboat place for every passenger and crew member. The provision was regulated by size, and yet size of ships had increased so rapidly but no provision had been made for very large ships in the regulations. Under the 1894 regulations, vessels of over 10 000 GRT with watertight transverse bulkheads, the Olympic class (to which *Titanic* belonged as the second ship of the class), had to provide lifeboat accommodation for 960 people.

The *Titanic* had room for over 3000 passengers and crew. That there was actually room in the lifeboats for 1178 was a voluntary bonus by White Star Line but on the night she sank there were 2227 souls on board. The original leader of the team that planned the Olympics, Alexander Carlisle had originally proposed sixty-four lifeboats, i.e. enough for everybody. This number was reduced in order to make more space available on the promenade deck (Gardiner and Van der Vat, 1995). There was supreme confidence in engineering in the early days of the twentieth century. Captain Smith of the *Titanic* is quoted as telling the *New York Times* in 1907 that: 'he had never been in trouble at sea in all his long career, though he had of course seen storms and fog; nor did he expect to be in the future. Modern shipbuilding has gone beyond all that' (Davie, 1987). It has often been said that the *Titanic* was considered unsinkable but the actual phrase from which this idea grew was 'practically unsinkable' (Gibbs, 1912).

The *Titanic* did have watertight doors but not to the same degree of protection as some other vessels, notably the Cunard's *Mauretania*, *Lusitania* and *Aquitania*. Full lifeboat protection for all those on board and effective watertight doors became mandatory in all jurisdictions very shortly after the Titanic disaster, as did improvements in communications. Marconi had demonstrated the practicality of wireless communications at sea as early as 1899 when messages were sent between two US Navy battleships twenty-five miles apart. By 1912, there were hundreds of vessels equipped with wireless apparatus but it was still a medium very dependent upon atmospheric conditions. Today every cruise ship carries a full communications fit using satellite systems to provide worldwide coverage for both routine and emergency communications.

Navigation techniques have also improved. The officers on the bridge no longer need to use a sextant to 'shoot the sun' to discover the ship's position. Global positioning systems (GPS) developed for military use in the first instance, and using satellite technology, are able to show a ship's position to a few metres. However, this does not always stop vessels running on to reefs and shoals as both Cunard with the *QE2* and *Royal Viking Sun* and RCI with the *Monarch of the Seas* found to their cost in the late 1990s. Radar, developed during the Second World War has also aided navigation but, like all technology, it can only assist the human beings on the bridge and not replace them. There must still be room for human as opposed to technological decision-making. Hoffer (1980) makes the point that had the *Andrea Doria* and the *Stockholm* not had radar they might not have collided. Without radar they would have passed each other in safety. It was a misinterpretation of the radar picture that caused the collision. To quote Hoffer:

> Each commander, interpreting his radar screen differently, came to an opposite conclusion. Each saw the situation as a mirror image of the other. Calamai [Captain of the Andrea Doria] thought he was to the left of the Stockholm. Carstens [Captain of the Stockholm] thought the opposite, that he was to the right of the Doria. In the last few minutes before visual contact both Calamai and Carstens manoeuvred their ships in the belief that they were moving away from danger. In actuality, at every turn they were coming inevitably closer to collision.
>
> (Hoffer, 1980)

Despite the impression given by the film industry it is not sinking through collision or grounding that is the major danger facing a cruise ship, nor the threat of terrorism, real as that is as shown by the taking of the *Achille Lauro* in 1885, but fire. Fire is the biggest threat to a large passenger ship. In the event of collision, modern pumps and watertight doors give the crew a good chance of getting the passengers into the lifeboats and abandoning the ship. Fire has been traditionally much harder to contain. Smoke can fill up spaces much more quickly than water and can travel through air-conditioning systems. Water is an imperfect medium to fight an on-board fire with. The water may put out the fire but will itself lead to instability. It was not the fire on board the *Normandy* (82 799 GRT) in New York harbour in 1942 that destroyed the ship whilst under conversion to a troop carrier, but the weight of water that was hosed on board causing it to capsize. Similarly, the loss of the *Empress of Canada* (20 002 GRT) in Liverpool in 1953 was as a result of fire and subsequent water damage. Both the sinking of the *Oceanos* (8000 GRT) in 1991 and the *Achille Lauro* (23 600 GRT) in 1994 were as a result of fire, fortunately without many fatalities.

Large numbers of passengers, many of whom may smoke, and a proliferation of electrical equipment – the Norway alone having 18 000 miles of electrical cabling on board – have produced vigorous standards of fire protection for cruise ships. This has culminated in the recent International Maritime Organization (IMO) requirement that smoke detectors be fitted in all passages, stairwells and escape routes.

The IMO, the requirements of the Convention on Safety of Life at Sea (SOLAS) and the insurance companies have made the modern cruise ship a very safe place, but only with constant vigilance. Ships now have far more lifeboat accommodation than passengers and crew in case access becomes blocked or restricted, and there is, by law, a requirement for a passenger safety drill prior to or just after sailing. Very little is now left to chance.

It might be thought that the success of the film *Titanic* in 1998 would have had a detrimental effect on the cruise industry – far from it. According to the UK magazine, *Woman's Own* (21/28 December 1998), the film 'was encouraging thousands to book cruise holidays'.

That the human aspect is still important was shown when the *Oriana* was designed with open bridge wings (the current trend being towards enclosed bridges) because her first Captain, Ian Gibb, believed that a captain should be able to feel the wind on his face (P&O, 1995)

Environmental considerations

Whilst the dumping of refuse and sewage into the sea may have been a standard practice at one time, it became completely unacceptable as knowledge of the damage such practices can do to the environment became wider spread. A modern cruise ship needs to be self-contained as far as the disposal of waste is concerned and thus has systems on board to ensure that material is only removed to designated disposal sites or, in the case of sewage, that it is properly treated before any discharge. Modern ships also need to cope with the vast demand for water for the passengers and crew. *Oriana*, the subject of the case study for this chapter can convert 600 000 litres of seawater into fresh water per day.

Case study

Oriana – P&O Cruises

The 69 000-ton **Oriana** which entered service in the spring of 1995 is unique in that she was the first vessel built specifically for the UK cruise market. As stated in Chapter 1, earlier vessels for the UK market had originally been designed for the liner service and had then been modified for cruise operations.

In 1974 P&O Cruises, the UK cruise operation of P&O, had refitted the 45 000 **Canberra** as a full-time cruise vessel. Built in 1960 the **Canberra** and her 1959 cousin the 42 000 ton **Oriana**, launched by the Orient Steam Navigation Company which merged with P&O in 1960, were designed for the UK–Australia liner service. By 1973 large passenger jets had decimated the liner trade and the ships commenced cruising mainly in the Pacific and Caribbean but without much success. **Oriana** spent much of her time in the Southern Hemisphere before being sold to Japanese interests as a floating tourist centre in 1986, but **Canberra** was allocated to the slowly re-emerging UK market where she built up a loyal following. In 1972 'The Great White Whale', as the Royal Navy nicknamed her, was hastily converted to a troopship to carry 3 Brigade comprising Royal Marines and elements of the Parachute Regiment to San Carlos Water in the Falklands Islands. Equipped with extensive medical facilities and helicopter landing pads, Canberra was in the first wave of the assault to recapture the Falkland Islands from the Argentinians. Despite her conspicuous white appearance (she was never repainted grey) and her vast bulk, she was not hit by intensive

Argentinian Air Force activity and spent three nerve-wracking days in the confined anchorage.

The British public had watched as **Canberra** had sailed out of the Solent on 9 April 1982 and they had cheered when she returned undamaged; the ship had entered the history books and possibly the psyche of the nation. The **QE2** also sailed south, but later and only as far as South Georgia, but **Canberra** went in harms way. At that time the **QE2** was regarded as the flagship of the British Merchant Marine and the government was unwilling to risk losing her (Hastings and Jenkins, 1983). The **QE2** transferred her troops to the **Canberra** and the ferry **Norland** on 28 May, and back to the war zone went **Canberra**.

Canberra became a quintessential British experience, Douglas Ward said: 'This ship provides a cruise vacation package in very comfortable, though not elegant, surroundings, at an affordable price, in good British floating holiday camp style, but with every strata of society around you' (Ward, 1994). **Canberra** built up a tremendous loyalty amongst many of her passengers. During research for this book we talked to many UK cruisers and amongst the over 50 age group, two ships were mentioned time and again, **Reina del Mar** (see Chapter 1) and **Canberra**.

By 1987, **Canberra** had captured 20 per cent of all cruises sold in the UK and a massive 45 per cent of all cruises that originated in UK ports (P&O, 1995). Despite the fact that she still had many inside cabins, no balconies and a proportion of cabins without en suite facilities, **Canberra** was still holding market share well into the early 1990s with regular 60 per cent repeat business.

As a brand, P&O Cruises was launched in 1988 based on **Canberra** and the smaller 29 000-ton **Sea Princess** (later renamed **Victoria**). Also in that year, P&O decided to investigate either a new running mate or a replacement for **Canberra**. As it turns out, **Canberra** operated for a short period with the new ship, the **Oriana**, before being replaced by the 63 500 ton **Star Princess** transferred from the Princess operation and renamed **Arcadia**.

There was nothing intrinsically wrong with the **Canberra** product other than she was an old ship that had seen much service. P&O Cruises were keen to retain the success of **Canberra** and went to great lengths to analyse why the ship had such a loyal following.

As mentioned earlier in this chapter, UK cruisers have different preferences to their transatlantic brethren. Robert Tillberg (see earlier) spent a considerable amount of time both on board **Canberra** and out and about in 'Middle England' finding out what people wanted. One of his discoveries, as we have stated earlier, was that UK cruisers prefer more smaller and intimate public rooms to those from North America. **Canberra** was a ship with a large number of smaller public rooms rather than the larger spaces found on US market ships. Barr and York (1982) have described this factor of **Canberra**'s success as 'disaggregation of space'. Tillberg and P&O also realized the importance of the 'comfort factor', comfort in this case being psychological; **Oriana** would have a semblance of **Canberra** in her appearance. The inset lifeboats and twin funnels were very characteristic of **Canberra** and a similar approach was taken for **Oriana**, although there was a single funnel cunningly fashioned to give an impression of two merged funnels. A cruiser transferring from **Canberra** to **Oriana** would begin to feel at home even seeing the ship from the main road leading to Southampton Docks.

The current generation of P&O Cruises and Princess ships could not be described as lacking in elegance (see the Ward quote about the **Canberra** earlier in this case study). Even a proportion of the Princess ships operated by P&O for the US market is sufficiently 'British' as to attract a loyal UK and Canadian following.

Margaret Robinson from the Wirral described **Canberra** after her first cruise as a four-star British family hotel with the best food and service she had ever seen.

Roger Cartwright has sailed on both **Victoria** and **Oriana** and had the opportunity to visit them when berthed together in Barbados. He describes **Oriana** as a 'swanky' London hotel with the West End and art galleries on the doorstep, whilst the **Victoria** is nearer to one of the elegant county-house venues in the Scottish Highlands, but both with a British atmosphere. This latter seems to strike a sympathetic chord with many UK cruisers who find some of the newer US market mega-ships rather too 'glitzy' for their tastes. It was this 'Britishness' that P&O Cruises wished to capture for their new ship.

The decision to order a new vessel is not one that P&O could take lightly. Although the UK market was growing in the late 1980s, it is a sobering thought that whereas a new ship for the US market needs to capture a mere 2 per cent of that market, a new P&O vessel for the UK market would have to assist in retaining **Canberra**'s massive share, once she was retired, plus gain 10 per cent on her own merits.

Originally entitled Project Gemini, planning for the new ship started in 1988. Certain key parameters in the design became clear very early on:

- The vessel needed a shallower draft than the **Canberra** in order to allow her to visit an increased number of ports.
- She needed to be fast. Designed for the UK home market, many of her cruises would be Southampton–Southampton, and yet Italy and the Eastern Mediterranean were popular UK market destinations so she would need to be able to get there and back within the traditional British fourteen- to sixteen-day holiday period, which would mean a service speed of 24 knots compared with P&O Princess's 70 000 ton **Crown Princess**'s and **Regal Princess**'s 19.5 knots, both ships being intended for the US market including the Caribbean.
- The ship would need the 'disaggregation of space' mentioned earlier to cater for British preferences.
- There would need to be a wide range of cabin options, again to cater for the UK market where many families are happy to cruise in three- or four-berth cabins.
- As British cruisers apparently sunbathe more than those from North America, generous open deck space would be required.
- As world cruises are an important January–March part of the P&O Cruises portfolio, the vessel must have a beam of no more than 34.2 metres, the maximum permitted for the Panama Canal.
- The vessel must be environmentally friendly to meet regulations and the increased environmental awareness of customers.

Initial designs were put out to tender in December 1989 but none of the twelve tender bids could meet P&O's budget. Project Gemini was one of only a number of large cruise ship projects being undertaken by P&O at the time. The company was investing heavily as Table 6.6 shows.

This represents a combined GRT of nearly 968 500 and, based on the figure of $4000 (£2500) per ton, represents a conservative investment of $3874 million (over £2,421 million). This is in addition to P&O's ferry and deep sea container operations and, as we will show when examining market share, P&O are only number three in the market behind the various interests controlled by Carnival and RCCL.

Project Gemini was put on hold until September 1990, by which time only two shipyards were in a position to bid for a revised, slightly smaller than originally intended, design. Unfortunately the three UK yards out of

Table 6.6   P&O/Princess new cruise ship building, 1989–2001

Ship	Company	Market	Size (GRT)	Max. no. of passengers	Debut date
Star Princess	Princess	US	63 500	1620	1989
Crown Princess	Princess	US	70 000	1910	1990
Regal Princess	Princess	US	70 000	1910	1991
Project Gemini (*Oriana*)	P&O Cruises	UK	69 000	1975	1995
Sun Princess	Princess	US	77 000	1950	1995
Dawn Princess	Princess	US	77 000	1950	1997
Grand Princess	Princess	US	104 000	2500	1997
Sea Princess	Princess	US	77 000	1950	1999
Aurora	P&O Cruises	UK	76 000	2000	2000
Ocean Princess	Princess	US	77 000	1950	2000
Sister to *Grand Princess*	Princess	US	109 000	2500	2001
Sister to *Grand Princess*	Princess	US	109 000	2500	2001

the original twelve were not interested and eventually the German yard of Meyer Weft in Pappenberg, Northern Germany, was able to produce an acceptable design at a price that met the P&O budget.

Soon the detailed design of **Oriana**, the name decided upon for the ship was underway. Much of the detailed design used the same technology as that employed by Boeing for the 777 airliner, namely computer-graphics aided three-dimensional interactive application (CATIA) and electronic pre-assembly in the CATIA (EPIC). These allowed a three-dimensional computer model of the vessel to be constructed and a check for interference between components, i.e. two components trying to occupy the same space (Sabbach, 1995). Both Boeing and Meyer Weft used the computer technology to make the design and building processes more efficient.

The basic statistics of **Oriana** are as follows:

Gross registered tonnage: 69 153
Crew: 760
Passenger capacity regular: 1760
Passenger capacity maximum: 1975
Passenger space ratio regular: 39
Passenger space ratio maximum: 35
Passenger decks: 10

Open deck space: 105 000 sq. ft
Cabins: 914 (comprising):
   Suites with balcony: 8
   Mini-suites with balcony: 16
   Staterooms with balcony: 94
   Staterooms: 66
   Outside cabins: 410
   Inside cabins: 320
Length: 260 m (853 ft)
Beam: 32.2 m (105 ft)
Draft: 7.9m (26 ft)
Service speed: 24 knots

On completion **Oriana** boasted the largest swimming pool afloat (one of three on the ship) and an unrivalled set of public rooms for a mainstream cruise liner. Douglas Ward described **Oriana** as:

> thankfully, quite conventional, and is evolutionary rather than revolutionary. Capable of speedy, long distance cruising. Has the largest stabilisers of any ship, covering an area of 231 sq. ft. She is a ship that takes Canberra's traditional appointments and public rooms and adds more up to date touches, together with better facilities and passenger flow, and a feeling of timeless elegance.

(Ward, 1998)

The latter comment is of vital importance. During the research for this book we had many opportunities to talk to UK cruisers from the **Oriana**-type marketplace and a wish for elegance came out strongly from many of them. **Oriana** is aimed at the upper end of the UK 'traditional' market, and her fixtures and fittings reflect that. As part of the design, cabins were more 'sea-going' than they would be on a US market ship. Indeed Princess Cruises, the P&O US operation, refer to all cabins as 'staterooms'. P&O Cruises reserve the 'stateroom' tag for a particular grade of higher-priced cabins – Britons appear to like the word 'cabin'. There are more cabins with baths and showers on **Oriana**, as opposed to the trend towards showers only in most US market accommodation, reflecting a cultural difference between UK and US tastes. Forty per cent of **Oriana**'s cabins have baths compared with less than 4 per cent on the **Dawn Princess** class.

Accommodation on board ships is smaller than that in land-based hotels, yet careful use of colour and design by Petter Yran, the architect responsible for cabin design, has given an impression of spaciousness. There are seven major types of accommodation on **Oriana:**

- Standard Cabins available as four, three or two berth inside and outside of approx. 150 sq. ft (also available as single cabins).
- Outside Staterooms with sitting area of approx. 190 sq. ft.
- Outside Staterooms with sitting area and balcony of approx. 220 sq. ft.
- Mini-suites with sitting area and balcony of approx. 360 sq. ft.
- Suites with a separate bedroom, lounge area and balcony of approx. 414 sq. ft.

In common with all new cruise ships, all accommodation has **en suite** facilities.

The use of wood within the accommodation has been extensive. This use of a traditional material with modern moulding and fire retardant techniques has allowed P&O Cruises to reintroduce the traditional opulence associated with the first class accommodation of the liner trade to the whole of their customer base, a trend which is being followed by the Princess operation and other cruise operators. As land-based package holiday hotels have improved their accommodation, so must the cruise operators follow suit.

In our opinion, the stateroom accommodation on the **Oriana**, with its sitting area and optional balcony, must rank amongst the best value for money on any ship and is the epitome of the designer's art.

Myer Weft assembled the ship in their huge erecting hall, sections being put together in one part of the shed and then craned into position like a gigantic construction kit, the maximum weight of any one section being limited to 600 GRT, the combined capacity of the two main cranes. The hall is 370 m long and over 100 m wide, an area equivalent to six soccer pitches – a large building indeed. The first part of the keel was laid on the huge floor on 11 March 1993. A total of 14 444 tons of steel was erected during the building of **Oriana**. As mentioned earlier, computer design played a major role in ensuring that the various subassemblies fitted together perfectly and that the holes for pipe runs etc. were all in the right places.

Between March 1993 and the floating out of **Oriana** on 30 July 1994 equipment and fittings arrived from all over Europe: engines from Germany; crockery from Staffordshire; stabilizers from Scotland; galley equipment from Poland; bathroom units from France; lifeboats and tenders from Holland; swimming pool equipment from Denmark; cutlery from Sheffield; gas boilers from Wakefield – the list seems endless. All of the equipment had to be fitted according to the carefully prepared plans.

Oriana's funnel was too large to be fitted inside and thus the ship was floated out into daylight on 30 July 1994 and, finally, on 7 January 1995 the funnel was fitted and final fitting out and finishing commenced.

Robert Tillberg made extensive use of lightweight materials for the upper parts of the ship to reduce topweight (see earlier), the aim being to create 'glass walls'. As Tillberg has stated: 'a window is a hole in a wall in which you put glass but on Oriana they really are glass walls, which give unrestricted views' (P&O 1995). The techniques to do this are relatively new and they allow designers much more latitude and creativity.

United Kingdom cruisers like to attend a proper theatre rather than the show-lounge concept prevalent on ships for the US market. To place a 'West End'-style theatre on **Oriana**, needing as it did a large room unsupported by pillars, gave the designers headaches but was eventually solved by strengthening the surrounding areas. This gave **Oriana** the first proper sea-going theatre.

It took the tugs, one of which had to be craned from the bow to the stern of **Oriana**, over four hours to gently manoeuvre her stern out of the building dock after the latter had been filled with 132 700 cubic metres of water (838 000 full bathtubs); **Oriana** was afloat.

When, later that month, **Oriana** sailed for her sea trials, it was necessary to dredge the River Ems – something that has to happen each time a large ship is launched at Pappenburg as the River is normally only 6.8 m deep and **Oriana** draws 7.9 m when fully loaded and even empty was far too deep for the 40 km of river. Not only had the Ems to be dredged but a railway bridge had to be dismantled to let the ship pass.

Extensive sea trials took place in the North Sea and in March 1995, **Oriana** was handed over to her owners. The Red Ensign of the British Merchant Marine was raised for the first time.

In April 1995, following an impressive naming ceremony by Her Majesty Queen Elizabeth II at Southampton, **Oriana** sailed on her maiden cruise and provided a large increase in available berths for the UK cruise market, increasing the P&O Cruises potential UK market by over 80 per cent.

Canberra was not withdrawn until the autumn of 1997 and was immediately replaced by the Arcadia (ex Star Princess) with no decrease in available berths. Canberra's last cruise was considerably overbooked and crowds lined the entrance to Southampton to mark the last arrival of the ship that had heralded the rebirth of the UK cruise industry and had become almost a national institution. Canberra was not sold on to another operator. She sailed later in 1997 for Pakistan and the ship breakers. Had she been refitted and sold, there was always the likelihood that in the short term, her loyal following may have gone with her.

Oriana has proved successful, but has not been without her problems. The replacement of her propellers early in her career did not completely cure a vibration in the stern, felt particularly in the aftermost of the two restaurants, the Oriental Restaurant, which commands excellent views of the ocean. However, a number of passengers have commented that it is a trade-off between the view and the vibration when deciding which restaurant to eat in (and thus which cabin to choose, as Oriana restaurants are allocated according to cabin position on the ship and not cabin grade as on the QE2).

We mentioned earlier that elegance is an important factor for the market segment Oriana is designed for, and elegant is an apt description of the ship. Whilst not as 'glitzy' as many of the new builds for the US market, there is a timeless feel about Oriana. The Curzon room on D Deck must rank as one of the most elegant rooms afloat with its spectacular chandelier, Steinway piano and chairs and sofas that reflect the lounge furniture found in many British homes, whilst Anderson's is the epitome of an up-market club. The library (with resident librarian) and reading room contain furniture especially commissioned from Lord Linley and designed to stand up to the rigours of the sea as well as being highly decorative yet functional. Oriana looks and feels British, an important comfort zone factor when marketing the product.

P&O Cruises commissioned a complete art collection for the Oriana, all of the works from UK artists. No less than 2882 pictures plus ceramics and sculptures were commissioned, more than are found hanging in the National Gallery in London. P&O Cruises actually sell a full catalogue of the art collection on board and it is more than a day's work to wander around the ship looking at each item.

With the QE2 effectively under US ownership from 1998 (following the acquisition of Cunard by Carnival) and marketed heavily towards the

US customer, **Oriana** is fast becoming the UK flagship, although this will change in the year 2000.

In April 1997, P&O Cruises ordered a new 76 000-ton vessel from Meyer Weft to be named the **Aurora** and due to debut in May 2000. The ship will be a larger version of **Oriana** with enhanced facilities, including a conference room and a business centre, but still designed for the UK market.

The philosophy behind **Aurora** gives a good indication of P&O Cruises' thinking about the UK market. To end this case study, we reprint below an interview conducted by Kay Davidson, the editor of 'The Dawning of Aurora', with Gwyn Hughes the Managing Director of P&O Cruises about the reasons and planning behind the decision to spend over £200 million on another new vessel. 'The Dawning of Aurora' is a series of pamphlets being sent to P&O Cruises 'POSH' Club members as the building of the ship progresses. These pamphlets not only provide information about the ship and the company, but also invite recipients' to submit views. **Aurora** is likely to be very successful if the 11 000 expressions of interest in the maiden voyage received by summer 1998 is any indication.

In the following extract the items in italics have been added by the authors to aid understanding.

THE BEGINNING OF AURORA

Ordering a new ship is not a decision that any shipping line takes lightly. It represents massive investment – £200 million in the case of Aurora – and there has to be confidence that enough people will wish to take cruise holidays over the life of the ship. And as the life of a ship exceeds 30 years, the predictions have to be accurate.

Kay Davidson conducted the following interview with Gwyn Hughes, Managing Director of P&O Cruises to find out some of the reasoning and planning behind the building of Aurora.

Q. Aurora is to be delivered in Spring 2000. Why then – why not earlier?

A. It was of paramount importance that the success of Oriana was ensured before we brought another new ship into the fleet. The retirement of Canberra last year *(1997)* meant that we needed to bring another first class ship in as soon as possible; the length of time that it takes to build a new ship meant that Arcadia *(ex Star Princess)* was by far the best option open to us at that time. Demand for quality cruises is rising steadily and so we are confident that we are introducing Aurora at the right time.

Q. Do you feel that P&O should have ordered Aurora at the same time as Oriana?

A. Hindsight is a wonderful thing! Yes, in the light of Oriana's success, we could have taken the plunge and ordered two ships but at the time it was more sensible to act with caution.

Q. When was Aurora first mooted?

A. We always have plans for new ships on the drawing board. Plans were made early in 1997 after Oriana's first two seasons.

Q. Are there plans for a sister?

A. As I said, there is a constant planning process in place. It is worth remembering that order books in the major shipbuilding yards are virtually full for the next two years.

Q. Did P&O Cruises consider taking another of the Princess Cruises' ships and refitting it as they did with Arcadia?

A. Princess' business is expanding as rapidly as our own and they need all their current ships for their expansion plans. In addition, building a new ship will allow us to incorporate all the latest developments in shipbuilding. This means that Aurora can bring world-class facilities such as round-the-clock dining to the British Cruise market.

Q. Will the British Cruise market absorb this increase? Especially in the light of increased choice now available to those wishing to take a cruise holiday?

A. We are confident that Aurora will be just as successful as our other ships. The growth in the popularity of cruising remains very strong and the type of ships that P&O has means we are in the best position to fulfil British Demand.

Q. What does this development mean for Victoria?

A. Victoria is an exceptionally popular and highly individual ship. Her presence in the fleet is assured for years to come.

Q. Will Aurora be British registered?

A. As with our other ships, it is our intention that Aurora will be registered in Britain.

Q. Where will Aurora be based?

A. Southampton is the homeport for P&O Cruises.

Q. Many people might have expected you to call the new ship Canberra. Why is this not the case?

A. That name is still clearly associated with one particular vessel that has not been out of service for very long. We know that there are many strong – and happy – memories of Canberra and we would not wish to cause confusion by giving another ship the same name so soon.

Q. Why build Aurora in Germany at Meyer Weft?

A. Prior to any decision, yards with the appropriate competencies were reviewed – both in the UK and world-wide. Meyer Weft built a very fine ship in Oriana and as Aurora is a development of Oriana, it was clearly of benefit to build her at the same shipyard. Meyer Weft have a very impressive record as one of the world's leading cruise ship builders; they have great technical expertise in building new-generation cruise ships and can deliver both on price and on time.

Q. In a nutshell, how will Aurora differ from the other ships in the fleet?

A. That's hard to summarise in a few sentences! Aurora will incorporate all the latest features introduced into new vessels world-wide plus a number of other innovations. As I mentioned earlier, she will have 24 hour dining as part of an extensive range of dining options, and other examples include an indoor/outdoor swimming pool and unsurpassed children's' facilities. This will make her a very forward-looking ship with a particular ambience. We are confident that the other ships will maintain their own unique appeal and will maintain our investment in all the ships and their onboard services so that we continue to offer the highest levels of passenger enjoyment.

(Reprinted by permission of P&O Cruises)

P&O obviously believe in the continuing growth and viability of the UK market, and it is an interesting reflection of that market that their repeat passengers identify so closely with the company and its vessels as to be interested in the technical progress of building etc.

7

Anatomy of a cruise

This chapter includes:

- booking
- setting off
- pre-/post-cruise stays
- embarkation
- who's who
- eating and drinking
- entertainment
- packages
- evaluation
- customer care
- staff
- case study: Royal Princess

This chapter is a case study in itself although there is a separate study at the end based on interviews conducted in 1995 on board the Princess Cruises vessel, *Royal Princess* (44 348 GRT). If occasionally the language is less academic and more flowery than other chapters, then we beg pardon but there is still something special about sea travel with its departures and landfalls, and it is that magic that the brochures attempt to convey and that we have attempted to analyse.

The case study in this chapter also introduces real people. They all assisted in a case study for a work on customer care, which has been adapted for this chapter.

It is too simplistic to think of a cruise as just being that portion of a holiday actually spent on the cruise ship. For the customer a holiday commences even before leaving home and may continue for some time upon return.

A commonly used term in customer care is 'value chain'. No product is entire in itself but is part of a chain in which each component adds value (Cartwright and Green, 1997). Whilst the cruise itself is the major component of the holiday, there are a whole series of experiences before, during and after the cruise that can add or detract from the main experience.

This chapter sets out to examine the value chain based on a generic cruise experience, synthesized from a series of actual cruises. It is not a description of a cruise *per se* but, rather, an analysis of the various factors and activities that go to make a cruise the experience that it is. To that extent the chapter follows a time line from the booking of a cruise to the return.

Before the brochure

It may seem trite to say it but before any booking can be made a customer or potential customer has to be informed of what is on offer – the Communications of the 4Cs (see Chapter 3).

Cruise companies plan two to three years ahead. People are booking earlier and earlier. Most of the year 2000 brochures were in circulation well before the end of 1998.

In order to offer a cruise to the public, the cruise company will have decided which of their ships will be operating how many cruises and in which areas, based on historical demand data. Detailed itineraries can then be planned. The companies have vast experience in ensuring that timings etc. meet both the requirements of customers and the economics of the operation. Maintenance and refits for vessels need to be programmed into the timetable. Great care has to be taken to ensure that these are realistic as more than one company has received bad publicity because a ship was not ready on time and customers were disappointed. If a new ship is being introduced, similar care has to be taken to ensure that it is ready in time for its first cruise. Many regular cruisers set great store by maiden voyages, despite the teething problems that can occur, and if the ship is not ready they may be reluctant to settle for a later cruise; there can only be one maiden voyage!

Ship's agents need to be contacted to ensure that base ports and visit ports can handle the itinerary. The political situation needs to be assessed to minimize any security risks (cruises can and are cancelled for geopolitical security reasons) and entertainment staff need to consider booking artists, the most popular of whom become booked up very quickly. Then, and only then, can the cruise be placed on sale and included in the brochure.

The brochure itself is a major piece of marketing and, despite the fact that many thousands will be distributed free, contemporary brochures have little expense spared in terms of quality of production. Companies are well aware of the various national legislations regarding advertising copy, and thus brochures are generally very truthful. Brochures certainly stress the advantages of cruising and the sumptuous accommodation and food.

The aim of any brochure is to transport the potential cruiser away from a dreary winter's day in Manchester or Des Moines on to a sundeck in the Caribbean with a pina colada in hand and a calm sea in the background. Attention, Interest, Desire and Action – Chapter 3; read the brochure, book the cruise.

Booking

As shown in Chapters 1 and 4, cruising is a holiday package at the top end, financially, of any holiday segment. It is not surprising, therefore, that the vast majority of our sample of cruisers spent a great deal of time prior to booking in order to make sure that their purchase met their needs. This is of considerable importance in the UK where deposits are non-refundable, unless for an insurable reason, and the 10 per cent that needs to be paid up front can be a considerable sum.

Our entire sample admitted to be avid readers of cruise brochures. All but first-time cruisers reported that they received regular updates on products from the companies they had cruised with in the past. Those who used the services of a specialist agent, e.g. Bolsover Cruise Club (see Chapter 3) received regular details of special offers.

A number of the UK sample also informed us that they scanned the relevant Teletext page (228) to see what offers were available. Being in the know, many of the sample were either early bookers (in the main these were people who were still in work and needed to book time off work) or, in the case of the retired, late bookers. All appeared very able to obtain the maximum discount.

First-time cruisers reported that they had studied brochures carefully before making a decision. Of our sample of nearly 100, only four couples booked directly with the cruise company. In both the UK and North America, mainstream travel agents or specialist cruise clubs were the preferred method of making a booking, the former by a visit and the latter over the telephone with a follow-up written confirmation.

On average the time lapse between booking and taking the cruise based on our sample, was found to be:

- Over a year: 12.
- Over six months: 20.
- Under a month; 8.

At the time of booking there are other choices to be made and information to be given. All but the cheapest of the Standard category cruises usually allow the cruiser some choice of the particular accommodation within their chosen price range. Airtours, Thomson etc. allocate cabins on embarkation in the same way as a hotel allocates rooms. Our sample preferred the choice given by the more traditional method but they were in the main regular cruisers, well acquainted with the layout of ships. For last minute deals, it is very often just one or two cabins that will be available within a price range and in that situation it is a case of take it or leave it. Regular cruisers often have favourite cabins and the earlier they book, the more chance there is that the cabin will be available.

In addition to the choice of cabin, where offered, there may well need to be decisions made concerning pre- and post-cruise stays. Many of the Standard products are now integrated with a land-based stay of a similar duration to the cruise and these will be examined later. There may also be an opportunity to arrive at the departure port early and leave the termination destination later. Many cruises may necessitate an overnight stay in a transfer location, for example, an Amazon cruise in 1993 on the *Pacific Princess* saw cruisers arriving from the UK and North America at Miami, being transferred to Fort Lauderdale, accommodated overnight and then joining charter flights down to Manaus. Most cruise companies offer discounted hotel stays both pre- and post-cruise at well below rack rates (standard hotel rates). Cruisers who have flown across a number of time zones often find a two- or three-night pre-cruise stay allows them to recover from jet lag so they are able to enjoy the nightlife on board their ship from day one of the cruise proper. Most of these extras need to be booked at the same time as the main cruise.

The majority of cruises still have fixed, two-sitting dinner arrangements and the customer will need to indicate their preference for first or main sitting (see later) and the size of table they require. Tables for two are in great demand but there are few of them, for the simple reason that four tables for two take up much more flow space (and staff time) than tables for six or eight.

This is also the time for the cruiser to inform the cruise company of any special physical or dietary requirements and of any birthdays or anniversaries (often the main reason for a cruise). Some companies offer cabin upgrades for major anniversaries.

Passport and insurance information will need to be provided. Cruise companies, in common with all package holiday providers, require customers to have adequate insurance cover. United Kingdom cruisers, who have the benefit of the free (at the point of delivery) National Health Service need to be aware that even a British doctor on a UK registered and owned cruise vessel will charge for his or her services. Cancellation for whatever reason also needs to be recovered if deposits are not to be lost.

If travelling with a company for the first time, there may be special inducements ranging from a welcome party to on-board credits to the cruiser's account on the ship.

For those living some distance from a gateway port or airport, arrangements need to be made to arrive at the 'jumping off point'. There has been a considerable growth in regional gateways and departure points in both North America and Europe. Unless the cruiser lives near to a major departure port there is likely to be an air component involved in the cruise. Given that some estimates say that over 18 million Americans suffer from fearing of flying (Eddy, Potter and Page, 1976: 203–4) and it must be presumed a similar proportion of Britons, it is no surprise that P&O, Fred Olsen and Direct Cruises cruise products that involve no flying are very popular, even though they mean a considerable drive in order to reach Southampton, Dover, Greenock or Liverpool.

For an increasing number of cruisers, however, cruising also means flying. The new entrants in the UK – Airtours, Thomson etc. – are well placed to offer regional departures (see Chapter 2) as they have the infrastructure and capacity to handle their own flights from a number of airports throughout the UK. The more traditional cruise lines need to rely on scheduled carriers for long haul and even inter-European flights. This involves the cruiser getting to a gateway, which in the UK will probably be London's Heathrow or Gatwick airport or Manchester. In the USA, New York, Houston and Atlanta act as major gateways.

Most of the companies using scheduled airlines offer some form of package for the cruiser. Princess have their 'headstart' package for UK cruisers, offering regional flights to Heathrow from Manchester, Edinburgh, Glasgow and Leeds/Bradford for £25 per person return and for £45 from other regional airports. This is considerably less than the scheduled rates but it most be noted that these flights were provided free up to 1997, as was an overnight hotel stay in London which is now charged at £25 by the company. Most of the traditional cruise companies offer similar free or discounted packages to their customers in the UK, Europe and North America. There are also discounted upgrades on scheduled airlines out of the gateway airports but the vast majority of cruisers travel economy (coach). Naturally those who can make their own way to the departure port can receive an air credit.

In addition to the use of scheduled airlines to and from gateways, increasing use is being made of charter operations. If a cruise company knows that it has a full aircraft load of cruisers from a particular point, it is able to arrange a charter. The use of a charter has some advantages and disadvantages to the customer. Part of the research for this book involved taking a cruise charter flight from the UK to the Caribbean. The flight was very late in departing, the legroom was much less than the scheduled equivalent and the food service and quality was poor. However, there was no need to collect luggage at the airport and on the return check-in was performed on board the ship. The return flight was with a different airline and service was much better. An advantage of using a charter operation is that there is much less danger of luggage going astray (see later).

As far as the value chain is concerned, for the cruise company it normally begins at the gateway airport. If there are sufficient cruisers through any one gateway it is likely that, in addition to the airline staff, the cruise company will have representatives on hand to deal with any problems.

As the companies usually provide their own hand baggage tags, the departure lounges sometimes resemble a children's game in which people try to identify others on the same cruise. One advantage of the charter-type operation is that the next time a cruiser sees their hold baggage after gateway check in will be in their cabin on board ship.

Assuming that the booking was not a last minute one, some two months before the commencement date, the cruiser will be required to pay the full amount of the cruise. In order to assist their cash flow, some companies will provide an extra discount if the total amount is paid in full at the time of booking or some time well before the due date. Some companies even provide a facility for the prepayment of gratuities with the final payment for the cruise.

Whilst this may seem strange to UK eyes where there is a different social perspective on 'tipping' it is less so for those from North America where tipping is much more a part of everyday activity.

Cruises to the less well-known tourist destinations may require the cruiser to obtain individual visas (group visas for those on organized excursions can often be obtained by the shipping company). Extra passports may be required if, say, the cruise is going to the Lebanon or Syria (both of which appeared on itineraries from the late 1990s) and the cruiser has an Israeli entry stamp in their passport.

Setting off

Like many journeys, much pleasure can be derived in the planning as well as the execution. Between final payment and departure many companies will send further details about the cruise including, in some cases, a list of shore excursions and the opportunity to pre-book and pay for them.

Currency needs to be obtained both as cash and travellers cheques. Most ships operate a cashless system based on a final cash or credit card system but incidentals (and gambling) need to be paid for in cash. German ships use the Deutschmark, Costa use the lira on European cruises and the US dollar on others. The UK-market companies use sterling, although the *QE2* is a US dollar vessel when cruising outside Europe, and the vast majority of other ships use the US dollar as their sole unit of currency.

Tickets normally arrive about two weeks prior to commencement and with passport and currency to hand, packing can begin and the journey to the airport or port planned.

Behind the scenes

Whilst it is the cruise company's staff on board the ship with whom the cruiser will have the most interactions, there is a large behind the scenes operation to support them. Cruiser details must be compiled and sent to the ship, special preferences noted and a careful check kept upon sales in order to decide when to discount certain cabin grades and by how much. The cruiser exists as a 'paper' customer long before he or she becomes an actual customer on board. On many ships restaurants need to be made ready, usually by the maître d'hôtel, as table sittings and allocations are one possible major source of friction.

Packing

Early in the Oscar-winning film *Titanic* there are scenes of Southampton with massive amounts of luggage being loaded on board the ill-fated liner. In the days of ocean liners being used as the main method of travelling between continents, luggage fell into two categories: wanted on the voyage and kept in the cabin; and not wanted on voyage and stored in the hold. Today there are still two types of luggage: hand baggage and aircraft hold luggage. Those who can drive to the departure port, and where the ship is returning to that port, can take as much luggage as they require; others need to follow airline baggage allowances.

The standard allowance for a long-haul flight is two suitcases and one for a regional flight. It is not possible, therefore, to take one's whole wardrobe on a cruise without incurring excess baggage costs and it is perhaps fortunate that shipboard life is much more informal than in the past. Nevertheless, as stated in Chapter 4, some formality is required and men will need at least a jacket and tie and ladies a reasonable dress for the formal nights on board. Products in the high Premium and Luxury categories may well have enforced dress codes in the evening and all companies ban bathing wear in public rooms.

Later in this chapter the problems of lost and delayed baggage will be considered as this can cause major problems.

Getting to the ship

As stated earlier, the vast majority of cruises require one or more flight components. These can be of considerable duration and may require stopovers on route, especially if the cruiser lives some way from their national gateway.

For example, in 1994 a cruiser from Scotland booking on the *Pacific Princess* for an Amazon cruise from Manaus to Fort Lauderdale would have the following flights:

> Edinburgh/Glasgow–London Heathrow
> Overnight in hotel
> London–Miami
> Coach to hotel in Fort Lauderdale
> Fort Lauderdale–Manaus via Caracas (charter)
> Miami–London (overnight)
> London–Edinburgh/Glasgow

thus adding two overnight hotel stays and a tiring overnight transatlantic flight to the holiday.

Pre- and post-cruise stays

To cope with the tiring aspects mentioned above, pre- and post-cruise stays have become very popular as a means of extending the value of a cruise holiday.

As mentioned earlier, two or three nights close to the embarkation port can give the long-haul traveller an opportunity to recover from any jet lag and to adjust to a new time zone. Our sample considered that it could take up to three days to recover from jet lag after a long-haul flight and this 'lost' time ate into their holiday. It is not unusual to find the very early morning light breakfast area on Caribbean cruising in the Caribbean populated by Britons whose body clock tells them it is nearly 11.00 a.m. when the ship's clock reads 6.00 a.m.!

Whilst both pre- and post-cruise stays are popular in major cities, one area in particular lends itself to such extensions (in addition to Florida which will be considered in the packages section) – Alaska. Much of the beauty of Alaska and British Columbia is inland and the main operators to the area have organized sophisticated cruise extensions in the region. Princess and Holland America have their own hotels, tour coaches and railroad operations. Between the two companies they have invested vast sums in the Alaskan tourist infrastructure (over $2250 million up to 1998) and HAL and their Westours operation are the biggest employers in the state (Ward, 1998). There are two types of tours usually offered in this region: Canadian Rockies tours covering the area from Vancouver to Calgary and often making use of the Rocky Mountaineer train; and Alaskan tours taking in the Denali National Park and often using railroad facilities, indeed Princess have their own fleet of 'ultradome' observation cars.

Alaskan cruises are usually only seven to ten days' duration and thus it makes sense for the long-haul traveller to add on an opportunity to see something of the hinterland and thus extend their holiday.

Most cruise companies will arrange flights to suit those who wish to book their own accommodation pre- and post-cruise but in such cases, airport transfers etc. need to be arranged by the cruiser.

Embarkation

Embarkation days are busy. Not only must new cruisers be accommodated but also those who are leaving the ship need to vacate cabins, be fed and then transported to the airport (see later). Crew may be going on or returning from leave and entertainers may be leaving or joining the ship (although this may also occur at visit ports for longer cruises).

Within the four to six hours between cruisers departing and leaving, cabins must be cleaned and the all traces of the previous cruise removed.

Passengers arriving by car or coach, e.g. at Southampton, will need to hand their vehicles over to one of the car parking agencies and those arriving by air (other than on a charter) will need to collect their luggage (hopefully it has arrived on the same aircraft) and clear any formalities before being assembled by staff recruited by the company's local agents and embarked on coaches for the journey to the ship. Luggage will sent on separately for delivery to the cruiser's accommodation.

At major base ports there are purpose-built embarkation terminals with cruise company staff and immigration officials to hand, examples being Miami, Fort Lauderdale, Venice, Piraeus (for Athens), Southampton, Dover, New York and Vancouver. Embarking on a cruise from a US base port can be a time-consuming business due to the strict US immigration policies.

At other base ports, temporary check-in desks will have been erected and manned by local staff and members of the purser's department, often aided by the entertainment team. Tickets must be checked and there is the obligatory photograph next to a lifebelt. No matter how bleary eyed after the journey, only the canniest of cruisers can escape this ritual, one of many staged photographic sales opportunities.

The first day

Finally, perhaps after a journey of many thousands of miles, the cruiser steps over the freehold of the ship. If using a major base port this will be along an airport style 'jetway', in other ports it may be up the gangway.

On certain Premium, and almost always on a Luxury product, a steward will be waiting in the reception area to escort the cruiser to his or her accommodation, where after a brief pause the cabin steward and, in the case of many suites, the butler will present their compliments and provide a guide to the accommodation's facilities.

All that remains is for the luggage to arrive. Missing or delayed luggage is a major problem for the staff of the purser's office. As stated earlier, cruising still involves some dressing up in most cases and nothing is more infuriating than delayed or missing luggage. Unlike shore-based hotels, the ship must sail to a schedule and it may be that luggage has to catch up with the ship. Luggage that is missing between gateway airport and base port airport is the responsibility of the airline, not the cruise company, but it is cruise company staff who need to provide assistance. According to one purser they can normally manage every item of clothing from the ship's shop or even borrowed from the crew, with the exception of ladies' shoes – these it appears are a very personal item indeed. Very little luggage actually goes missing but our sample reported very high anxiety levels over the possibility of arriving without luggage and waiting for it to catch up with the ship.

Entertainment is normally muted for the first night on board as there may be the excitement of sailing. Seven-day cruises normally sail as soon as possible on the evening of day one but many longer cruises will spend the first evening in port and sail at midday or mid-afternoon on day two.

The days when the departure of an ocean liner was major events are long gone. When liners were the only way to travel between continents, sailings were a major occasion with bands and crowds on the pier (McAuley, 1997). P&O Cruises' sailings out of Southampton still provide a uniformed band to see the ship on her way down the Solent but most departures in the modern cruise industry are now very low key. Occasionally something unusual happens to bring back the magic of a traditional 'sailing'. In the summer of 1996, the 69 153 GRT *Oriana* became the largest ship to tie up in the Northern Spanish port of La Coruna. At 2000 hours when the ship sailed, to the strains of a Gallacian bagpiper, it seemed as though the whole town had come out to see the sight. Not only was the pier crowded but so was the main road of the town and the outlying jetties, 3000–4000 people waving and the passengers of the Oriana lining the decks and waving back – some actually moved to tears. Such moments are rare and cannot be programmed but are worth all the more for the glimpse they give of the days when a sailing was often the parting of loved ones. More often than not, cruisers are still unpacking as the ship slips away into the dusk with little fanfare and only the obligatory pilot cutter for company.

Within the first twenty-four hours of a cruise, maritime law requires a full muster of passengers at their emergency stations. Whilst some cruisers treat this as an added entertainment, it is a serious activity as lives may depend on it. Emergency drills are demonstrated, safety information imparted and cruisers shown how to don lifejackets. It was not always this organized and there has been at least one reported case of a liner in the 1950s where little information was given out at the obligatory muster. The liner was the *Andrea Doria* and she sank after a collision on the approaches to the USA, sadly with the loss of a number of lives (Hoffer, 1980). Since the loss of the *Andrea Doria*, passenger-shipping companies have taken emergency drills very seriously and each cruiser is obliged to attend.

Who's who on board and ashore

The first evening and the second day of a cruise provide a chance to explore the ship, meet one's dining companions and attend the various introductory talks by the entertainment staff. The second evening is often the occasion for the first of the formal evenings – the Captain's welcome. The captain of a passenger ship has a legal position far in excess of that held by any shore-based manager – he is 'Master under God'. Much of the controversy of the *Titanic* centres around whether the chief executive officer of White Star Line, J. Bruce Ismay, ordered Captain Smith to sail as fast as possible (Davie, 1987; Gardiner and Van der Vat, 1995). In law Ismay had no rights on board the ship other than the common law rights of every other passenger; the Captain holds sole legal responsibility, even when the ship is being navigated by another officer or a civilian pilot. It is a tradition of cruising that the Captain meets his 'guests', one party for each sitting, with cruisers dressed in their best and a selection of ship's officers in white mess undress uniform. The Captain will take the opportunity to introduce the ship's heads of department and the all-important cruise director. On ships with a large percentage of repeat business, these parties may conclude with a 'where are they now?' session letting the cruisers know where their favourite captains have gone. Naturally the ship's photographer will be in attendance to capture that moment with the Captain.

The Captain needs to be more than a superb navigator. He or she is the main representative of their company and needs public relations skills as much as seamanship, but a seaman or woman they must be because of their legal responsibilities.

Derived from the old rank system of the Royal Navy, many merchant officers wear coloured strips in between their gold braid to denote the department they represent; deck officers have no coloured strips, pursers and entertainment staff wear white, electrician's green, doctors red and dentists pink. Bar staff will wear distinctive company uniforms.

A cruise ship provides a good fit to the Argyris (1960) definition of an organization: 'Organisations are complex human strategies to achieve certain objectives.' The objectives of the crew are threefold:

1 To provide a pleasurable cruise experience in safety for the customers.
2 To so delight the customers as to produce repeat business.
3 To generate profits.

The organization required to do this is very complex. First, there is the onshore organization. In order to operate even a single cruise ship, the company needs to market the product, sell the product by supporting agents and direct sales, and to handle bookings. There need to be staff with expertise in every aspect of marine operations and safety. Agents need to be in place in ports and supplies ordered. There may be a franchise department dealing with food, which as will be shown later is a vital part of any cruise, and there needs to be an entertainments section – all this in addition to the human resource and finance functions of any large organization. These people may be many thousands of miles away from their product – the cruise.

On board there is a large hierarchy under the Captain and this is divided into a series of departments covering certain aspects of the ship's operation.

Staff captain and deck department

The second in command on a cruise liner is the staff captain who has responsibility for the human resource management of the ship as well as being a deck officer in his or her own right. Staff captain is usually the final stepping stone on the road to full command.

The deck department is responsible for the navigation of the ship, i.e. getting the cruisers from port A to port B in safety. Modern passenger vessels, cruise ships included, are fitted with the most up-to-date technological aids to navigation and communications. Global positioning systems have done away with the need for sextants etc., but it still takes many years of training to become a deck officer and it is not all technology. Despite the most modern aids, ships do still run aground and, as the first Captain of *Oriana* stated when insisting that the bridge of the ship had open not enclosed bridge wings, 'a Captain still needs to feel the wind on his face' (P&O, 1995).

The deck department is also responsible for the operation of the lifeboats and tenders, and thus come into regular contact with cruisers at ports where the ship cannot tie up alongside, when ferrying them to and from the shore.

The deck staff monitor anchors and mooring ropes. They ensure that the latter are eased to account for the rise and fall in the tides, and that the 'rat guards' – circular pieces of metal at the top of a mooring rope just before it comes aboard the ship – are in place to stop any unwelcome rodent visitors.

Engineering department

Unlike the days of coal-fired ships when vast armies of stokers needed to be on board, the engine rooms of a modern ship are very labour efficient. However, in addition to tending to the means of propulsion, the engineers on board have to tend to the infrastructure of what is in effect a small floating town. Not only must the town move from A to B as efficiently as possible using the minimum amount of fuel but pollution must be minimized – indeed zero tolerance of pollution is now the norm – and the various needs of the population met. Fresh water and electricity in vast quantities must be supplied. *Oriana* (69 153 GRT) requires 600 000 litres of drinking water per day and the equivalent of a small power station to generate the electricity to light the ship, power elevators and other passenger equipment, operate the air-conditioning, run the navigational systems and provide heating (P&O, 1995). All this must be monitored and maintained by the engineers.

Security department

Since the hijack of the 23 639 GRT *Achille Lauro* and the murder of a passenger in October 1985, security has become a major concern of the shipping companies. The announcement, 'all ashore that's going ashore' may still reverberate around the ship about an hour or so before sailing but the only visitors in today's security-conscious world are likely to be official ones. It no longer possible to have friends and relations on board without prior permission, and then only rarely. Cruisers are issued with identity cards that also serve as a means of signing items to their shipboard account and these cards must be shown every time a cruiser enters or leaves the vessel. On the gangway, and ashore at tender ports there will normally be found a member of the ship's security team. Whilst they can and do investigate any crimes on board, their main function is to ensure that no terrorist or petty thief is able to gain access to the ship. The Captain has considerable legal responsibilities but in the event of a major crime or incident, police from the port or even police from the ship's country of registry or ownership will join it to carry out an investigation. As an example, when an elderly UK passenger disappeared off a UK-registered ship in the Caribbean in the spring of 1998 two officers from a UK police force joined the ship for the final sector of its cruise to carry out an investigation.

With large multinational crews aboard, the security staff also act as internal police dealing with similar problems to those found anywhere ashore – petty theft, fights and, increasingly, drug use – although all cruise companies have extremely strict regulations in this regard.

Medical department

It is rare today to find a cruise ship that does not have at least rudimentary medical facilities staffed by experienced doctors and nurses, although there are no regulations insisting on this. In general, the longer the duration of cruises a ship is engaged upon, with resultant less frequency of ports of call, the more extensive the facilities. As mentioned earlier, medical treatment for cruisers on board is not covered by national health schemes (except for ships registered in Russia or the Ukraine) and insurance is vital. The medical facilities are usually sufficient to carry out at least minor surgery and will be serving not only the cruisers but the crew as well. In the event of major surgery being required the cruiser or crew member would probably be landed ashore either as soon as the ship docked or by medical evacuation. Many cruisers are elderly and the cruise companies do ask on their booking forms for details of any medical problems. One ship, the 11 563 GRT *Aegean Dolphin* has a dialysis station on board. As a matter of interest, ship's doctors are technically self-employed and spend much of their time dealing with minor accidents and seasickness, easily cured by injections in severe cases.

Purser's/hotel manager's department

On ships and companies with a British or European ancestry, the head of the major 'passenger department' is the purser. On ships with a North American background this may be the hotel manager who has a purser reporting to him or her. In this book we shall remain with the Anglicized form. The purser's department is very much the front end of the organization. The department is usually based in the reception or front desk area of the ship. Many regular cruisers still refer to it as the purser's desk but in fact it is the marine equivalent of a hotel reception (front desk in North America). The desk will be staffed on a twenty-four hour basis and is the main point of contact for cruisers.

Whilst the Captain may be the titular head of a ship's hierarchy it is the purser's department and the cruise director's staff that have most interaction with the cruisers, forming an inverted hierarchy (Cartwright and Green, 1997).

The major areas that the department have to deal with (excluding food and entertainment which will be dealt with later) are as follows.

Accommodation

The vast majority of cruisers are perfectly happy with their cabin but many first-time cruisers have concerns about the space in non-suite accommodation. The use of curved surfaces and creative photography can make cabins appear more spacious than they actually are and whilst many of the brochures state the size, very few people can actually visualize 150 sq. ft. Second, there is the problem of restricted views. Lifeboats and other safety equipment can partially or entirely obscure the view from an outside cabin. The top range of Standard grade products upwards are quite explicit about this in their brochures and such accommodation is usually cheaper than a similar cabin with an unobstructed view. The customer can thus choose such a cabin, balancing view against cost. They do not have this option where the cruise company allocates cabins, as with some cruises at the lower end of the Standard category. Third, cabins may be in a noisy part of the ship. If the customer has a choice and they choose a cabin directly under a discotheque, then that is a choice they have made but, otherwise, they may wish to remonstrate with the purser's staff.

Most cruisers are happy with their accommodation and it is rare, but not unheard of, for a cabin not to be habitable. In cases of complaint it is for the purser's department to negotiate with the cruiser and to offer a change of accommodation within the chosen grade, if such accommodation is available. If the ship is full to capacity, advice will need to be sought from corporate headquarters as to any refund or future discounts.

Housekeeping

With ships carrying up to 3000 cruisers, there is a mammoth task in keeping cabins clean. Each cabin will have one or two allocated stewards who have responsibility for ensuring the cleanliness and tidiness of the cabin – not always easy as holiday-makers tend to strew their belongings around. Not only must the staff make up the cabin each morning and replenish toiletries etc. but on all but the most basic of cruises they will turn the beds down at night, subdue the cabin lighting and even leave a sweet on the pillowcase. One 'eccentric' couple we spoke to, who always travel with two teddy bears (they are not alone, as the television documentary *The Cruise* showed in 1998), returned at night to their cabin on one particular cruise to find the bears in different places and occasionally with a bottle of spirits in front of them!

Towels and bathrobes, where provided, need to be replaced and laundry collected and returned. The steward will also be required to deal with room service when on duty. There needs to be a minimum of one steward to approximately every twenty cruisers, plus relief stewards etc., making this together with the restaurant operation a major employer on the ship. Cabin stewards come from a variety of national backgrounds but many are from Third World countries where the salaries received are comparatively good compared with local standards. On those ships where tipping is allowed stewards can make up to $60 (£40) per day in addition to their wages.

Any problems with cabin maintenance are dealt with through the purser's department and then forwarded to the relevant engineers.

Cash

Cashless cruising (the signing for on-board purchases) relieves the cruiser of needing to carry cash. However, trips ashore, postage stamps and gambling need paper currency. Some ships operate a separate Bureau de Change but usually it is a function of the purser's desk to carry out this function.

Shore excursions

Shore excursions may appear a lucrative additional income market for cruise companies but according to Ward (1998) the average mark-up per person per tour is only 25 per cent and therefore only marginal when it comes to contributing to the total profit for a cruise. However, cruisers expect the company to provide excursions. A separate section under a shore excursion manager and port lecturer reporting to the purser's department usually handles these. Arranging suitable excursions within a budget and the time frame of the period in port is a specialist task and one that requires liaison with local tour operators through the ship's agents. Most cruisers take at least one organized excursion whilst on a cruise and the quality of excursions, which can be anything from a walking tour or snorkelling to an excursion by air either locally or regionally, varies greatly. Some are no more than a trip to a local souvenir shop, others really satisfy the Dipper by allowing him or her to gain a meaningful experience. The worst excursion reported to us involved a four-hour round trip through the Costa Rican rain forest to a village that appeared to consist of three rather tacky souvenir shops, and one of the best was a full day in Florence with an exceptionally knowledgeable tour guide. Tours can often be pre-booked and there is always an on-board booking facility. One advantage of taking a tour is that the ship will not sail unless all organized tours have returned.

A difficult task that falls to the purser's department is that of cruisers who fail to make it back on board at a visit port. Those not on organized tours are responsible for getting themselves back on board. If they only just miss the ship, the pilot boat can bring them back (they may charge) but otherwise the local agents need to liaise with the ship to effect a return, at the cruiser's cost.

Special needs

The purser's department is also responsible for ensuring special needs are met. Very often this will be as simple as ensuring that pre-ordered flowers are placed in a cabin or that an anniversary is remembered. It may also require providing assistance to cruisers with disabilities. More and more ships, especially the newer ones are equipped with a small number of cabins that will accommodate a wheelchair. Ramps and sliding doors also make access easier and the only real barrier to the disabled cruiser is when the ship cannot tie up, as tenders and wheelchairs are not always compatible.

Children

Unless a ship is especially advertised as having no facilities at all for children (as many of the luxury and niche ships are), there will be at least one trained children's counsellor or activity supervisor and an area set aside for play. Many of the newer ships are designed to be children friendly, the epitome of which must be the Disney ships with their special zones for children and their unique appeal to children of all ages! Most ships will provide a baby-listening service but, as with land-based hotels, there are often restrictions on children in public rooms after a certain time and the youngest have special meal times.

Disembarkation

Disembarkation is as big a task as embarkation. Sometimes the only difference is that the cruisers at least know their way around the ship (or should do).

Bags will have been packed the night before, collected from outside cabin doors and stored whilst hoping that no cruiser has left their travel documents or medication in their suitcase. On a ship with 3000 cruisers there will be a minimum of 3000 suitcases, and possibly up to 6000, to be stored. When the *Andrea Doria* sank in the collision with the *Stockholm* in 1956, there was conjecture that the weight of baggage placed on one side of the ship prior to docking in New York the next day was enough to increase the list to a fatal 20 degrees (Hoffer, 1980). Packed suitcases can weigh a great deal, especially when there are several thousand of them.

On those cruises where gratuities are the norm (and this is the majority), these will be given out, often in envelopes (thoughtfully) provided by the company. The average gratuities are in the order of $3 (£2) per person per day for the room steward, $3 (£2) per person per day for the waiter and $1.50 (£1) for his or her assistant, the bus boy. Even without a tip for the restaurant management staff, a fourteen-night cruise for two can cost upward of $210 (£130) in tips alone. Tipping is not obligatory but it is expected, especially in the North American market where it is the normal way of making up low wages. Some staff working for cruise lines reported to us that their wage levels were set taking the likely level of tips into account, and in the UK the Inland Revenue assume a certain level of gratuities for those working in industries where tipping is the norm.

During the packing process the cruiser will have been asked to place tags on their luggage indicating the time and method of the onward journey. These tags correspond to various flights or post-cruise stays and allow the shore-side staff to place luggage together in convenient groups.

Those cruisers who are using a charter operation, especially if it is the whole complement of the cruise, may have their baggage taken directly to the airport and loaded aboard the aircraft, the necessary security questions having been asked on board the ship.

As accommodation has to be vacated after breakfast on disembarkation day, most of the public rooms are in use as waiting areas; cruisers being called forward to disembark according to their onward arrangements. Ships staff are usually present at the main doors to say goodbye, and porters and assistance are provided quayside where necessary. The later disembarkees will overlap with those arriving and for a time the ship is a very hectic place. Those taking a back-to-back cruise, i.e. rejoining the ship for a second cruise are well advised to take an excursion and stay out of the way.

Items that have been inadvertently left behind need to be labelled and arrangements made for them to be forwarded.

Transport to the airport or package hotel will be provided for all those not making independent arrangements and the cruise will be over, although luggage can still go astray and flights can be delayed. These are all part of the value chain.

Many of our sample reported that one of the first things they do on returning from a cruise is to scan the brochures (many collected on the ship) in order to plan the next cruise.

Food and beverage department

Cruises are renowned for the quantity and perceived quality of their food. Airtours offer six snacks/meals per day and if one is so minded it is possible to have four breakfasts on most ships.

217

Breakfast can be taken either on deck or in the dining room and there is usually an early riser light breakfast available before the main cooked offering. It is also possible to have a continental breakfast delivered to one's cabin. Following morning coffee, lunch too can be eaten in the dining room or out on deck, usually in the form of a large buffet. There is afternoon tea – served, according to many of the brochures, by a white-gloved steward – the main meal of the day, dinner, and finally a late night buffet for those who still have an appetite. Ward (1998) estimated that for a Standard product the company spends between $7.50 (£5) and $17.50 (£11.50) per cruiser per day on food. This will be much higher on Luxury products.

There are national differences. Ships operating in the US market will often have a pasta course for dinner whilst this is omitted on UK market ships. Overall there is usually plenty of food of a reasonable quality to be had. Many of the companies employ famous 'executive' chefs to prepare their menus although the ship's chefs in the galley on board actually cook the food.

In the 1960s it was not unusual to see the catering officer in a local market buying fresh produce but today many of the supplies are purchased centrally and delivered to the ship in pre-packed and sometimes pre-positioned containers. In keeping with the growth in healthy eating, menus now contain low fat etc. options in addition to the more traditional fare.

Not only food (including items for special diets), but drinks in huge quantities are required to be stored for cruises. Cruisers, perhaps more than land-based holiday-makers seem to wish to try the more exotic. Two of our sample who never have more than an occasional glass of wine admitted to trying nearly every possible cocktail whilst on a cruise in addition to a brandy after dinner on most nights.

Alcoholic drinks have a mark-up placed on them in lieu of a gratuity to the steward, and whilst it is possible to have this removed in the case of bad service we have had no such instances reported to us.

One paradox of the cruise industry is that a UK-registered ship operating in the North American market will operate to US alcohol laws. Thus an eighteen-year-old Briton on board will not be able to buy an alcoholic drink, despite this being legal in the UK as the US law stipulates a minimum age of twenty-one for the purchase of alcohol.

This department has the most staff, a vast army of waiters and bus boys being needed to provide a swift service. On two-sitting ships, which still comprise the majority, the first sitting have about an hour and a half to eat before their tables are cleared for the next sitting.

A recent trend has been towards open dining – choosing the table, the time and even the venue for dinner. This seems likely to be a continuing trend and our sample reported positively on the opportunity to have a change of scene and of not being with the same dining companions throughout the cruise.

Equally recently has been a trend for cruise companies to subcontract their food operation to major concerns within that field. This has the advantage that the cruise company can concentrate on the shipping and entertainment aspects of the product but the disadvantage is that, in the case of complaint, the cruise company will still be held responsible by the customer.

Cruisers in the Luxury and some Premium categories are able to eat *en suite* if they so desire.

Entertainment department

Modern cruising has progressed far beyond a crew cabaret, fancy dress parades and passenger talent competitions. In the days of the ocean liner trade, little entertainment beyond music was provided. Today entertainment is an important component of a cruise.

Shows

All but the most basic of cruise ships has a show lounge and the most modern (see the case study on *Oriana* in Chapter 6) have a theatre. Casts are formed from professional entertainers although, unlike on shore, singers and dancers may well have to look after children, escort shore excursions and run quizzes.

There is considerably more interaction between entertainers on a ship than on shore, with the exception of holiday camps. The girl in the feathers and sequinned costume the cruiser saw on stage last night may well be sitting in the next sun lounger in the morning; in effect, they are always on stage.

Modern shows tend to be high-tech and make use of pre-recorded singing in many instances. In addition to the chorus line of male and female dancers there will normally be a male and female lead singer, one of whom, Jayne MacDonald shot to stardom when her experiences were profiled in the 1998 UK television documentary, *The Cruise*. The lead artists tend to rotate around ships depending on the bookings made by their agents, and some spend a considerable part of their careers afloat.

In addition to the Las Vegas/West End shows – two performances of a different show every two or three nights – the ship will also carry a succession of cabaret artists, usually a comedian and a magician, who together with the lead singers will provide a series of more intimate cabaret performances. Many of the upper Standard and Premium UK products also provide a classical artist to perform concerts during the cruise.

Gambling

In the 1960s the *Reina del Mar* (see Chapter 2) had a set of slot machines at a time when they were illegal in the UK. Today all bar a handful (mainly German, and Swan Hellenic's *Minerva*) of cruise ships, including some in the niche market, have a casino of some type. Many of the Standard US market ships have a huge almost non-stop casino operation, although this must close whilst in port.

Indoor and outdoor sporting facilities have become *de rigeur* on the vast majority of ships. As more and more people join shore-side health clubs, so they wish to continue their fitness regime during the cruise, and properly equipped gymnasia have become the norm in addition to the obligatory swimming pools, including some indoor ones. Nearly every ship has a designated mile circuit where the less energetic can ensure that they at least obtain some exercise in between meals.

The social hostess (see later) is often required to facilitate classes on social skills ranging from napkin folding to a thousand and ones things to do with a headscarf, and then there are the quizzes.

Most cruise ships hold a series of trivia quizzes and some of these, especially on UK-market ships, can become very serious occasions with thirty or so teams vying for a very mundane prize. P&O Cruises' quizzes are very popular and a whole lounge can be taken up, often late in the evening, with the same teams competing night after night.

There is usually a current affairs or similar lecturer. Some cruises, especially those from Fred Olsen, Page and Moy, NCL and P&O Cruises, are themed around a variety of subjects from antiques to jazz and specialist guest lecturers are available to increase the cruiser's knowledge of the subject. On cruises of a cultural nature (see Chapter 4), eminent experts may be on board.

The cruise director and/or social hostess

Whilst in law the Captain is the most important member of the crew, much responsibility for the enjoyment of the cruiser lies with the cruise director. Often recruited from the ranks of the entertainment industry, the cruise director is responsible for the activities on board, working within the laid down corporate guidelines. Cartwright and Green (1997) have profiled the work of a cruise director and the very great contribution this individual, by acting as host, compere and friend, can have on the ultimate enjoyment of a cruise cannot be overstressed. It is a job for the gregarious extrovert as they are 'on stage' almost the whole time and, whilst every cruiser will know the name of the cruise director, he or she must make it appear that they know every cruiser as an individual. Where the cruise director is male, he may have a social hostess as a deputy who also assists the Captain in hosting parties etc.

Ports of call

The geography of cruising was covered in an earlier chapter but there are those who do not always go ashore and thus a range of activities, albeit reduced, is usually provided on board as are the full range of meals.

Sales opportunities

Shops and merchandising

The vast majority of cruise ships have some form of shop on board selling not just essentials – combs, toiletries etc. – but also a range of merchandised products often bearing a logo of the ship. There is a huge range of products, including perfumes, gifts and clothes from the humble T-shirt to formal outfits. Custom's regulations prohibit the opening of on-board shops whilst in port in order to remove competition from local suppliers but they will be open from sailing well into the evening. Their standard varies but newer ships often have quite extensive arcades of shops whilst older ships may have just one small outlet. Many of the shops are run, under the direction of the purser's department, as franchises usually managed by major high street names.

Beauty

Franchises such as Steiner cater for the beauty element of a cruise. With at least two formal occasions on each cruise, there is a good opportunity to merchandise hairdressing and beauty products. All but the most basic of cruise ships also offer massage and a whole range of toning services, and many of our sample reported that a visit to the beauty salon was a must on a cruise even if they did not use such facilities at home.

As with all holiday-makers, cruisers drink concoctions on holiday that they would never touch at home!

Photographs

Ship's photographers are adept at never letting a photo opportunity pass by. They will photograph cruisers embarking, at every port, at the Captain's parties, at dinner, on the dance floor, in fact anywhere. The photographs are then displayed with a view to the cruiser making a purchase, and many do. The ship's photographers will also sell film and carry out a developing and printing service but their main function is to photograph the cruiser and sell the result.

Disembarkation

Due to the needs of airlines, the disembarkation process usually commences about two-thirds of the way through a cruise with a request by the purser's office to confirm flight times. There is something sad about thinking about going home so soon after arriving but the purser's department have a massive task to get everybody off the ship prior to the arrival of the next set of cruisers, and planning has to start early. In general, those with the longest daytime journey are disembarked first and those whose onward journey requires a night flight are disembarked last.

Packages

A development of the cruise industry in the 1990s was the cruise and stay package, often based on a seven-day cruise and a seven-day hotel stay. The hotel element of such packages is often very inexpensive and allows a short cruise to be extended at little extra cost. Many of these packages are offered by the newer companies that have expertise and resources in the land-based package holiday business. In addition to Florida, the base for so many cruises, the Dominican Republic, the Canary Islands, Majorca, Cyprus and Thailand are becoming increasingly popular cruise and stay destinations.

Disney has made the cruise and stay package a basic element in their product with the cruise on the Disney ship being part of a combined Disney resort package.

More up-market packages, often cruises on the *QE2* or the *Oriana*, involve a trip on the Orient Express; the cruise itself and a flight on Concorde, and specialist companies offer a series of such packages. Canadian and Alaskan packages have already been mentioned and these are becoming increasingly popular.

Evaluation

Throughout the holiday industry, ratings are used to inform potential customers of the standard of a product be it stars, rosettes etc. Tourist authorities often have their own ratings as do major package operators, e.g. Thomson with their T ratings. These may conflict with each other, especially where there is not a comparison with other operators, hence the importance of ratings that look at a comparison of provision.

Official evaluation

Port navigation and health authorities are obliged to ensure that the ship's entering or leaving their jurisdiction are both safe and hygienic. The US government is especially vigilant in this. Whilst there have been very few cases of ships being unsafe, the US does have a rating system for hygiene standards, the results of which are published, and if the ship has not reached a high enough standard, permission to sail may be refused.

Guides

The main guides to cruising are Fodor's and the Berlitz guide, the latter edited by Ward and mentioned many times in this book. Ward gives a clear indication of how the numerical scores and stars are awarded, and feels that those who undertake this work are owed a debt of gratitude from cruisers as they do help to ensure good standards.

However, what makes one ship better than another to an individual cruiser may well, as we have indicated earlier, be a matter of personal choice. All a rating system can do objectively is to say whether certain physical attributes, e.g. swimming pools are present; it can only be subjective about the experience.

Not only must the number of stars be considered but also the category of cruise, and thus it is possible to find certain apparent anomalies whereby a Standard product receives a higher rating than a Premium one. It must be remembered that the category of product relates to items such as space as well as ambience. Thus according to the 1998 Berlitz guide (Ward, 1998), Carnival's 70 637 GRT *Ecstasy* (one of a series of sister ships), a Standard product, receives four stars whilst P&O's *Pacific Princess*, a Premium product, receives only three stars plus. Amongst our sample were those who would have been overwhelmed by the *Ecstasy* and bored stiff on the *Pacific Princess*. Rating systems are only truly effective when they compare like with like.

The Fodor guides to cruising, e.g. *Fodor's 99: The Best Cruises* (Fodor, 1999), contain a large amount of information but it is directed almost exclusively at the US market. There are details not only of companies and ships but also of visit ports. However, operations such as P&O Cruises are only mentioned in passing; even *Oriana* (Chapter 6) receives only two lines. Both the Berlitz guides (Ward) and the Fodor guides are widely available in the US and the UK.

Internal evaluation

All organizations like to know how they are doing in the eyes of their customers. Holiday companies regularly ask customers to evaluate their experience at the end of a holiday, often offering a prize draw as an incentive to fill in a questionnaire.

Cruise companies set great store by the evaluations, the re-hiring of some entertainers being contingent on their receiving high scores. Discussions with our sample suggested that North American's rate the same experience higher than Europeans, a finding that the companies need to consider when setting success criteria.

However well constructed a questionnaire, it cannot supplement a senior member of staff, the Captain, purser or cruise director walking around the ship and talking to the cruisers, this is where the true information is to be found. Management by wandering around (MWBA) was seen by Peters (1987) as a key managerial skill and one that the best staff on cruise ships appear very adept at using.

Customer care

There are those who would argue that the true test of business success is repeat business and that is generated by good customer care. Looking after and delighting customers should be second nature but, as Cartwright and Green (1997) have shown, there are at least as many cases of bad customer care as there are good ones.

Complaints should be dealt with on the spot if possible and that is where the purser's department comes in. It should rarely be necessary for corporate headquarters to be involved. Most pursers' departments have a degree of latitude in providing recompense in the case of complaint, anything from a bottle of champagne to a discount on a future cruise.

Princess Cruises runs a scheme (as do other companies) whereby cruisers can nominate staff for an award. The Princess scheme also allows those staff in the public eye to nominate staff behind the scenes for a similar award thus ensuring that everybody is aware that customer care is their business. The internal customer is just as important in the value chain as the external one (Cartwright and Green, 1997).

Customer behaviour

Customers (and cruisers are just a sub-branch) behave in different ways, Jones and Sasser (1995), writing in the *Harvard Business Review*, postulated five types of customers and our research found good examples of at least four amongst our sample:

1 Apostles.
2 Loyalists.
3 Mercenaries.
4 Hostages.
5 Terrorists.

Apostles

Apostles are the cruise companies' greatest allies. They carry out the advertising for the company, they tell all their friends and business colleagues and encourage others to try the product. There are two problems associated with Apostles: first, their friends etc. may have different tastes and what suits the Apostle may be a disappointment to others; second, the Apostle may be delighted by the company but if anything goes wrong then 'hell hath no fury . . .'.

A disappointed Apostle will be very disappointed indeed. Our sample contained a couple who had undertaken many cruises with a particular company. They had a problem not of their making on one cruise. It was not resolved to their satisfaction and the company has lost two customers and, perhaps worse, a competitor has gained them.

Loyalists

Loyalists are very satisfied and come back again and again. They may not be as vocal as the Apostle but disappoint them at your peril. Our sample contained a large number of loyalists and it was quality not loyalty clubs that kept them with the same company.

225

Mercenaries

The mercenary is driven by price. There is little a company can do to keep them. If a similar product is cheaper elsewhere, then that is where they will go. They are satisfied but they have a low loyalty threshold. They will fill in a questionnaire with very high satisfaction scores but cruise with a competitor next time. Our research suggested that the US market was more susceptible to this category than the UK market, which contained a high number of loyalists.

Hostages

The hostage stays with a company because there is no alternative. For much of the 1970s and 1980s, UK cruisers who did not wish to fly had very little choice of cruise company. Many migrated from Union Castle and the *Reina del Mar* to *Canberra*, and it is to the credit of P&O Cruises that many have proved not to be hostages but have stayed with the company despite offers from the competition. As far as low-cost cruising in the UK is concerned, fewer people are hostages as there are now a number of competitors in the marketplace. As with all hostage/monopoly situations, competition drives up quality.

Terrorists

An Apostle scorned can become a terrorist, not by committing criminal acts but by making sure that the company receives bad publicity. Television consumer programmes are a haven for terrorists; they have been so let down that they want to tell the world.

Without customers no organization can flourish. Cruising is a growing sector of the tourism market and the cruise companies are taking increasing care to ensure that customers not only take further cruises but that they remain loyal to one company.

Staff

The staff employed by the cruise industry fall into five main categories:

1 Permanent 'crew'.
2 Hotel operation staff,
3 Entertainment staff,
4 Shore-based staff,
5 Indirect personnel.

Permanent staff

The officers and technical members of the crew of any cruise ship are highly trained individuals who will normally be working their way up a career ladder. Many of the navigation staff will have a 'Master's Ticket', that will eventually enable them to apply for a captain's position. Many of the officers will have started their seagoing career as cadets, whilst technical staff will have completed a college or university programme in their specialism together with continuous professional development (CPD) whilst at sea. The current trend is for staff to stay with a company but not necessarily a brand, for example, officers switch between P&O Cruises and Princess.

Hotel operation staff

The large numbers of male and female waiters, bus boys, stewards, croupiers etc. make up a considerable proportion of the crew of any cruise ship. Some of these staff make a career out of being at sea, for others it is a way of seeing the world whilst they are young (Cartwright and Green, 1997). Recruitment is often via agencies that specialize in supplying staff for the cruise industry, training then being provided by the operator. Where the catering operation is franchised, as on an increasing number of vessels especially in the US market, the franchisee supplies the staff. P&O Cruises have inherited the tradition of their liner trade predecessors and recruit many of their staff from Southern India, in particular Goa, having an office in Bombay.

Staff training, linked as it is to customer care, has become an increasing feature of modern cruise operations and this is conducted both ashore and on board.

Entertainment staff

Entertainment staffs are recruited using agencies and dedicated company teams ashore. Entertainers usually undertake short contracts, flying out to join ships for their contract period.

Behind the scenes of any cruise ship is a vast staffing logistics exercise designed to ensure that the crew are able to join the ship for new contracts or after a leave period, or are able to leave. Whilst the majority of the crew embark and disembark at base ports, it is not unusual for entertainment staff to join and leave the ship at visit ports.

Further details of the role of staff and life aboard cruise ships can be found in Dickinson and Vladimir (1997).

Case study

Royal Princess

(Adapted from Cartwright, R. and Green, G. (1997) **In Charge of Customer Satisfaction.** Oxford: Blackwell, by permission of the authors.)

There is a complex organization chart for a vessel such as the **Royal Princess.** Indeed, the ship could be regarded as an organization in its own right, from the passenger's point of view, and there are four main areas of operation with the Captain in overall control and accountable for the first three.

1 Transportation/safety aspects connected with the ship. Under the direct control of the Captain, the navigation, engineering, electrical etc. staff ensure that the voyage is completed on schedule, in safety and with as little inconvenience to the passengers as possible.
2 Hotel aspects. Over 1200 passengers need to be accommodated and fed. One can never complain about the quantity of food offered on a cruise, eating can start at 0600 and finish with the midnight buffet, with any number of meals and snacks in between. Laundry facilities need to be provided; staterooms kept clean and made up, indeed a whole range of housekeeping activities. Passengers need to acquire foreign currency, they may need medical attention, their accounts need to be kept up to date. Under the accountability of the Captain this role falls to the purser's department, a very large department indeed.
3 Entertainment. Cruise ships provide a full range of entertainments and activities ranging from quizzes, deck games and cabaret to full-scale shows. There are shore excursions to be arranged, shops to be run and photographic services to be provided. Modern cruise ships have a full entertainments team, again under the ultimate control of the Captain but organized through the cruise director. The cruise director is one of the members of staff that the passengers will come to know most closely. No less than twenty-four nationalities (twelve different nationalities of passengers and twenty-four different nationalities of crew) were represented aboard the ship, all with their own cultural norms and needs.
4 Pre- and Post-cruise. Passengers have to travel from home to their ship and return home again after the cruise. The vast majority of passengers will be making an air journey. So will their luggage and so, indeed, may crew who are joining or leaving the ship.

Travel to and from the ship is arranged by Princess Cruises but is not under their direct control. When a passenger who has travelled on two different airlines finds that their luggage has not arrived at the same time as they have and he or she goes to the purser's office, the company cannot (and to their credit do not) say that this is not their problem. Every effort is made to track down the luggage prior to sailing and if it is not found immediately, toiletries and clothing vouchers are provided. This is always a problem for any organization that has to rely on third parties meetings their needs. An excellent organization will take ownership of these issues on behalf of the customer.

It may not be Princess Cruises' fault that the luggage is lost but it is their responsibility to find an acceptable solution and if this means helping out with clothes and accessories, then so be it. The pursers' staff are adept at making up wardrobes but as Alersandro Bologna, a purser, has pointed out, ladies' shoes are the major problem. At least the passenger has something to wear and a toiletry kit, and most luggage does turn up although it can require considerable liaison between the ship and the airline concerned. The airlines are equally as concerned because it is their reputation that is at stake. As John McSorley, a duty manager for British Airways at London's Heathrow airport remarked in 1995: 'Just because the passenger is booked on a group ticket (i.e. taking a cruise or package holiday with the ticket booked and purchased by the travel company) does not mean that they are any less your customer.' This is a good example of our purchaser–end user relationship. Indeed, the airline staff are well aware that companies like Princess Cruises are major customers themselves through the tickets that they book for their passengers, and that valuable business could be lost if the airline's service affects the quality of a holiday.

All the organizations involved with getting the traveller to and from the ship and with his or her comfort when ashore – airlines, hotels and excursion companies – need to get it right first time if the experience is to be both enjoyable and memorable, and not memorable for the wrong reason. In the case of third party activities booked by the company, it is the company who are likely to receive the blame if things go wrong even if the problem is beyond their control.

There can be tensions between the four areas. The ship may have to sail before a missing item of luggage is recovered. Passengers on shore excursions may, through their own fault, miss the ship. Essential maintenance may mean that some facilities are temporarily unavailable.

Sailing times and meal times may conflict. The organization needs to function in a holistic manner. Most passengers never realize the depth and complexity of planning that occurs to ensure that the logistics work. All staff need to be **functionally competent**. The Captain needs to be an expert seaman or woman, the chefs need to be able to cook properly, the singers need good voices, the shore excursion staff need to know about the ports of call.

The organization needs **organizational competence**. It needs to be committed to its customers; it needs systems and procedures in place to deal with foreign immigration and customs procedures, effective staff rotas and training programmes. Given the cultural mix of passengers the entertainments and activities need to reflect this so that nobody feels left out. Whilst functional and organizational competence should be assumed as being present, **personal competence** is a different matter. At this stage it is necessary to give a few examples of the level of service provided by referring, with their permission, to specific individuals and their philosophies of customer service The people we are concentrating on are not in the main the senior officers of the ship but those with whom the customer comes into regular contact, waiters, stewards and entertainers.

The maître d'hôtel on the **Royal Princess**, Renzo Rotti, who was in charge of the dining room operation had to ensure that everybody was seated at a table that suited them. Unlike land-based hotels, dining room meal times are set and on the **Royal Princess** they were divided into two sittings. He needed to ensure that the numbers were comparable for both sittings, requiring considerable diplomatic and negotiation skills. As Renzo said, 'a smile and a pleasant manner can cut through many potential problems'. Through his seven head waiters he needed to ensure that the table teams, waiter and bus boy, worked well together. He learnt names of cruisers and went around to every table, every night checking on the quality of the food and the service. He has been in the catering/service business for over forty years, having started as a footman at Blenheim Palace in Oxfordshire (UK), the family seat of the Marlboroughs and birthplace of Sir Winston Churchill. Food is one of the main attractions of a cruise and Renzo and his team needed to get it right every time if the customer was to take away pleasurable memories. Passengers cannot choose another restaurant, although the latest generation of cruise ships is installing more choices for dining as seen earlier.

Passengers have the opportunity to express a table and sitting preference at the time of booking. Sometimes they forget or they change their mind and want to sit with new friends. There are only a finite number of spare places and Renzo's smile and accommodating manner went a long way to satisfying those passengers who required a change. Even if it is not possible, they know that everything that could be done has been done.

The bar staff and stewards have a job many of us would, at first sight, envy until we think about the long hours and, as with all the crew, the fact that you cannot but take work home with you when work is home. Passengers and crew, whilst having separate areas, are together for up to three weeks at a time; hence the vital importance of effective customer relationships. Also because the ship is by definition self-contained, each member of the crew is normally another member's internal customer.

Cartwright and Green (1997) define an **internal customer** as somebody within the organization for whom you satisfy a want or need that is required for them to satisfy their internal or external customers. Under this definition, Renzo Rotti was an internal customer to the staff who look after the computer records showing meal preferences.

When we order a drink from a steward or stewardess we do not see the internal transactions that may occur. Samantha Knight was a trained accountancy technician taking a two-year break and seeing the world and her colleague, Steve Britton, who spent much of his working day in the Horizon Lounge at the base of the ship's funnel, was intending to make a career at sea. Both recognized the need to build up a relationship with the customer and take the informal feedback they receive very much to heart. As Samantha put it: 'A smile may be all the encouragement you need.' They were both internal customers for the bar staff. They did not mix the drinks but it is they who received the complaint if all was not to the customers liking. Both saw themselves as important sources of information. They are the people cruisers were likely to ask, 'where are the toilets?' or 'how long is the Panama Canal?' and both stressed the need for patience and a sense of humour. At times they had to go beyond their duties. Certain cruises may have a large number of senior citizens or people with disabilities. They did not just tell people where to find something, if possible they took them. It is these little 110 per cent actions that are remembered and can make all the difference.

Cathy Webster, a Junior Assistant Purser on the ship made a very vital point: '**You have to remember that to the passenger they are one of one not one of 1200.**'

Everybody wants to be thought of as individuals and one of the greatest contributions that an employee can make to an organization's customer service is to treat people as 'one of one' and not just as another customer. Using their name, remember their needs, smiling: all these go a long way to providing that added extra and it costs nothing but can gain a great deal. As Cathy Webster noted, 'you can tell how somebody is feeling by the way they greet you'. Be sensitive.

The key staff in the entertainment product on a ship like the **Royal Princess** are the cruise director, the social hostess and the entertainers themselves.

Billy Hygate, the cruise director of the **Royal Princess** for part of 1995 has a background in the entertainment business, being a very competent singer. It was his job to devise a package that will entertain a wide range of customers, both in terms of age and nationality, but still keep within the show schedules laid down by the company. These major productions formed the nucleus of the package but the order of presentation was left to him, in consultation with the Captain. A job like Billy's is high visibility; he had to be seen around the ship and passengers greeted him like an old friend. As an entertainer since the age of thirteen he is used to being in the public eye; but all those at the sharp end need to make a positive presentation of themselves. It is interesting that the Disney Corporation refer to staff as 'cast' and to their working environment as a 'stage'.

Billy Hygate was empowered to make changes to the programme provided it did not deviate too far from that laid down. What he did before making any changes was to listen to what the customers wanted.

Working alongside and reporting to Billy was Caroline Day, the social hostess. She was very visible about the ship talking to the customers; as Tom Peters put it: 'Management by wandering about' (see earlier in this chapter). The role of talking to the customers must never be underestimated. It requires skill; Caroline had not to be intrusive, she needed to remember a large number of names, what the last conversation with that person was about. It is a job with a great deal of autonomy and responsibility. The person who talks to a customer is the one who can solve the problem there and then without it becoming a major issue.

We all like to be entertained and many people harbour a secret desire to be an entertainer. How do the entertainers on board view their relationships with their customers, or audience as common parlance would have it?

Jill Galt is a pianist/singer specializing in piano bar incidental songs and music, and cabaret. In such an intimate environment a good relationship with the customers is vital. Jill (and her husband who is also a musician) work on cruise ships on a regular basis and having the same audience night after night has advantages and disadvantages. If you do not relate to your audience you are still stuck with having them around for quite a long time but, if all goes well, you are able to build up a good relationship. This allows Jill to greet people not only by name but also with their favourite piece of music. As she pointed out, she makes a large number of transient relationships but you cannot let the fact that these friendships are transient get in the way. They live on through the songs, indeed you can buy the tape! She sees her role as being 50 per cent entertainer and 50 per cent public relations.

As in all situations, there will always be the customer who does not like the product and insists on telling you, but for an artist like Jill, 'you just have to turn the other cheek, don't react and remember the vast majority who do like your work, but you do need to listen'.

Senior staff often grow up within the company, something successful organizations like Emirates (Airline of the Year in 1994) and British Airways also encourage; they have been with the company for a long time and understand its culture and mission. Junior staff in Princess come from diverse backgrounds. A wine steward with a BA (hons) in hotel management gaining experience for a few years, a shop assistant waiting to join the Royal Navy, a Mexican waiter sending money home; how do they achieve the necessary customer service skills?

The driving force must come from the top, from the standards set throughout the fleet by the corporate headquarters in Los Angeles, from the P&O traditions and, most important when one considers that there are a growing fleet of ships separated by thousands of miles, by the example set by the Captain and senior officers. Whilst we have concentrated on the staff at the 'sharp end', it is from their superiors that the ethos and standards of the organization comes. However, it is the contribution of the junior staff that is most visible to the customer. The Captain of the **Pacific Princess** in 1994, Captain David Christie, in conversation was only too clear that it is these staff that make or break a company. They need and have adequate accommodation, they appear to be valued by the company and they make the passenger experience not just good but excellent.

233

All new Princess staff follow a company induction:

1 There is a safety induction as passengers will assume that any crew member is fully conversant with all safety aspects, perhaps not realising that the crew member may have just joined their new ship.
2 There is a task induction where they are trained in what may be very new tasks.
3 There is an induction that deals with the personal competencies; what the company stands for, pride in the ship, meeting the needs of customers.

The impression gained after talking to a large number of the crew on board **Royal Princess** was that the success of the product is directly related to the calibre and motivation of the staff on board, a finding that confirms the work of Peters and Waterman (1982) in their study of successful US companies.

8

Niche cruising

This chapter includes:

- cultural cruises
- sailing cruises
- freighter cruises
- mini-cruises
- river cruises
- coastal cruises
- expedition cruises
- land/air cruises
- case study: MV Hebridean Princess

Thus far in this book the main consideration has been the traditional type of cruise, albeit in many cases in contemporary ships. However, the tourism career of a growing number of people leads away from the majority type of holiday.

In this chapter a series of different types of cruises are considered, all of them, with the exception of river cruises, making up only a small percentage of the total but with increasing growth rate.

Cultural cruises

Mention has already been made, in earlier chapters, of the P&O Swan Hellenic operation based on the 12 000 GRT *Minerva*. *Minerva* in common with many German cruise ships has no casino operation but, as stated earlier, her cruises include contributions by distinguished experts, thus meeting the needs of Seekers as introduced in Chapter 4. Whilst the intensity of such a cruise might appeal to only a minority, there has been a trend from the late 1990s in the UK market for increased emphasis on a cultural aspect to certain cruise holidays by introducing a theme to the experience.

Minerva, whilst having many of the facilities of a mainstream cruise ship (with the exception of gambling), does not provide Las Vegas or West End type shows. However, she does have a library of over 4000 volumes and is a class of cruising that provides an interesting link between mainstream cruises and expedition cruising (to be considered later in this chapter). With size and accommodation nearer to mainstream than expedition cruising, operations like those of Swan Hellenic provide a means by which older cruisers of a Seeker nature can see less visited parts of the world in considerable luxury, albeit at a slightly higher price than a mainstream cruise in the same category.

In 1998, Fred. Olsen's ship *Black Prince* (11 209 GRT) and *Black Watch* (28 492 GRT) operating in the UK Standard market offered golf, food and drink, comedy, antiques, photography, sport, classical music, television personalities and even retirement planning themes on certain cruises, the latter being a good marketing idea given the age range of many of their base market. The *Ocean Majesty* (10 417 GRT) chartered UK operations of Page and Moy offer cruises in association with the UK National Trust. The visiting of stately homes etc. has boomed in both Europe and North America, and its extension to the cruise industry is entirely logical.

Silversea operates certain cruises in association with National Geographic and the 1999 P&O Cruises brochure showed no less than thirty-five themed cruises on a whole series of topics, a number of them associated with popular television and radio programmes. The themes included:

- classical music
- birds and wildlife
- sequence dancing
- antiques (hosted by television personalities)
- cooking
- the 1960s
- the 1970s
- golf
- comedy
- motoring

- bridge
- jazz
- comedy
- maritime (including talks from a *Titanic* survivor!)
- sport
- homes and gardens
- The Archers (a very popular UK radio soap opera).

Whilst the applying of the word 'culture' to the above could be questioned, and indeed the actual content of the theme is but a very small part of the cruise, there is no doubt that a substantial part of the UK market is looking for something in addition to the traditional cruise experience. The provision of themed cruises is meeting that need.

Using the classic former transatlantic line *Norway* (ex *France*, 76049 GRT), NCL offer a series of music-themed cruises featuring jazz, the Glenn Miller sound etc., appealing to a very wide audience.

The cultural content of a *Minerva* cruise is an integral part of the experience, but the themed cruises on offer are marginal activities and do not impinge on the overall experience to the extent that they would diminish the holiday for somebody disinterested in the theme topic.

The Disney Cruise operation mentioned in earlier chapters could be considered in the themed cruise category, given the decidedly Disney atmosphere on board their super-liners and the close connection between stays in Disney resorts and a short cruise. Disney have been very careful to ensure that their ships have considerable adult only areas on board and in most respects resemble Premium products within the mainstream market, albeit with excellent facilities for families.

Sailing cruises

There is a certain poetic majesty about a fully rigged sailing ship underway, an impression captured on countless artist's canvasses.

By the end of the First World War, there were very few commercial sailing ships left to ply the world's oceans. The notion of harnessing the wind, cheap though it was, had been made obsolete by the speed and thus competitive advantage that the steam and then the diesel engine gave.

By the 1980s the only large sailing ships left in the world were either serving as museums – HMS *Victory*, USS *Constitution*, *Cutty Sark* etc. – or were in service as sail training ships either as part of national merchant/ military schemes or as youth projects.

However, in 1986 a new breed of sailing ships came into existence with the introduction of the 5350 GRT *Wind Star* and her sister *Wind Song* in 1987. These were joined by the *Wind Spirit* in 1988. Carrying up to 148 cruisers the trio are sailed using a computerized sail-setting and trimming system and have all the facilities that would be expected of a modern cruise ship, including a casino and slot machines.

In 1990 and 1992, Club Med entered the cruise market with two very large sailing ships, *Club Med 1* and *Club Med 2* (both of 14 745 GRT), also highly computerized and boasting normal cruise ship facilities. Club Med had long been known for the particular ambience of their land-based holidays and the use of specially trained gentile ordinaires (GOs). In 1998, Windstar by then part of the Carnival group acquired both the Club Med cruise operation and both vessels, *Club Med 1* being renamed *Wind Surf* in 1998 and equipped for up to 312 cruisers.

These vessels could be described as in the mainstream tradition but with sail propulsion. With the major cabins of approximately 188 sq. ft, the accommodation is similar to that on mainstream motor cruise vessels but without a huge show lounge. There are gambling facilities and, in line with the current trend in Luxury and top-end Premium products, dining is not to set sittings or table allocations.

Windstar itineraries are very similar to those of mainstream cruises, Panama Canal, Caribbean, Mediterranean on seven-day cruises, with the exception of a fourteen-day transatlantic cruise for each vessel.

Costs are somewhat higher than for an equivalent Premium motor cruise. Ward (1998) rates the ships at four stars to four stars plus, and in the Premium category, but it is difficult to equate this type of cruise with more mainstream varieties because of the different facilities and ambience on board. Nevertheless, a comparison between the per diem price for *Wind Surf* and the much more traditional *Pacific Princess*, in the Mediterranean in 1999 shows that the former is more expensive although it is, as stated above, a very different product.

A range of sail cruises has developed in a manner that parallels that of mainstream cruising. Of a more traditional nature as far as the design of ships is concerned is the operation of Star Clippers operating in the Caribbean, Mediterranean and the Far East, including trans Indian and Atlantic Ocean crossings – traditional sailing ship routes. Originally operating with two ships, *Star Clipper* and *Star Flyer*, each 3025 GRT and of modern construction but traditional appearance (indeed the first 'true' clipper ships to be built and classified as sailing passenger vessels since the early 1900s), the company has announced the building of the world's largest sailing ship to a conventional design, *Royal Clipper*, to debut in June 2000 carrying 228 cruisers. Unlike the Windstar ships, the Star Clipper fleet use conventional square-rigged sailing methods and those cruisers who wish can attend sailing lessons.

Royal Clipper, fully rigged on all five masts, is the culmination of design techniques that saw the birth of the elegant tea clippers such as the *Cutty Sark* of the nineteenth century and currently preserved at Greenwich, London. Like the Windstar vessels, cabin accommodation and dinning arrangements are in line with mainstream motor cruise vessels. We quote below, with permission from Star Clippers, the advanced information on the *Royal Clipper* from their 1999 brochure:

> In the year 1910, the largest sailing ship the world had ever seen was launched. With five towering masts and scores of enormous sails, the *Preussen* flew over the seas faster than any ship – sail or steam – had ever gone before. In her time, which was to last only a few short years, she was the ultimate sailing vessel, capturing the hearts of those who were fortunate enough to see the *Preussen* as the winds drove her through the waters at astonishing speeds of 20 knots or more. [Authors' note: there may be some literary licence here for, fast as the *Preussen* was in the most favourable wind conditions, it is doubtful whether she could have reached the speeds of the 1909 British destroyers of the F Class – in excess of 34 knots (Dolby, 1962) – or the British battlecruiser *Lion* of 1910 – 27 knots – or the German battlecruiser *Moltke* of 1908 – 25.5 knots – or indeed the Blue Ribbon winning *Mauretania* of 1907 – speed of 26 knots recorded in 1909 – all of which were equipped with Parson's turbines.]
>
> Today (1999), on the cusp of the millennium, a new era in sail is being inaugurated with the launch of *Royal Clipper*. She is the dream of Star Clippers' owner whose heartfelt wish is to share the joy of sailing on a magnificent full-rigged ship with those, like him, who love the romance and adventure that the era of the great sailing ships embodied. Like her illustrious ancestor, the *Preussen, Royal Clipper* will be 439 feet in length, the largest true sailing vessel in the world. A fully rigged sailing ship with 5 masts carrying 42 sails, *Royal Clipper* is also expected to achieve speeds of 20 knots, or more!

Unlike the *Preussen*, but just like *Star Clipper* and *Star Flyer*, she carries the latest navigational and stabilising devices guaranteeing no more than a 5 degree heel, and she offers open seating dining, tastefully appointed public rooms and comfortable accommodations in a traditional nautical atmosphere. *Royal Clipper* will also have some extraordinary features that are truly unique. They include a three-story glass enclosed atrium that funnels sunlight into the heart of the ship, a marina platform and a floating dock that drops down from the stern, allowing swimming and watersports right from the ship. The ship will have three swimming pools, including a glass-bottomed pool that adds to the special ambience in the piano bar.

The *Royal Clipper* is the first authentic sailing ship to offer an undersea view. The aptly named Captain Nemo Club is a lookout lounge at the very bottom of the ship, where you can watch fish and the sea bottom through thick glass portholes (think of 20 000 Leagues Under the Sea!). Underwater floodlights will light up the area and attract fish at night when the ship is anchored, and they'll be just as curious and incredulous as you!

Royal Clipper is scheduled for delivery in June 2000 to cruise for that year in the Mediterranean until winter and then from Barbados on 7 and 14 day voyages to the lower Windward Islands and the Grenadines. With dependable trade winds all year round, this is a particular opportune area to experience the exhilarating thrill of sailing downwind under 56 000 sq. ft of billowing sail on the world's largest and newest, true sailing ship.

(Star Clippers 1999 brochure)

Although the former Club Med vessels are bigger, Star Clippers claim that *Royal Clipper* is the largest 'true' sailing ship because of her traditional design and that whilst, in common with the other members of the fleet, she has the latest in navigation and stability devices, she is still sailed in a traditional manner rather than by computer. As with all large sailing vessels, such a ship makes a truly thrilling sight when underway with all sail set.

Windjammer Cruises operate a fleet of much smaller sailing vessels plus one small converted motor freighter in the Caribbean. These are more hands on cruises where accommodation is much more basic (there are a number of upper berths) and cruisers are able to assist in operating the ship. As such the product, although not cheap, is geared to a younger age group of cruisers. The cruises are about half the Windstar price although the products are geared at different markets.

Germany has had a reputation for sail training ships in the past and there are a number of cruise-type sail vessels operating within the German market plus a small number for French-speaking cruisers.

Sail training ships such as the *Lord Nelson* are not strictly part of the cruise market but differ from those operated by marine training organizations in that individuals can book trips on them, but often in spartan accommodation and as a part of the crew. A growing trend, exemplified by the *Lord Nelson* has been facilities for the disabled enabling them to be full and active members of the crew of such ships.

As can be seen above, sail cruises have also undergone considerable market differentiation. There has been a growth in sail cruising since the mid-1990s with a differentiation in the market ranging between a more activity-style cruise and a more mainstream-style cruise where the use of sail is a means of moving a cruise ship from A to B, with Star Clippers being in the middle of this range. Most of the recent products of the sail cruise operations are in the Premium bracket. The arrival of the major player in the cruise market, Carnival, into sail cruise operations (Windstar) most probably presages a rapid growth in the sail cruise sector, especially given the importance of environmental considerations.

In terms of the categories of cruisers introduced in Chapter 4 (PRESSED), sail cruising appears to appeal to Enthusiasts (including what Dickinson and Vladimir, 1997, term 'ship buffs'), Partygoers, especially on the smaller more informal ships and 'soft' Explorers (Ward, 1999). The concept of a 'soft expedition' will be explored later in this chapter.

Freighter cruises

Up to the 1960s many of the freight ships on regular routes carried a small number of passengers. As the ships were sailing a regular routine, unlike most of today's freight ships which, like tramp steamers of old, follow the cargoes, it was possible to plan a voyage using this means. Manchester Liners from Manchester to Canada, Blue Star Line and Blue Funnel Line were just three of the UK operators who offered a limited number of berths with few if any entertainments but superb food.

Today this form of cruising has all but vanished although there are a few ships still operating regular services that offer a cruise-type experience. By the end of the 1990s, Ward (1998) was listing only two freighter-type cruise operations. First, that of Iveran Lines using the 19 203 GRT container ship *Americana* carrying a maximum of 108 cruisers complete with a well-stocked library and gentlemen hosts for single female cruisers and a huge minimum PSR of no less than 177.8. The second listing is for the much smaller Royal Mail Ship (RMS) *St Helena* (6767 GRT) operated by Curnow Shipping on a regular UK–Capetown service via Tenerife, St Helena, Ascension Island and Triton Ad Chula. The vessel, one of the few left that is genuinely a Royal Mail Steamer carries a maximum of 128 passengers on six round-trip sailings per annum (1998).

Mini-cruises

Modern car ferries can be as large as a cruise liner and the trend has been for them to offer facilities similar to the cruise industry, especially on overnight sailings. The ferry companies have tapped into a growing market for leisure trips without motor vehicles.

By 1980, the largest car ferries were approximately 12 000 GRT, as shown in Table 8.1 the size has increased dramatically, especially in Scandinavian waters.

Table 8.1   **Scandinavian car ferry sizes, 1979–89**

Year	Ship	GRT	Pass B/U	Cars
1979	Diana II	11 671	714/986	555
1980	Wasa Star	14 919	1100/850	515
1980	Finlandia	25 678	1601/399	480
1984	Svea	33 829	1625/375	350
1988	Athena	40 012	2090/110	620
1989	Cinderella	46 398	2810	480
1989	Silja Serenade	50 376	2614	450

Note: B/U = berthed passengers/unberthed passengers

A fivefold increase in GRT has not seen a corresponding increase in capacity but in providing berths for all passengers, and the decrease in car carrying capacity has been compensated by increased facilities.

The comparative luxury of such ships has allowed the companies to offer three- to four-day round-trip mini-cruises. Those from the North Eastern ports of the UK to Scandinavia and Northern Germany are especially popular. The trend began in the 1960s and 1970s when facilities were sparse but today the products are marketed as mini-cruises in their own right. The *Blenheim* (10 420 GRT) of Fred Olsen Lines was a joint car ferry/cruise liner and their *Black Prince* (11 209 GRT) began life with two names – in winter she was the *Black Prince* cruise ship and in summer she operated as a Scandinavia–UK car ferry service, *Venus*, for Det Bergenske D/S. She was converted to a pure cruise ship in 1986.

A number of car ferries have been converted into cruise liners by removing the vehicle decks and replacing them with cabin accommodation. They are normally easily recognized by their slab sides and comparative lack of outdoor deck facilities. *Delphin* ex *Belorussiya*, *Hebridean Princess* ex *Columba* (see later) and NCL's *Leeward* are examples. Indeed, Ward (1998) predicts that the *Leeward* (25 000 GRT) may undertake a Miami–Cuba ferry operation if the political situation permits, and she has retained her ramps whilst operating short cruises for NCL.

P&O operate a series of mini-cruises to the Orkney and Shetland Islands in the North of Scotland embarking passengers on the scheduled Aberdeen–Stromness (Orkney)–Lerwick (Shetland)–Aberdeen ferry service, a cruise that comes complete with organized shore excursions as an optional extra.

River cruises

An ocean cruise can only touch the seaward fringes of a country; a river cruise can delve deep into the hinterland with no problems of rough seas.

Up to the political changes in the former Soviet Union in the late 1980s and early 1990s, the most popular areas for river cruising were the Nile and the Rhine. The former (according to the BBC in 1999) is still the most popular river cruise destination for UK cruisers despite attacks on Western tourists in Egypt in the late 1990s.

A number of companies, including Swan Hellenic operators of the *Minerva* (see above), operate river cruises either using their own vessels or the vessels of local operators.

The Nile

The Nile is devoid of bridges and thus the limiting factor on the size; especially the height, of river cruise vessels does not apply. It might be expected that Nile cruises, given the wealth of antiquities in the area would be primarily aimed at Seekers (Chapter 4) but the relative inexpensive nature of many of the cruises also attracts first-time cruisers, especially Partygoers.

Nile cruises have featured in the portfolio of European package holiday companies for a considerable number of years, often as part of a two-centre package.

Many Nile cruises are centred around the Luxor area with its close proximity to the Valley of the Kings and optional excursions to Abu Simbel. The cruises operate between Aswan and the Sohag area, with flights between Cairo and Luxor, or travelling the full length of the river between Cairo and Aswan and the Aswan High Dam.

Nile cruise ships need to be of very shallow draft to cope with the river at its lowest, and accommodation is similar to mainstream cruise vessels. As with the mainstream cruise products, there is a wide variety of price ranges and Standard, Premium and Luxury applies as much to the Nile market as to the mainstream cruise market.

In 1998, the traditionally styled but very modern *Prince Abbas* began operations on Lake Nasser, on the other side of the Aswan High Dam. Carrying 128 cruisers and, equipped with both a plunge pool and a gymnasium, this vessel has added an extra segment to the traditional Nile area cruising. Owing to the sheltered nature of Lake Nasser it is able to operate with a high superstructure on a low draft. *Prince Abbas* looks like a traditional Victorian paddle steamer from the area, which belies its modern nature and facilities.

The Rhine and Moselle

The Rhine has long been a river cruise destination, encompassing as it does historical sites and a major wine-producing area. Passenger riverboats have provided a service up and down the Rhine for generations and companies such as KD (Köln–Dusseldorf), established in 1826, operate extensive cruise operations on the river.

The Rhine is navigable from The Netherlands up to Basle in Switzerland and remains a major commercial artery of Western Europe. There are no locks and thus river cruise vessels have uninterrupted passage up and down the river with the advantage that the equally attractive Moselle joins the Rhine at Koblenz and provides an alternative cruising area.

Rhine cruises accommodate between 100 and 200 cruisers using long and low vessels. All accommodation is outside and the vessels usually have three passenger decks with a lounge, restaurant etc. as the main public rooms. Vessels cruise during the day, visiting one or two riverside towns and then tying up for the evening, cruisers either finding entertainment in the town or enjoying a drink with music in the lounge. The relatively small size of the vessel precludes mainstream cruising type entertainment and thus this is not a product for Partygoers and, due to the informality, is not really for Strollers.

Rhine/Moselle cruise itineraries tend to be Amsterdam (The Netherlands)–Basle (Switzerland) or Strasbourg (France) taking in most of the navigable length of the river over eight days and seven nights; round trips to Düsseldorf–Strasbourg–Düsseldorf, again eight days or shorter three- and four-day variations on the above. The major visit towns in addition to Amsterdam, Basle, Düsseldorf and Strasbourg are Nijemegen, Volendam, Kampen, Arnhem (The Netherlands), Köln (Cologne), Koblenz, Rüdesheim, Boppard (Germany) with coach excursions to historic cities such as Heidelberg often included. Major Moselle visits are to Cochem, Bernkastel and Trier. A number of cruises also take in part of the River Main to visit Frankfurt and Wurzburg.

Given the large number of castles and vineyards along the middle Rhine, this area remains a firm favourite with holiday-makers from both the UK, the rest of Europe and North America who would, perhaps, not consider themselves cruisers as described in this book but who want more than an average package holiday. As a destination it appeals to the older Dipper who can make a leisurely progression up or down one of Europe's mightiest and most historical rivers. As with mainstream cruises, hotel extensions to the cruise package are freely available.

Rhine/Moselle cruising is not a cheap option. Per diem prices for a mid-range cabin for 1998–9 from UK (by air) ranged from £59 to £150.

The Danube

The other 'mighty' river of Western Europe is the Danube navigable by cruise craft from Kelheim in Germany to the Black Sea (theoretically). For socio-political reasons most cruise ships tend to operate only as far as Budapest in Hungary, the former Yugoslavia and Romania not being, as yet, part of the itineraries.

The opening of the Main–Danube canal has also provided a link between the Rhine and the Danube, thus allowing through cruises such as the Danube–Moselle cruises offered by, amongst others, Europe Cruise Line. Danube cruises use vessels similar to those on the Rhine with visits being made to Regensburg, Passau (Germany), Linz, Melk, Vienna (Austria), Bratislava (Slovakia) and Budapest.

Other Western European river cruises

The popularity of river cruising with 336 000 cruisers in 1996 (Ward, 1998) has led to an expansion of cruising areas with cruises in Western Europe being offered on the Seine and Rhône in Northern and Southern France respectively, the Douro in Portugal and the Po in Italy. Closely linked to Rhine cruises are those operated on the waterways of The Netherlands and Belgium, especially in the spring when the bulb fields of the former are in flower. There has even been a small operation on the Thames in the UK, up to Oxford, but the low bridges and narrow locks have restricted this to a very small vessel.

The reunification of Germany in the 1990s together with the liberalization of many Eastern European regimes also led to the development of the River Elbe from what was the Deutsche Demokratische Republik (the former East Germany) down to Prague in the former Czechoslovakia, now the Czech Republic.

Russia and the Ukraine

The demise of the Soviet Union in the early 1990s has led to an easing of travel restrictions in many of the former Soviet republics. Cruises are now available from St Petersburg (formerly Leningrad) and Moscow, in part on the mighty Volga and taking in the Golden Ring of historic cities, and from Kiev (Ukraine) to the Black Sea on the Dnieper. The Russian cruise vessels are very similar to those on the Western European rivers albeit slightly larger (up to 260 cruisers), whilst the Dnieper is able to accommodate even larger vessels.

Most of these cruises are operated by Western European companies in association with local enterprises, thus being able to assure their customers of a high standard of accommodation and cuisine.

North America

Given that the stern-wheel paddleboat has featured in many, many Western films and that generations of children were brought up (in the English-speaking world) on Mark Twain, it is surprising that the Mississippi only became a major international cruise destination in the 1990s. Traditionally designed vessels accommodating over 400 cruisers now operate a series of three- to fourteen-day cruises up and down the river, from New Orleans to Minneapolis/St Paul via Memphis. This area is becoming very popular given both the historical and musical connections. In the past the Mississippi was a major exploration route into the US hinterland and Civil War enthusiasts find a wealth of historical sites especially around the buffs at Vicksburg. The Mississippi was described during the US Civil War as an arrow pointing right into the heart of the Confederacy (Dupuy and Dupuy, 1960) and thus, just as certain Rhine sites are a priority for Second World War enthusiasts, so the Mississippi attracts those interested in US history.

A potential growth area in North America is the Hudson River from New York to the state capital of Albany especially during the fall foliage season. Clipper Cruises offers ten-night New York–New York cruises on the 1471 GRT *Nantucket Clipper* carrying 102 cruisers in informal surroundings. The same company also offer cruises on the Great Lakes (Erie, Michigan, Superior and Huron) and down the St Lawrence Seaway in Canada, as well as the Amazon and coastal cruises in North and South America plus the Antarctic (see later).

Far East

The two main river cruise destinations in the Far East, both developed in the 1990s, are the Irrawaddy in Mandalay (originally called Burma) and the Yangtze River in China. Irrawaddy cruise vessels are of similar design to those on the Rhine and cruise between Mandalay City and Bagan, and often offering an option of a rail cruise (see later).

The Yangtze River has been opened up to tourism as a result of changes in policy by the People's Republic of China although damming of the Three Gorges may cause changes to itineraries. Cruises tend to operate between Wuhan and Chongqing through the Three Gorges on vessels that have a similarity to those on the Nile. Many optional excursions, often by air, to sites such as Xian are normally available.

The Murray River in Australia also has a small cruise operation using vessels similar to those on the Mississippi. In 1999 river cruises began to be offered on the Yenisey River in Siberia, well into the Arctic Circle.

Coastal cruises

We are defining a coastal cruise as one that leaves the estuarine areas for a considerable portion of the cruise and uses vessels smaller than mainstream cruise ships. Therefore, round-UK cruises, Alaskan cruises, Amazon–South America or the Caribbean, West Coast USA and St Lawrence–East Coast USA and Norwegian cruises originating in the UK or the Baltic are excluded from this section as they are considered mainstream cruises operating around a particular coastal area. A number of cruises that could fit into this category are considered in the section on expedition cruises.

As early as the 1960/70s, British Rail (as it then was) was offering UK coastal cruises on the car ferry *Avalon*. The 2112 GRT *Hebridean Princess* (ex car ferry *Columba*) and converted for cruising during 1988/89 operates a series of six-to fifteen-night cruises around Scotland, Northern Island and Norway, being based at Oban in Western Scotland. The product is most definitely a Luxury one based very much on a Scottish country house hotel. Unlike many cruise operations, the *Hebridean Princess* does not sail at night and visits many of the remote islands off the Scottish coast (see case study at the end of this chapter). The *Hebridean Princess* is an example of what we describe as a 'soft expedition'; using inflatable boats to get ashore and being one of the few ships to be equipped with ship's bicycles. A number of other companies offer similar round-UK cruises (see Caledonian Star later).

There are also coastal cruises on the US East Coast, Mexico and the Orinoco area of Venezuela using small vessels that can visit places inaccessible to the larger mainstream vessels.

One of the oldest coastal cruises, although using scheduled services (and as such has an affinity with the freighter and mini-cruises covered earlier in this chapter) is that along the Norwegian coast. Whilst most Norwegian cruising is undertaken by mainstream operations, the vessels of the Norwegian companies OVDS and TFDS, known collectively as the Norwegian Coastal Voyage® (NCV) and founded by Richard With, form an informal and interesting alternative to a conventional cruise. NCV classify their vessels as traditional, mid-generation and modern with price differentials between the three types, the modern being the most expensive. In 1999 the size of vessels varied between the traditional TFDS *Harald Jari*, 2558 GRT with 169 berths (and a capacity of 410 passengers and four cars), and the same company's 12 000 GRT *Polarlys* of 1996, with 482 berths and a capacity of 691 passengers and fifty cars. The ship is one of five similar vessels; three operated by TFDS based in Tromsø and two by OVDS based in Narvik.

The service exists to link the coastal towns and fjords of the Norwegian coast, but for cruisers a north-bound cruise, Bergen–Kirkenes and a south-bound Kirkenes–Bergen of eight days each are offered together with a round trip, Bergen–Kirkenes–Bergen over thirteen days and a five-day mini-cruise Måløy–Bergen.

Accommodation ranges from basic inside cabins to suites on the modern ships but without suite options on the others. Given the scheduled nature of the vessels, entertainment tends to be of the quiet, self-organized variety, although some concerts are arranged. However, the cruise does give the opportunity to visit a series of ports bypassed by the mainstream cruise ships up to and beyond the Arctic Circle and there is a range of shore excursions.

The 1999 per diem rate for an average outside cabin on a modern ship was around £150, in line with the rates for many Standard mainstream products.

Expedition cruises

There are many remote parts of the world, off the standard tourist tracks, that can only be visited by sea. There are two types of cruises to these areas, 'soft' and 'hard' expeditions. We define a soft expedition as one being undertaken on a vessel that offers mainstream standards of accommodation, but on smaller vessels, and a hard expedition is one undertaken in the most basic of conditions. Very few, if any of the latter are on offer as packaged cruises, although they can sometimes be purchased on local ships normally undertaking scientific or freight work.

The 1990s saw a considerable increase in the number of soft expeditions offered, products that are very attractive to Seekers and especially Explorers who prefer a comfortable bed and a good meal in much the same way as the safari holidays in East Africa have developed. Indeed, one product that fits in between expedition and main stream cruising is that of the African Safari Club's *Royal Star* (5360 GRT) that operates Indian Ocean cruises coupled with East African safaris, with entertainment on board provided by the crew and a resident band.

More remote areas now visited by smaller cruise vessels include the Galapagos Islands, famous for wildlife and regulated as to the number of ships allowed to visit, the Bering Sea and Straits between Siberia and Alaska, and the Antarctic regions. Former Soviet navy icebreakers such as the 12 288 GRT *Kapitan Khlebnikov* are able to take cruisers, in a fair degree of comfort over the top of the world. In 1999 the ship completed the first ever Arctic circumnavigation for cruise passengers. A number of such icebreakers have been put into service allowing those with Explorer tendencies to visit remote areas in comfort and safety, although not cheaply. A number of nuclear-powered former Soviet icebreakers, e.g. *ib Yamal* (20 646 GRT), have been converted and used for expedition cruising – the only nuclear-powered vessels that have appeared within the cruise market. The West's only nuclear-powered merchant vessel was the *Savannah* (13 599 GRT) of States Marine Lines, built in 1959 and capable of carrying sixty passengers in addition to freight. She was not a commercial success, carrying her last passenger in 1965 and being converted to a museum ship in Charleston (South Carolina) in 1981 (Kludas, 1992).

The 3095 GRT *Caledonian Star* operates a number of cruises in South America, the Caribbean, around the UK, up into the Arctic Circle and in the Mediterranean and, like all expedition vessels, replaces the mainstream cruise director and entertainment with experts on the areas to be visited, such vessels often having lecture facilities.

Smaller Caribbean and Pacific islands receive visits from the smaller expedition cruise vessels that can use their inflatable dinghies to ferry cruisers in and out of remote areas.

The Antarctic is the latest growth area for cruising with all the environmental problems entailed by such growth. The Falkland Islands off the southern end of South America had no tourist industry before the 1982 conflict between Britain and Argentina following the latter's invasion of the islands that year. Lord Shackleton's 1976 report into the future of the islands (Shackleton, 1976) suggested that tourism could have a role in developing the local economy but the first 'cruise ship' to arrive in the islands was not carrying a group of happy cruisers. Instead, P&O's *Canberra* (44 807 GRT), requisitioned for war service (STUFT – ships taken up from trade), dropped anchor in San Carlos Water in the early morning of 21 May 1982 carrying not only her civilian crew but the 3500 men of the British 3rd Commando Brigade (Hastings and Jenkins, 1983). For a number of years after the end of the conflict in June 1982 the only ships and aircraft operating around the Falkland Islands were those of the Royal Navy and the Royal Air Force. As South America developed as a cruise destination in the 1990s, Port Stanley, the capital of the Falkland Islands, became a new and interesting visit port for mainstream cruises rounding Cape Horn.

The Falkland Islands – Ushuaia in Argentina and Punta Arenas in Chile – are the furthest south that mainstream cruise ships call but some smaller expedition ships, e.g. Society Expedition's 3153 GRT *World Discover*, cruise into the margins of the Weddel Sea and visit South Georgia (of Falkland's conflict fame where the *QE2* transhipped the British 5th Brigade to the *Canberra*), and the South Orkney and Shetland Islands as well as the Antarctic Peninsula itself. Such cruises carry resident naturalists and geologists, and are definitely for the Explorers and Seekers. *World Discover* operates in the Antarctic in the Austral summer (November–February) when there is nearly twenty-four hours of daylight. A typical itinerary from UK for the year 2000 is shown in Table 8.2.

Table 8.2 *World Discover* **itinerary WD01501, January–February 2000**

Date	Place
13–14 January	Fly London–Buenos Aires, stay overnight
15 January	Fly Buenos Aires–Ushuaia, embark *World Discover*
16 January	At sea
17 January	West Falkland
18 January	Port Stanley, East Falkland
19 January	At sea
20 January	At sea
21 January	South Georgia
22 January	South Georgia
23 January	South Georgia
24 January	At sea
25 January	South Orkney Islands
26 January	Elephant Island
27 January	Antarctic Peninsula
28 January	Antarctic Peninsula
29 January	Antarctic Peninsula
30 January	Antarctic Peninsula
31 January	At sea–Drake Passage
1 February	At sea–Drake Passage
2 February	Ushuaia, disembark; Fly Ushuiai–Buenos Aires
2–3 February	Fly Buenos Aires–London

Prices indicated for the above are £223 per person for a three-berth cabin, £287–£451 per person for a two-berth cabin and £507 per head for a suite, but these exclude the £1395 quoted round-trip air fare to and from London (Noble Caledonia Ltd, Antarctic 1999–2000 brochure).

As more and more expedition-type vessels enter service, it is clear that there is a growing market for this form of soft exploring and that more areas will be opened up to tourist development with all the concerns for the environment that this generates. The Antarctic is an especially sensitive area and governments are carefully monitoring tourism in the area.

Land/air cruises

One of the advantages quoted by our sample of cruisers was that suitcases had only to be unpacked once on a holiday that took in a number of places. Coach tours have been a staple of the tourist industry since before the Second World

War but those on coach tours often use a succession of hotels. Thus coach tours cannot even be considered as a land cruise in the sense that the word 'cruise' is used in this book.

Since the introduction of the Orient Express holiday package in the late 1970s, a number of other rail cruise style operations have been developed in Spain, Canada, Hungary, Russia, India, Malaysia, China and the USA (the American Orient Express). A number of these are offered in conjunction with sea cruises. It is not the intention or purpose of this book to explore rail cruises save to comment that they may, in time, come to form a possible alternative cruise package for Seekers and Strollers, offering as they do an opportunity to penetrate even deeper into an area than a river cruise.

No current commercial aircraft offers proper sleeping accommodation, although this has not always been the case as the famous Douglas DC3 (Dakota) began life as the Douglas Sleeper Transport (DST) with curtained-off sleeping berths as in North American railroad sleeping cars (Eddy, Potter and Page, 1976). Thus the few 'air cruises' that were offered in the 1990s (often using chartered and reconfigured DC10 aircraft – descendants of the DST) also do not fit our definition of a cruise, although it is not impossible that this could change and a true 'seven-day world cruise' could be offered.

Many aspects of niche cruising have similarities with mainstream cruising and it is not easy to draw definitive lines and say where one ends and the other begins as the case of Disney illustrates. However, the market for Seekers and Explorers is growing and one can expect to see more developments and growth in the specialized types of cruise.

Case study

MV Hebridean Princess

Oh isle of my childhood I'm dreaming of thee, As the steamer leaves Oban and passes Tiree.

(Scottish ballad)

The busy fishing and ferry port of Oban lies where the Forth of Lorne meets the seaward end of Loch Linnhe opposite the island of Mull on the West Coast of Scotland. The railway reached Oban in the 1870s through the endeavours of the Callender and Oban Railway company and for many miles from Crianlarich to Oban, much of it by the shores of Loch Etive, the railway and the 'Road to the Isles', the A85 Perth to Oban road, run alongside each other twisting and turning through wild and spectacular scenery.

The harbour at Oban is no stranger to the black-hulled, red-funnelled ferries used to link a number of the Western Isles with the mainland. Oban together with Ullapool to the north and Rothesay and Ardrossan to the south has long been a centre for ferry operations. Travel between the Western Isles and the mainland has always been problematic and the development of regional air services has not removed the need for ferry links. Hebridean farmers even receive discounts when taking livestock to the mainland giving rise to stories in 1998 that some were taking a sheep on the first part of their holiday and leaving it on the mainland to be picked up on their return. The inhabitants of the island, like those off New England and British Columbia use the ferries and air services as mainland dwellers use buses and trains. These are a vital part of the economic infrastructure. Operated latterly by the Caledonian MacBrayne company, whose name (CalMac) is emblazoned upon the ships' hulls, weather permitting they maintain a year round service.

Between March and early November a similar vessel, slightly older than the current generation of ferries and with no ownership proclaimed on her sides, can be observed either in Oban harbour or anchored off one of the islands. Those not interested in ships would presume that this is just another of the ferries linking the islands and the mainland but in fact the ship, the 2112 GRT **Hebridean Princess** has been described as 'one of the world's most well-kept travel secrets' (Ward, 1999).

As stated in Chapter 5, the UK as a cruising area is a current growth area (a star in the Boston matrix terms introduced in Chapter 3). Scotland has 69 per cent of the UK coastline within its borders due to the contorted and convoluted coastline and 166 islands, if one includes Skye now linked by a bridge to the mainland (Haswell-Smith, 1996). It is no surprise, therefore, that Scotland is playing a central role in the development of the UK as a cruise destination.

The **Hebridean Princess** was built by Hall Russell (Scotland) in 1964 as a passenger cargo ferry named MV **Columba** destined for service in the west of Scotland where she served until the late 1980s when she was displaced by newer tonnage with more vehicle capacity. Purchased by Hebridean Island Cruises Ltd, she reappeared in 1989 as the **Hebridean Princess**, an almost unique niche product for the cruise industry.

Scotland has long been a major tourist destination for Europeans and North Americans, and indeed for other inhabitants of the British Isles. Many North Americans have Scottish roots and the mix of scenic grandeur and stirring history make for a successful tourist destination. Figures from the World Tourism Organization in February 1999 showed that the UK received over 25 million visitors in 1998 and was the fifth most popular tourist destination in that year.

There has long been a tradition of country house hotel operations in Scotland and the **Hebridean Princess** has taken the country house concept into the cruise industry.

There are much newer small ships offering exclusivity for their cruisers, those of the Cunard **Sea Goddess** operation, Seabourne and even Silversea reflect the top end of the market, but **Hebridean Princess** is an old ship that has been decorated in a country house style and offers activities not dissimilar to those one would associate with being a guest at a stately home or castle.

The cruising itineraries are mainly around the Scottish islands with forays to Norway and Northern Ireland. The ship has a maximum capacity of fifty cruisers in thirty cabins. The accommodation comprises:

Suite: 1
Veranda twin cabins: 4
Twin cabins: 14
Single cabins: 11

Amazingly for a Luxury product and indicative that cruising is about much more than just accommodation, two of the single cabins have a shared toilet and bathroom and are inside cabins with no portholes or windows, another single and three double cabins also being inside.

The accommodation is not large, the suite has a total area including balcony of 340.1 sq. ft (about the same as a suite on the **Pacific Princess** or **Island Princess** – 360 sq. ft but no balcony), non-balconied twin cabins range from 121.5 sq. ft to 243. 2 sq. ft, the former being small by mainstream cruise standards whilst the latter is quite large. Single cabins range from 64.5 sq. ft to 162.5 sq. ft. Up to this point it could be concluded that the accommodation is nothing special and is highly priced. A June 1999 seven-night cruise (undiscounted) per head in the smallest single cabin cost £2650 ($4240), a mid-range twin cabin cost £4075 ($6520) and the suite cost £6195 ($9912). A North American cruiser also needs to pay for a transatlantic flight.

The reason the company can charge the rates they do is connected with the uniqueness of the itineraries, the ambience on board, the cuisine and the high standard of fitting out. All accommodation is named not numbered and is fitted out to the highest specification in a manner resembling that of a bedroom in a country estate. The company has also received much praise for the high-quality care provided by the all-British staff.

The ship does not cruise during the night and provides an itinerary that takes in some of the least known but most beautiful parts of the UK, a sample being shown in Table 8.3.

Table 8.3 *Hebridean Princess*: **The True North itinerary, June 1999**

Day 1	Embark Oban and depart 1900 to anchorage
Day 2	Cruising then Tanera Mor (Summer Isles) then cruising
Day 3	Cruising–Orkney
Day 4	Cruising–Shetland
Day 5	Shetland–cruising
Day 6	Fair Isle–Shetland–cruising
Day 7	Cruising–Invergordon–disembark

The ship is certainly one of the few to carry bicycles for cruisers to use on shore and the thirty-seven all-British crew provides excellent service. Cuisine is Scottish, local and freshly prepared. Everything with the exception of alcoholic beverages (although a free non-alcoholic and paid for alcoholic mini-bar is provided), and purchases from the shop is provided in the cruise price including excursions and entrance fees. There is a real opportunity to get away from it all as mobile telephone reception is poor in the Scottish Islands and there is only an emergency link from the ship to shore.

The weather in Scotland can be very wet and the seas rough but the ship was built for those waters, and with a draft of only ten feet she is able to approach the more isolated islands closely enough to ferry passengers ashore. Whilst mainstream companies have been offering round-Britain cruises for some time, none of their ships can visit the more remote areas. Listed below are the ports on the **Hebridean Princess**'s 1999 cruise season:

Scotland: Oban, Tobermoray (Mull), Salen (Loch Sunart), Sound of Sleat, Skye, Loch Torridon, Plockton, Kyle of Lochalsh, Muck, Corpach, Torosay Castle, Loch Craignish, Tayvallich, Gigha, Jura, Colonsay, Iona, Staffa, Barra, Eriska, Canna, Loch Coruisk, Loch Ceann Traigh, Rum, Eigg, Harris, Trehnish Islands, Loch Ewe, Handa, Fangamore Bay, Lochinver, Ullapool, Shaint Islands, Tiree, Coll, Vatersay, Glenelg, Inverie, Lewis, St Kilda, North and South Uist, Orkney, Shetland, Fair Isle, Invergordon, Loch Fyne, Arran, Ailsa Craig, Holy Island, Mull of Kintyre, Crinan, Islay.

Northern Ireland: Rathlin Island, Strangford Loch.

Isle of Man: Port St Mary/Port Erin, Douglas.

Norway: Eivindvik, Vik, Gudvangen, Flåm, Undredal, Fjaerland, Bergen, Jondal, Folgefonn Glacier, Ulvik, Utne, Rosendal.

These are most unusual destinations on a most unusual ship designed for Seekers and Enthusiasts who have more than a little Explorer in them. That Hebridean Island Cruises have been able to take a nondescript redundant inter-island ferry and turn it into a product that meets the needs of their customers and also blends in so well with the cruising area visited, shows the importance of market research and listening to the customer – and then providing what they want in a manner that delights them.

9

The future of cruising

This chapter includes:

■ predictions
■ the markets
■ the companies
■ the cruising areas
■ the ships
■ World City
■ case study: **Mistral**, Festival Cruises.

This book has considered the cruise industry up to the year 2000 but what does the future hold in store for what has been a remarkable success story?

Predictions

In making predictions for the development of the cruise industry in the first decade of the twenty-first century, two basic assumptions need to be made:

1 The downturn in the Asian economy of the latter part of the 1990s will be reversed.
2 there will be no major global conflicts.

Whilst the second might be optimistic, there is evidence that the Gulf War of the early 1990s affected the inclination of US citizens towards foreign travel and thus any such conflict may have a disproportionate effect on the industry given the preponderance of the US market. The late 1990s saw a number of horrific attacks on tourists in Egypt and Uganda and the former, a massacre at Luxor, had a very detrimental short-term effect on River Nile cruises.

Assuming the above is correct, by looking at current trends as discussed in this book it is possible to make some general predictions under the following broad headings:

■ the markets
■ the companies
■ the cruising areas
■ the ships
■ the *World City* project.

The market will continue to differentiate and it is possible that the UK package operators, Airtours, Thomson, First Choice etc. will continue to expand their cruise operations. They will need to update their vessels, as some of them are quite elderly. Given the amount of cruise-ship building since the 1980s, there is likely to be tonnage made redundant by the more established operators.

The views of our sample were that those undertaking their first cruise on one of the newer operators may well upgrade to a Premium product for later cruises. Our sample was of the opinion that 'cruising gets in the blood' and this is verified by the high repeat business percentages generated by the industry. At present the newer operators offer a product that links closely with their established land-based package operations and whilst this is a good entry-level product it may well be that customers require a more traditional and up-market product as part of their 'cruising career'. If this is the case, it augers well for the more traditional operators in so far as the package holiday type cruise appears to have generated a new demand rather than just split an existing market, and that new demand may provide additional customers for the traditional operators at a later stage.

As the market that grew first, the US market appears to be showing signs of saturation (see Chapter 3) and whilst it will continue to grow, the growth will be slower than in the 1970s and 1980s. In 1996 the percentage of US citizens taking a cruise was 1.8 per cent and we would predict that this will reach 2.2 per cent by 2005.

The UK market grew consistently in the 1990s and such growth looks set to continue, especially with the links between cruising and traditional package holidays as the providers of the latter enter and expand their cruise operations. Taking a cruise was for many years 'a once in a lifetime' experience for many holiday-makers in the US and UK. By 1999 it had become less exceptional as the prices of the lowest priced cruises became nearer to the norm for package holidays. By 1996, 1.1 per cent of the UK population were cruising and, considering the huge growth in foreign holidays undertaken from the UK, the room for market growth is apparent.

The market for the rest of Europe will grow. Whilst there has been a distinct UK, and to lesser extents German and Italian markets, companies such as MSC and Festival Cruises have been targeting the European customer (see case study at the end of this chapter). It will be interesting to see whether UK cruisers see themselves as part of this market causing a merger of the markets or whether the UK market will remain distinct. The German market was the beneficiary of a number of new builds in the 1990s, a trend that seems likely to continue (see Table 9.1).

Table 9.1 New building for the German market, 1996–9

Ship	GRT	Date	Company
Aida	38 600	1996	Arkona Touristik
Columbus	14 903	1997	Hapag–Lloyd
Deutschland	22 400	1998	Peter Deilmann Reederei
Europa (replacement for 1982 vessel)	28 600	1999	Hapag–Lloyd

The period 1999–2001 will see the introduction of new purpose-built tonnage for the European and the UK markets (*Mistral* – see case study at the end of this chapter – and *Aurora* – see case study at the end of Chapter 6), indicating that the companies see the markets as distinct, although marketing of *Mistral* commenced in the UK at the end of 1998.

The Asian economies were badly hit by recession in the later 1990s, the newly formed Indonesian company, Awani Cruises, never actually starting its operation. The capacity for regeneration in the region is such, however, that the market was already showing signs of recovery in 1999 and looks set to grow both for the indigenous market and a growing UK/European market for Star and Sun Vista Cruises. Star Cruises plan to have six vessels in operation by the end of 1999.

The market for families and younger adults shows great potential for growth. All of the newcomers to the UK market in the latter half of the 1990s stressed the facilities for families, especially when combined with a hotel stay. The Disney product is especially designed for families, although great pains have been taken to provide child-free zones. It can be predicted that the Standard and Premium markets may well develop to comprise two distinct sectors each – family and older couples/singles – catering for quite different motivations.

Young adults also provide considerable growth potential as realized by the Carnival Cruises product (see Chapter 4) and as cruising loses its 'fuddy-duddy' image it can be expected that this sector of the market will grow considerably.

Discounting seems set to continue. Our sample was of the general opinion that certain aspects of cruise operations were being affected by cuts from the operators. Certain companies had ceased providing free regional flights and London hotel stays for UK cruisers on fly cruises, and a particular 'bone' of contention was the quantity if not the quality of food provided.

The companies

One could be tempted to begin this section with 'how large will Carnival become?' The trend in the 1990s was that small companies did not succeed – Delphin, American Family Cruises etc. – whilst the larger ones grew by new building, acquisitions and mergers. There were exceptions. In the UK, Fred Olsen maintained a small single-ship operation for many years (although the company had other interests) until *Black Prince* was joined by the *Black Watch* (28 492 GRT, ex *Star Odyssey*, ex *Westward*, ex *Royal Viking Star*) in 1996. Festival commenced as a single- and rapidly two-ship operation in 1995, and the debut of the *Mistral* (see case study at the end of this chapter) underlines the company's faith in itself.

The Big Four – Carnival, RCI, P&O/Princess and NCL – had 64 per cent of the market by 1999 with Star Cruises, Royal Olympic (an amalgamation of Sun Cruises and Epirotiki Lines), Festival and Louis Cruise Lines (in their own right and as operators for Thomson) beginning to grow considerably. With the new ships they have on order, the Big Four look set to continue to dominate the market. All four have developed distinct segments of the market with Carnival having operations in the Standard, Premium, Luxury and Niche markets giving them coverage of a wide customer base which allows cruisers to upgrade whilst still remaining (perhaps without knowing it) with the same corporate group. Smaller operators will remain vulnerable to takeovers by the larger operators.

It is to be expected that the new entrants to the UK market will continue to develop their products. Indeed, it was announced in early 1999 that Airtours had acquired the *Song of America* (37 584 GRT) from RCI, a purchase that would increase their capacity considerably.

Newer companies will continue to be vulnerable to takeovers and mergers unless they are part of a larger grouping. The strength of Airtours and Thomson is in their diverse holiday and flight operations – they have been major players in these sectors and are only vulnerable to a very large predator although the acquisition of nearly 30 per cent of Airtours by Carnival is worthy of note.

Given the investment required it is difficult to see a major new player entering on to the scene. Disney's cruise operation is just a small part of their worldwide operations and is complementary to their other tourism and film interests. One name does spring to mind as a possible player – Virgin, under Richard Branson. The company already has rail and air operations and a move into the tourism industry might not be a surprise, although up to 1999 they had made no such move.

The cruising areas

Cruising now offers a wide variety of cruising areas as detailed in Chapter 5. Much of the development has been incremental from traditional cruising areas, a development that is expected to continue for a considerable proportion of the market.

Caribbean cruises have been extended to the Mexican and Colombian/ Venezuelan coast, and there are indications that the ports on the Gulf of Mexico are beginning to receive increased calls by cruise ships, capable as they are of acting as both base and visit ports. Increasing numbers of ships are likely to operate a cruise route from the St Lawrence down the Eastern Seaboard of the USA and the Maritime Provinces of Canada. In terms of history, culture and scenery these itineraries mirror those of the Baltic and Norway and, whilst research showed that many repeat cruisers alternate between the Mediterranean and the Caribbean, in future there could be a similar alternation between Northern Europe and the north-west of North America.

By 1999, South America was a feature of itineraries from a number of companies. Commencing in the early 1990s as an Amazon to the Caribbean package, voyages around the continent seem set to increase, although the weather around Cape Horn will make this a seasonal trade.

Incremental growth from the Eastern Mediterranean is dependent on the political situation in the area, but it is likely that Lebanon and Jordan will see their cruise business increase. Syria joined the cruise destinations in 1999 with Festival itineraries featuring what had been, until recently, a closed country for Western tourism. Relatively few itineraries took in the Gulf region at the turn of the century, but the Gulf states have seen a massive increase in land-based tourism and the cruise industry cannot be far behind, although the seas of the region will need to free of the threat of war.

The states comprising the former Yugoslavia have hosted cruise ships since the beginnings of the industry but political instability and outbreaks of hostility more or less killed the trade in the 1990s. By 1998, however, Dubrovnik was again featured in brochures and, given the ease of reaching the area from the base ports of Venice and Piraeus, it is likely that more Croatian and Yugoslavian ports will be visited.

Apart from the Atlantic visit ports in Morocco and the resorts of Tunisia, the North African coastline has seen little cruise activity, with the exception of Port Said and Alexandria in Egypt. Algeria and Libya remained closed to Western tourism (Algiers did feature as a visit port for the *Reina del Mar* in the late 1960s) but, again, political developments may open these areas up and lead to the Southern Mediterranean/North Africa becoming a growth area.

The Atlantic Islands are nearly all part of an established cruising area but their development as base ports could lead to fourteen-day cruises that take in the Azores to the north-west and West Africa to the south. In 1999–2000 Princess Cruises offered a small number of round-Africa itineraries and Dakar should certainly be able to be visited on a fourteen-day cruise out of the Canaries. East Africa, with its associated safaris, has long been a favourite European long-haul tourist destination and it might be expected that there will be a growth in Indian Ocean cruises in this area, currently featured on only a few mainstream itineraries plus the small Royal Star operation (see Chapter 5)

As the Asian market recovers from the downturn of 1998, it is possible to see a scenario whereby India becomes a cruising region in its own right. The logic of this is derived from possible incremental moves southwards from the Eastern Mediterranean and westward from the Singapore area. Long a provider of crews for liners (especially P&O), the subcontinent has many coastal attractions and good berthing facilities, often developed as part of the expansion of British trade routes in the nineteenth century.

South East Asia including China, Japan and Australasia has been the latest area to develop as a cruise market. Whilst the journey times both from Europe and North America are long, the latest heavy jets have cut hours from the journey. Therefore, more mainstream companies are offering itineraries in the region in addition to those currently offered by the Japanese cruise industry and companies such as Star and Sun Cruises who offer cruises for a mixed Western/ South East Asian market. Thomson now include Star Cruises packages in their UK brochure and, given the growth of Thailand as a European resort area, there appear to be good prospects for the further development of South East Asian cruise and stay holidays marketed in Europe.

Northern Europe has also seen incremental developments. The Norwegian area has been expanding to include the North Cape, Greenland and Iceland, whilst the growth in round-Britain cruises has been exceptional. In 1998, thirty-one cruise ships called at Invergordon on the Dornoch Firth in the Highlands of Scotland with no fewer than thirty-nine visiting Lerwick in the Shetland Islands (local figures). Whilst the UK and Scotland in particular cannot match the Mediterranean and Caribbean for weather, the history, culture and family links with North America appear to be attracting an increasing market share.

Alaska is probably saturated as far as a major development of the cruise industry is concerned but the Antarctic remains the great unexplored region. As discussed in the previous chapter, only niche cruises visit the area and it is expected that any attempts to make the region into a mainstream destination will meet with strong international opposition on environmental grounds.

The ships

The future for the 17 000–35 000 GRT ships, except in the Luxury sector of the market, looks bleak unless new entrants to the industry acquire them. The traditional operators have been building larger and larger ships and it is likely that by 2010, if not earlier, the 200 000 GRT barrier will be broken. The introduction of the *Mistral* (see case study at the end of this chapter) is, to over half our sample, a welcome break in the trend, as they preferred a smaller ship. It must be stressed that the *Mistral* is not small *per se* at 48 000 GRT but is when compared with the *Carnival Destiny* at 101 000 GRT and the *Grand Princess* at 109 000 GRT.

The Luxury sector of the market seems set to grow as shown by the ordering of two new vessels by Silversea (see case study at the end of Chapter 4). Many Premium products are approaching the facilities of the Luxury sector with the exception of PSR and intimacy. Discussions with our sample showed that those who are used to cruising are becoming more sophisticated in their wants and are demanding facilities which exceed many of those in package holiday hotels.

The building of larger ships will impact on cruising areas (see earlier). Just as the US Navy has always maintained separate Pacific and Atlantic fleets (transfers being effected via the Panama Canal), so those cruise companies using ships too big for the Panama Canal will need to split their operations into distinct East (Caribbean/Mediterranean/Northern Europe) and West (Alaska/Far East) operations, with any transfer of tonnage using Cape Horn.

Larger ships will increase the strain on the infrastructure of many smaller visit ports and thus the niche market for soft expeditions into such ports is likely to grow. The trend has been for the larger ships to operate on a 'bus route'-type scheduled service, especially in the Caribbean, and this trend is expected to continue.

On-board facilities will continue to be developed to cater for a wider range of cruisers. Family facilities are the norm on most new building, especially in the Standard category, and Premium and Luxury category ships are increasingly being provided with business communication facilities. Those ships operating in the Japanese market can also be used as conference centres and it is likely that this market will become more developed, linked to the short-cruise market.

World City

Knut Kloster, of NCL fame, heads a project, originally known as Phoenix and later as World City, to build a floating city that would be the largest cruise ship, indeed the largest ship, ever contemplated. The vessel is planned to be of a minimum of 250 000 GRT, capable of carrying over 5200 cruisers and would include its own 400-capacity day cruisers that would dock inside it. The plan is for the vessel to split its time equally between the Mediterranean and the Caribbean (Miller, 1992). Whether the cruise industry is ready for such a huge vessel is not yet certain and the investment required to build it would be huge. Such a doubling of size in one swoop is not unprecedented. When Brunel launched the *Great Eastern* (18 915 GRT) in 1859, she dwarfed any other ship ever built; even by 1874 the latest Cunard vessel, *Bothnia* was only 4555 GRT. By 1884 the Cunarder *Umbria* registered 7718 GRT, and it was not until 1889 that a ship comparable in size to the *Great Eastern* was launched – the White Star liner *Oceanic* at 17 274 GRT (Davie, 1987). *Great Eastern* was criticized because of her size (Eddy, Potter and Page, 1976) and the critics proved to be right. Underpowered for her great bulk despite having a propeller, paddle wheels and sails, she was a failure as a passenger ship. However, she laid the first transatlantic telegraph cable before being used as a floating exhibition centre – for which redundant passenger ships are still used – before being scrapped in 1889.

If the *World City* is launched, there should be no problems with power as modern technology can cope with the increase in size; the problem will be in the ship generating enough customers to fulfil its economic potential.

Another plan generated in the later 1990s by Swiss interests was to build a replica of the *Titanic* and operate it as a cruise ship, banking perhaps on the success of the film *Titanic*. The idea of re-creating the ambience of an Edwardian liner may have some market advantage although such a project would need to re-create only the palatial first class accommodation and not the steerage berths used for immigrants.

The role of aircraft in the demise of the liner trade and the eventual development of the cruise industry has been discussed earlier in this book. There have been experiments with air cruises based on chartered aircraft and hotels. However, these lose many of the attractions of cruising with continual transfers between airport and hotels and the inability to relax properly, even on an aircraft configured for many less passengers than would be found on a scheduled service. In February 1999, the *Sunday Times* reported on a military development by Lockheed of an 800 ft long 'airship' able to carry 500 tons (the payload of fourteen Boeing 747s) together with the suggestion that there might be a tourist role for such craft akin to that of luxury trains such as the Orient Express (*Sunday Times*, News Section, 28 February 1999: 9). Such an 'airship' cruise may be someway in the future but it could provide a novel way of seeing the grandeur of the Antarctic and other wilderness areas without the environmental problems that ships could cause.

Cruising, which began, as very much an upper-class holiday is now a part of the mainstream tourism industry employing large numbers of people and requiring vast sums in investment. The steady growth from the late 1970s onwards seems set to continue and, even when (or if) the market becomes saturated, the cruise sector will remain an important part of the tourism industry.

This book has examined the cruise sector and has endeavoured to paint a picture that those working in or studying in the industry will find useful and informative. It seems fitting to conclude the text with a case study that looks not only at the introduction of a new vessel but which also depicts a company altering its market position. The fact that the product is designed to be a generic European one to be introduced in the year following the introduction of the first tranche of currency union within the European Union adds an extra political and social dimension.

Case study

Mistral, Festival Cruises

The launch and naming of a new ship is always an exciting and emotional affair for those involved. The naming of **Oriana** (Chapter 6) involved Her Majesty the Queen, the band of the Scots Guards, the choir of Westminster Abbey and the Bishop of Winchester – pomp and circumstance at its best. However, in the days when mega-ships of 100 000 GRT are taking to the seas, the launch of a medium-sized liner might not seem a fitting finale to a text on cruising.

Mistral (48 000 GRT), however, may well be an important milestone in the history of the cruise industry as she is the first ship to be built to cater for a generic European market. As has been shown throughout this book, the North American and UK markets have been well served in recent years by a growing number of cruise vessels designed to cater for their specific needs; other European nationalities have been less well served. As well as the UK market there have been German and Italian sectors in addition to small French operations but, other than the predominantly Italian MSC cruises, European union has not been evidenced within the cruise industry.

Festival Cruises was founded by George Poulides in 1993 (Ward, 1998) whose operations had previously owned **The** (sic) **Azur** (14 717 GRT, ex **Eagle**) which had latterly been under charter to Chandris. The vessel, built in 1970, had been converted from a P&O cross-channel car ferry to a cruise ship in 1981 (Kludas, 1992) and had gained a good reputation, especially amongst UK cruisers, for inexpensive cruises. The ship is the largest that can pass through Greece's Corinth Canal and this was a marketing USP for her owners. **The Azur** was joined by **Bolero** (16 107 GRT, ex **Starward**), originally one of the earlier NCL Miami-based cruise liners. Known in Europe as Festival Cruises, the operation was marketed in North America as Azur–Bolero Cruises (now being known as First European Cruises) and gained good reports from Ward (1997; 1998; 1999) for a modestly priced product delivered well but without the facilities normally to be found on the current generation of vessels, especially those for the US market. A third ship was acquired in 1997 with the purchase of the **Flamenco** (17 042 GRT, ex **Southern Cross**, ex **Starship Majestic**, ex **Sun Princess**, ex **Spirit of London**), originally ordered by Kloster but purchased whilst building by P&O in 1972.

The evolution in design referred to in Chapter 6 is shown by the side elevations of the **Flamenco** and the **Mistral** in Figure 9.1.

Famenco

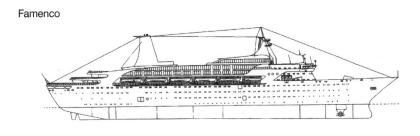

Mistral

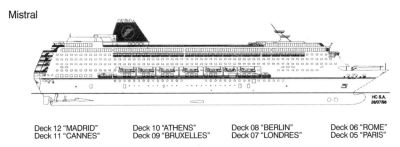

| Deck 12 "MADRID" | Deck 10 "ATHENS" | Deck 08 "BERLIN" | Deck 06 "ROME" |
| Deck 11 "CANNES" | Deck 09 "BRUXELLES" | Deck 07 "LONDRES" | Deck 05 "PARIS" |

Figure 9.1 Side elevations of **Flamenco** and **Mistral**.
Courtesy Festway Cruises. Reprinted with permission.

At this point Festival appeared to be a small operation using vessels primarily displaced from the US market and operating in the lower to middle range of the Standard product segment (Chapter 4).

A prediction as to the future development of Festival might have suggested that they would either continue to acquire older ships or that they could be vulnerable to a takeover by a larger operator, perhaps one of the new UK entrants to the cruise industry. It would have been hard to predict that they would charter the **Bolero** to the UK package holiday company of First Choice from the spring of 1999, and that they would also introduce a brand new 47 900 GRT vessel and move themselves into the top end of the Standard market and perhaps knock on the door of the Premium categories.

Mistral had been laid down, unnamed, for another cruise company. The builders were to be Chantiers de l'Atlantique in France, the same yard that built the **Norway** ex **France** – still the world's longest passenger ship. The incomplete vessel was acquired by a group of French investors and placed on long-term lease/charter to Festival in 1997 (Ward, 1999) at a very early stage in construction and named **Mistral** with a debut date of July 1999.

As soon as Festival acquired the hull, still in its early stages of building, the design philosophy was to build a ship that would appeal to a generic European market, providing a high-quality cruise experience at afford-able prices and with a European ambience.

Whilst Festival as a company is a newcomer to the market, its principals have been in the ship-owning market for over fifty years and thus they have a body of knowledge upon which to base their design philosophy.

January 1999 saw a major political change in Europe. In addition to enlargement of the EU throughout the late 1990s, 1999 saw the first group of countries including France, Germany and Italy (but excluding the UK) embark upon monetary union with the introduction of the 'Euro'. The idea of a common European identity was gaining ground, although more slowly than many of those committed to a united Europe might have wished but, apart from the MSC operation mentioned earlier, the European cruise market was still delineated into nationality-based sectors.

Fodor's (1999) guide comments that many of the ships operating in the European cruise market were older vessels displaced from the North American market. The only really new vessels that had been built exclusively for European-based cruisers were the German vessels listed in Table 9.1 and **Oriana** plus **Aurora** (see Chapter 6) for the UK market.

Mistral is one of the first ships built for the European Standard or Premium markets to include balcony cabins (others being **Oriana**, **Aida** and the later Costa vessels), now a feature of nearly all new builds in the North American market. **Mistral's** accommodation is listed in Table 9.2.

Table 9.2 *Mistral*'s **accommodation**

Accommodation	Number
4-berth inside cabins	18
2-berth inside cabins	218
2-berth outside cabins	282
Mini-suites and balcony	80
Total	598

Based on full occupancy of the four-berth cabins and two sharing the other accommodation, this gives Mistral a normal cruising complement of 1232 on a 47 900 GRT hull, although it must be stressed that according to Festival's brochure, all of the two-berth cabins can accommodate a third or fourth cruiser. This brings the maximum possible occupancy up to 2275, but it is highly unlikely that every cabin would be occupied by a family to its fullest extent and Festival have informed us that the maximum number of berths to be sold will not exceed 1580. We quote the figures, however, in order to be consistent with other occupancy figures used in this book. These figures put the Mistral in line with Carnival and RCL vessels in terms of PSR but with, according to Festival, cabins that are above average size for Standard products.

Passenger accommodation has been kept away from the main nightlife areas of the ship as a matter of policy. As another deliberate policy, no suites are available; the space they would have occupied being used to increase the number of mini-suites with balconies available as these have a greater appeal to European passengers.

Décor, especially artwork is of a general European ambience and the library includes volumes in the main European languages. Language is a problem on multi-nationality ships; Ward (1999) comments on the number of announcements needed in order to relay information to all cruisers. To mitigate against too many announcements in differing languages, Festival developed an interactive, fibre-optic, in-cabin television system to relay much routine information.

As discussed in Chapter 6, the lowest two passenger decks contain the public rooms with all accommodation being above them, the balcony cabins being situated on the highest accommodation deck. In this respect, Mistral follows the pattern set by Royal Princess.

The naming of decks and public spaces reflects the generic European concept of the ship. The decks are named; Paris, Rome, London, Berlin, Brussels, Athens, Cannes and Madrid respectively, whilst there is a Mayfair Lounge, San Marco Room, L'Etoile Restaurant, Richelieu Library and Caff'e Grecco etc – truly European!

All outside cabins have picture windows – there are no portholes in passenger cabins – and with mini-suites closely resembling the superb examples on **Oriana**, both in size and layout, the accommodation should join that on **Oriana** and **Aurora** in setting a benchmark for the European market.

In 1999 the currency on board Festival ships was the Italian lire and it will be interesting to see if, eventually, the **Mistral** adopts the Euro as the usual means of pricing on board. Given that the ship is registered in France – indeed she is one of the few, if not the only, cruise ship registered in France – use of the Euro might be a useful way of avoiding any 'national preferences' and problems that might occur with operating in a different currency to the other vessels in the fleet.

Mistral will also be one of the first (**Edinburgh Castle** introduced the trend in Europe) vessels for any purely European market to offer alternative dining, with the Rialto Grill being available as a matter of course to mini-suite customers and at a supplement to all others. In this the ship follows the precedent of the **QE2** where different restaurants are used for different cabin grades.

Mistral operates a series of seven- to twelve-day Mediterranean itineraries based on Venice, Genoa in the summer and autumn (including Lebanon and Syria). She then crosses to the Caribbean for the winter offering seven-day figure of eight cruises based on Martinique or Guadeloupe (French islands – French ship) bringing two new base ports into the area.

Fitting neatly into the price bracket between the Standard products of Thomson and Airtours and the Premium P&O product, in addition to offering a 'national' ship for the French market, **Mistral** seems to be well placed within the market.

The decision to move to the upper end of the Standard product is deliberate policy by Festival. The research for this book suggests that there will be market share to be captured from those cruisers trading up from other Standard products plus new cruisers who wish for a product that is linked less directly to the package holiday sector.

The importance of ships like **Mistral** (and **Oriana**, **Europa**, **Aida** and the latest Costa vessels) is that they bring cruising for the European market more into line with the facilities offered by companies operating in the North American market. Our UK sample were of the general opinion that having cruised on a North American market upper-Standard/Premium vessel, the offerings in terms of facilities of many of the European market companies in the Standard range was considerably inferior.

Although still a relatively young company, Festival intend to enter the twenty-first century with five ships (including **Bolero** on charter to First Choice) and were certified to ISO 9002 (Quality Assurance) in 1994 and the International Safety Management Code (ISM) in 1994/5 – the first cruise line to be certified for both areas.

The **Mistral** offers cruising for the smaller European markets including The Netherlands (although many Netherlanders still use HAL despite the company being owned by Carnival), Belgium, Spain, Portugal etc. in addition to the UK, French, German and Italian markets. This gives the company the whole of the EU as a marketplace – the trick will be to convince each national group that they are not a minority. In that respect the success of **Mistral** may well be closely linked to the progress of closer European unity.

In seeking to capture a percentage of the UK market, Festival must consider the cruising patterns of the British. Our research showed that whilst those new to cruising appeared satisfied with seven-day cruises or seven-plus-seven days cruise and stay packages, more experienced cruisers preferred longer cruises, especially in the Caribbean. A number of the established companies in the area run back-to-back packages, normally but not always using the same vessel, which are very popular with UK cruisers. **Mistral** does offer some longer cruises but the majority of itineraries are for seven days. The 1999 itineraries for **Mistral** following her introduction in July comprised:

    16 seven-day Greek Islands from Venice with a possible seven-day
        break on Rhodes
    2 ten- and 1 eleven-day Eastern Mediterranean from Genoa
    1 fifteen-day transatlantic, Genoa–Guadeloupe
    1 seven-day Caribbean Islands (Christmas)
    1 ten-day Caribbean Islands (millennium cruise).

Whilst competitors may not always welcome a new player into the marketplace, the advent of a new upper-range Standard product for the European market can only drive up standards overall. Given the pan-European nature of the **Mistral** operation it is likely that the ship will serve to introduce new people (and nationalities) to cruising, thus growing the overall European market.

Appendix 1
The chronology of cruising
1819–1998

1819   First steam assisted crossing of the North Atlantic by the Savannah

1839   Cunard commence North Atlantic operations

1837   P&O commence mail and passenger operations

1881   Oceanic Yachting Company commence cruises on the ex P&O Ceylon

1906   *Mauretania* launched

1912   *Titanic* disaster

1914–18 First World War

1920   US Prohibition introduced leading to 'booze cruises'

1934   German, 'Strength through Joy' cruises begin operations

1939–45 Second World War

1958   *Andes* converted cruising only vessel

1961   *Canberra* delivered

1964   *Reina del Mar* enters cruising market first for Travel Savings Association and then Union Castle

1965   Princess Cruises formed. P&O and Orient Steam Navigation merge

1966   Kloster and Arison form partnership

1968   *QE2* delivered to Cunard

1969   RCCL (now RCI) formed

1970   Royal Viking Line formed

1971   Cunard sold to Trafalgar House

1972   Arison breaks with Kloster's and forms Carnival Cruises. *Mardi Gras* goes aground on first cruise

1974   P&O purchase Princess Cruises. *Reina del Mar* withdrawn

1979   Kloster's Norwegian Caribbean (now NCL) buy the *France* and rename her *Norway*

1982   Falklands conflict

1983   Unsuccessful bid by Trafalgar house for P&O. Trafalgar House buy Norwegian America Lines

1988   Sitmar purchased by Princess (P&O). Carnival acquire Holland America

1990   Chandris re-brands its US operation as Celebrity Cruises. Japan Cruise Lines formed

1994   Trafalgar House acquire Royal Viking Line. Festival Cruises formed

1995   P&O introduce *Oriana* into service. Airtours commence cruise operations. Star Cruises commence Asian operation

1996   Carnival purchase 29.6% share of Airtours. Trafalgar House purchased by Kvaerner

1997   Carnival acquire Costa Cruises. Thomson commences cruise operations. *Canberra* scrapped. *Star Princess* transferred from Princess fleet to P&O Cruises as *Arcadia*

1998   RCI acquire Celebrity. Carnival acquire Cunard. Direct Cruises commence operations and then acquired by Airtours. P&O announce order for *Aurora*. Festival announce *Mistral* for 1999 operations

Appendix 2
The Big Four cruise fleets, 1998–9, and Star Cruises (Asia)

Star Cruises is one of the fastest growing cruise lines in the late 1990s. Dates given are when the ship was first launched/joined the current company. Vessels due to be sold in 1999 are included with the original company.

Ship	GRT	Date	Ship	GRT	Date
CARNIVAL GROUP					
CARNIVAL			COSTA		
Carnival Destiny	101 353	1996	*Costa Allegra*	28 430	1992
Carnival Triumph	101 353	1999	*Costa Classica*	52 950	1992
Celebration	47 262	1987	*Costa Marina*	25 441	1990
Ecstasy	70 367	1991	*Costa Riviera*	31 500	1963/83
Elation	70 367	1998	*Costa Romantica*	53 049	1993
Fantasy	70 367	1990	*Costa Victoria*	75 200	1996
Fascination	70 367	1994			
Holiday	40 052	1985	HOLLAND AMERICA		
Imagination	70 367	1995	*Maasdam*	55 451	1993
Inspiration	70 367	1996	*Nieuw Amsterdam*	33 930	1983
Jubilee	47 262	1986	*Noordam*	33 390	1984
Paradise	70 367	1998	*Rotterdam*	59 652	1997
Sensation	70 367	1993	*Ryndam*	55 451	1994
Tropicale	36 674	1982	*Statendam*	55 451	1993
			Veendam	55 451	1996
			Volendam	63 000	1999
			Westerdam	53 872	1986

Ship	GRT	Date	Ship	GRT	Date

CARNIVAL GROUP (*Continued*)

CUNARD			SEABOURN		
Queen Elizabeth 2	70 327	1969	Seabourn Legend	9 975	1992
Royal Viking Sun	37 845	1988	Seabourn Pride	9 975	1988
Sea Goddess 1	4 260	1984	Seabourn Spirit	9 975	1989
Sea Goddess 2	4 260	1984			
Vistafjord	24 492	1973/84	Airtours (and Direct Cruises) (29.6%)		
			Carousel	23 000	1971/95
WINDSTAR			Seawing	16 607	1971/95
Windsong	5 703	1987	Sundream	22 945	1970/97
Windspirit	5 736	1988	Ex Song of America	37 584	1982/99
Windstar	5 703	1986	Apollo	28 574	1962/88
Windsurf	14 745	1990/98	Edinburgh Castle	32 573	1966/97

ROYAL CARIBBEAN INTERNATIONAL

RCI			CELEBRITY		
Enchantment of the Seas	74 137	1997	Century	70 606	1995
Grandeur of the Seas	74 137	1996	Galaxy	76 522	1996
Legend of the Seas	70 950	1995	Horizon	46 811	1990
Majesty of the Seas	73 941	1992	Mercury	76 522	1997
Monarch of the Seas	73 941	1991	Zenith	47 255	1992
Rhapsody of the Seas	78 491	1997			
Song of America	37 584	1982			
Sovereign of the Seas	73 192	1988			
Splendour of the Seas	69 130	1996			
Viking Serenade	40 132	1982/92			
Vision of the Seas	78 491	1998			
Voyager of the Seas	142 000	1999			

Peninsular & Oriental

Princess			P&O Cruises		
Crown Princess	69 845	1990	Arcadia	63 564	1989/97
Dawn Princess	77 000	1997	Oriana	69 153	1995
Grand Princess	109 000	1998	Victoria	27 670	1966/79
Island Princess	19 907	1972/74			
Ocean Princess	77 000	1999	P&O Holidays		
Pacific Princess	20 636	1971/75	Fair Princess	24 724	1956/97
Regal Princess	69 845	1991			
Royal Princess	44 348	1984	Swan Hellenic		
Sea Princess	77 000	1998	Minerva	12 500	1996
Sky Princess	43 692	1994			
Sun Princess	77 000	1995			

Ship	GRT	Date	Ship	GRT	Date
Norwegian Cruise Lines					
NCL			Orient Lines		
Leeward	25 000	1980/95	*Marco Polo*	20 502	1966/93
Norway	76 049	1962/80			
Norwegian Capricorn	28 000	1973/98			
Norwegian Crown	34 250	1988/96			
Norwegian Dream	41 000	1992			
Norwegian Dynasty	19 069	1993/97			
Norwegian Majesty	32 396	1992/97			
Norwegian Sea	42 276	1988			
Norwegian Sky	76 000	1999			
Norwegian Wind	41 000	1993			
Star Cruises					
Star Aquarius	40 022	1989/93			
Star Pisces	40 022	1989/93			
Superstar Capricorn	28 000	1973/97			
Superstar Gemini	19 076	1992/95			
Superstar Leo	74 500	1998			
Superstar Sagittarius	18 556	1972/98			
Superstar Virgo	74 500	1999			

Appendix 3

The decimation of the liner trade in the 1955–80

The chart only covers vessels built pre-Second World War and in regular liner service in 1955, or those built for the liner trade post-Second World War up to 1966. Only the original and final names are given; many vessels were renamed and changed owners several times. For a full history of these ships see Miller (1995). This list does not include ferries or vessels that were built directly for the cruise industry.

Original name	Company	Launched	GRT at launch	Route	Final name/ 1999 name	Fate
France						
Jean Mermoz	Cie de Navigation F & C	1956	12 460	France–Far East	Mermoz	Cruising 1970, in service 1999
Ancerville	Cie de Navigation Paquet	1962	14 224	France–W Africa	Ming Hua	Cruising 1981, sold as hotel ship 1986
Pasteur	Companie de Sud l'Atlantique	1939	29 253	France–S America	Filipnas Saudi 1	Sold 1957, cruising 1972, laid up 1974–7. Accommodation ship 1977–80, sank en route to breakers 1980
Antilles	French Line	1952	19 828	France–W. Indies	Antilles	Ran aground and burned 1971
Flandre	French Line	1952	20 469	France–New York	Pallas Athena	Sold for cruising 1968, burned and scrapped 1995
France	French Line	1961	66 348	France–New York	Norway	Laid up 1974–9, sold for cruising 1979, still in service 1999
Ile de France	French Line	1927	43 153	France–New York	Ile de France	Scrapped 1958
Bretagne	Transports Maritimes	1951	16 335	France–S America	Brittany	Sold for cruising 1961, burned and sank 1963
Provence	Transports Maritimes	1951	15 889	France–S America	Symphony	Sold for cruising 1965
Felix Roussel	Messageries Maritimes	1930	16 753	France–Far East	Arosa Sun	Sold 1955, accommodation ship 1960, scrapped 1974

Ship	Company	Built	Tonnage	Route	Later name	Fate
Ferdinand de Lessops	Messageries Maritimes	1951	10 881	France–Mauritius	*La Palma*	Sold for cruising 1970, laid up 1997
La Marseillaise	Messageries Maritimes	1949	17 321	France–Far East	*Bianca C*	Sold 1957, cruising 1958, burned and sank 1961
Pasteur	Messageries Maritimes	1966	17 986	Germany–France–S America		Sold 1972. Sank after fire 1985
Germany						
Berlin	N. D. Lloyd	1925	15 286	Germany–New York	*Admiral Nakhimov*	Seized by USSR 1944, sank after collision 1986
Europa	N. D. Lloyd	1930	49 746	Germany–New York	*Liberte*	Handed over to France post-Second World War, scrapped 1962
Potsdam	N. D. Lloyd	1935	17 528	Germany–Far East	*Safina–E Hujjaj*	Seized by UK, 1945, troopship, sold 1960, scrapped 1976
Pretoria	German–East Africa Line	1936	16 662	Germany–S Africa	*Tanjung Pandan*	Seized 1945, troopship, pilgrim ship 1958, sold to Indonesia as training ship 1979, scrapped 1987
Patria	Hamburg–America	1938	16 595	Germany–S America	*Rossia*	Seized by UK 1945, handed to USSR, scrapped 1985
Romanza	Hamburg–America	1938	16 595	Germany–S America	*Romantica*	Acquired by Canada, cruising 1970, scrapped 1996
Greece						
Olympia	Greek Line (Liberian flag)	1953	22 979	S. Europe–New York	*Regal Empress*	In service 1999
Israel						
Shalom	Zim Lines	1964	25 320	Haifa–New York	*Regent Sun*	Sold 1967, cruising 1973, laid up 1995
Zim	Zim Lines	1955	9 831	Haifa–New York	*Dolphin IV*	Sold for cruising 1972, in service 1999
Italy						
Ausonia	Adriatica SpA	1956	11 879	Italy–Lebanon	*Ausonia*	Converted for cruising 1978, in service 1999
Eugenio Costa	Costa	1966	30 567	Italy–S America	*Edinburgh Castle*	Cruising 1967, still in service 1999
Federico C	Costa	1958	20 416	Italy–S America	*Sea Breeze*	Sold 1983, still in service 1999
Oceanic	Home Lines (Panamanian flag)	1965	39 241	New York–Nassau	*Oceanic*	Cruising 1966, still in service 1999
Andrea Doria	Italian Line	1953	29 083	Italy–New York	*Andrea Doria*	Sank after collision with *Stockholm* 1956
Augustus	Italian Line	1952	27 000	Italy–S America	*Asian Princess*	Laid up 1990
Cristoforo Colombo	Italian Line	1954	29 191	Italy–S America	*Cristoforo Colombo*	Hotel ship 1977, scrapped 1983
Giulio Cesare	Italian Line	1951	27 078	Italy–S America	*Giulio Cesare*	Scrapped 1973
Leonardo Da Vinci	Italian Line	1960	33 340	Italy–New York	*Leonardo Da Vinci*	Cruising, 1977, laid up 1978, burned and sank 1980
Michelangelo	Italian Line	1965	45 911	Italy–New York	Not available	Sold 1977 to Iranian Navy, scrapped 1992

Original name	Company	Launched	GRT at launch	Route	Final name/ 1999 name	Fate
Raffaello	Italian Line	1965	45 933	Italy–New York	Not available	Sold 1977 to Iranian Navy, sunk by missile attack 1983
Saturnia	Italian Line	1927	23 940	Italy–New York	*Saturnia*	Scrapped 1965
Vulcania	Italian Line	1927	23 970	Italy–New York	*Caribia*	Sold 1965 for cruising, scrapped 1974
Conte Biancamano	Lloyd Sabaudo	1925	24 416	Italy–New York	*Conte Biancamano*	Scrapped 1960
Conte Grande	Lloyd Sabaudo	1927	25 661	Italy–New York	*Conte Grande*	Scrapped 1961
Guglielmo Marconi	Lloyd Triestino	1963	27 905	Italy–Australia	*Costa Riviera*	Sold for cruising and rebuilt 1980, in service 1999
Galileo Galilei	Lloyd Triestino	1963	27 907	Italy–Australia	*Sun Vista*	Sold for cruising 1979. Sank after fire in 1999
The Netherlands						
Maasdam	Holland America	1952	15 024	Rotterdam–New York	*Stefan*	Sold 1968, laid up 1990
Nieuw Amsterdam	Holland America	1938	36 287	Rotterdam–New York	*Nieuw Amsterdam*	Cruising 1971, scrapped 1974
Rotterdam	Holland America	1959	38 645	Rotterdam–New York	*Rembrant*	Cruising 1969, sold 1996
Ryndam	Holland America	1951	15 015	Rotterdam–New York	*Copa Casino*	Sold 1962 for cruising, sold 1992 as floating casino
Statendam	Holland America	1957	24 294	Rotterdam–New York	*Regent Star*	Laid up 1996
Johan van Oldenbarnevelt	Nederland Line	1930	19 040	Amsterdam–E Indies	*Lakonia*	Sold for cruising 1962, sank after fire off Madeira 1963
Oranje	Nederland Line	1939	20 017	Amsterdam–E Indies	*Angelina Lauro*	Sold 1964, cruising 1972, burned and sank *en route* to breakers 1979
Willem Ruys	Royal Rotterdam Lloyd	1947	21 119	Rotterdam–East Indies	*Achille Lauro*	Sold 1964, mainly cruising, burned and sank 1994
Norway						
Bergenfjord	Norwegian–America	1956	18 739	Norway–New York	*Rasa Sayang*	Sold for cruising 1971, burned and sank 1980
Oslofjord	Norwegian–America	1949	16 844	Norway–New York	*Fulvia*	Cruising 1967, burned and sank 1970
Sagafjord	Norwegian–America	1965	24 002	Norway–New York	*Saga Rose*	Cruising 1966, sold 1983 and 1997
Portugal						
Infante Dom Henrique	Companhia Colonial	1961	23 306	Portugal–Africa	*Seawind Crown*	Laid up 1976–88, sold for cruising, in service 1999
Santa Maria	Companhia Colonial	1953	20 906	Portugal–S America	*Santa Maria*	Scrapped 1973
Vera Cruz	Companhia Colonial	1953	21 765	Portugal–S America	*Vera Cruz*	Scrapped 1973
Principe Perfeito	Companhia National	1961	19 393	Portugal–Africa	*Marianna 9*	Sold 1967, accommodation ship, laid up 1992

		1965	19860	Leningrad–Canada		
Soviet Union						
Alexandr Pushkin	Baltic Shipping Co.				*Marco Polo*	Cruising then sold and renamed Marco Polo, still in service 1999
Sweden						
Gripsholm	Swedish–America	1957	23 191	Sweden–New York	*Regent Sea*	Sold for cruising 1975, laid up 1995
Kungsholm	Swedish–America	1928	20 223	Sweden–New York	*Imperial Bahama Hotel*	Sold 1947, cruising 1960, floating hotel 1964, scrapped 1965
Kungsholm	Swedish–America	1953	21 141	Sweden–New York	*Columbus C*	Sold 1964, cruising 1981, sank 1984
Kungsholm	Swedish–America	1966	26 678	Sweden–New York	*Victoria*	Sold for cruising 1975, in service 1999
Stockholm	Swedish–America	1946	11 700	Sweden–New York	*Italia Prima*	Sank the Andrea Doria 1956, sold 1960, rebuilt 1990, in service 1999
UK/Canada						
Oxfordshire	Bibby	1957	20 586	Troopship	*Fairstar*	Sold for cruising 1963
Nevasa	British India	1956	20 527	UK–India (troopship)	*Nevasa*	Educational cruising 1964, scrapped 1975
Uganda	British India	1952	14 430	UK–India (troopship)	*Uganda*	Educational cruising 1968, scrapped 1986
Duchess of Bedford	Canadian Pacific	1928	20 123	UK–Canada	*Empress of France*	Scrapped 1960
Duchess of Richmond	Canadian Pacific	1928	20 022	UK–Canada	*Empress of Canada*	Burned and sank 1953
Empress of Britain	Canadian Pacific	1956	25 516	UK–Canada	*Topaz*	Sold 1964, cruising 1975, still in service 1999
Empress of Canada	Canadian Pacific	1961	27 284	UK–Canada		Sold for cruising 1974, still in service 1999
Empress of England	Canadian Pacific	1957	25 585	UK–Canada	*Ocean Monarch*	Sold for cruising 1970, scrapped 1975
Empress of Japan	Canadian Pacific	1930	26 032	Canada–Far East	*Hanseatic*	Rebuilt and sold for 1958, burned and sank 1966
Britannic	Cunard	1930	26 943	UK–New York	*Brittanic*	Scrapped 1961
Carinthia	Cunard	1956	21 947	UK–Canada	*Fair Princess*	Sold for cruising 1968, still in service 1999
Caronia	Cunard	1948	34 183	UK–New York	*Caribia*	Converted for cruising, sold 1967, scrapped 1974
Franconia	Cunard	1923	20 158	UK–New York	*Franconia*	Scrapped 1956
Georgic	Cunard	1932	27 759	UK New York	*Georgic*	Scrapped 1956
Ivernia	Cunard	1955	21 717	UK–Canada	*Feodor Shaplin*	Cruising 1962, sold 1973, laid up 1997
Mauretania	Cunard	1939	35 738	UK–New York	*Mauretania*	Scrapped 1965
Media	Cunard	1947	15 465	UK–New York	*Flavian*	Sold, 1961, burned and scrapped 1989
Queen Elizabeth	Cunard	1940	83 673	UK–New York	*Seawise University*	Sold 1970 to be floating university, burned and sank 1972
Queen Elizabeth 2	Cunard	1968	65 863	UK–New York	*Queen Elizabeth 2*	In service 1999
Queen Mary	Cunard	1936	81 235	UK–New York	*Queen Mary*	Sold as museum/hotel 1967

Original name	Company	Launched	GRT at launch	Route	Final name/ 1999 name	Fate
Samaria	Cunard	1921	19 602	UK–New York	Samaria	Scrapped 1956
Saxonia	Cunard	1954	21 637	UK–Canada	Leonid Sobinov	Cruising (renamed Carmania), 1962, sold 1973, laid up 1996
Scythia	Cunard	1921	19 730	UK–New York	Scythia	Scrapped 1958
Sylvania	Cunard	1957	21 989	UK–Canada	Albatros	Sold for cruising 1968, in service 1999
Tuscania	Cunard	1922	16 991	UK–New York	New York	Sold 1939, scrapped 1961
Aureol	Elder Dempster	1951	14 083	UK–W Africa	Marianna 6	Sold as accommodation ship 1974
Monarch of Bermuda	Furness–Bermuda	1931	22 424	New York–Bermuda	Arkadia	Caught fire 1947, rebuilt and sold 1958, scrapped 1966
Queen of Bermuda	Furness–Bermuda	1933	22 575	New York–Bermuda	Queen of Bermuda	Scrapped 1966
Rangitane	New Zealand Shipping Co	1949	21 867	UK–New Zealand	Oriental Esmerelda	Sold 1968, scrapped 1976
Rangitata	New Zealand Shipping Co	1929	16 737	UK–New Zealand	Rangitata	Scrapped 1962
Rangitiki	New Zealand Shipping Co	1928	16 755	UK–New Zealand	Rangitiki	Scrapped 1962
Rangitoto	New Zealand Shipping Co	1949	21 809	UK–New Zealand	Oriental Carnival	Sold 1969, scrapped 1976
Ruahine	New Zealand Shipping Co	1951	17 851	UK–New Zealand	Oriental Rio	Sold 1968, scrapped 1974
Orcades	Orient (Later P&O) Line	1948	28 164	UK–Australia	Orcades	Scrapped 1973
Oriana	Orient (Later P&O) Line	1960	41 923	UK–Australia	Oriana	Museum ship in Japan, 1986
Orion	Orient (Later P&O) Line	1935	23 371	UK–Australia	Orion	Scrapped 1963
Oronsay	Orient (Later P&O) Line	1951	27 632	UK–Australia	Oronsay	Scrapped 1976
Orontes	Orient (Later P&O) Line	1929	19 970	UK–Australia	Orontes	Scrapped 1962
Orsova	Orient (Later P&O) Line	1954	28 790	UK–Australia	Orsova	Cruising, 1969, scrapped 1974
Orranto	Orient (Later P&O) Line	1925	20 032	UK–Australia	Orranto	Scrapped 1957
Arcadia	P&O	1954	29 734	UK–Australia	Arcadia	Cruising 1975, scrapped 1979
Canberra	P&O	1961	45 733	UK–Australia	Canberra	Cruising 1973, scrapped 1998
Canton	P&O	1939	15 784	UK–Far East	Canton	Scrapped 1962
Chusan	P&O	1950	24 215	UK–Far East	Chusan	Cruising from 1960s, scrapped 1973
Himalaya	P&O	1949	27 955	UK–Australia	Himalaya	Scrapped 1974
Iberia	P&O	1954	29 614	UK–Australia	Iberia	Scrapped 1972
Maloja	P&O	1923	28 037	UK–Australia	Maloja	Scrapped 1954
Mongolia	P&O	1923	16 385	UK–India	Acapulco	Sold for cruising 1951, scrapped 1965
Mooltan	P&O	1923	20 847	UK–Australia	Mooltan	Scrapped 1954

Strathaird	P&O	22 544	1931	UK–Australia	*Strathaird*	Scrapped 1961
Stratheden	P&O	23 722	1937	UK–Australia	*Marianna Latsi*	Sold as hotel/pilgrim ship 1963, scrapped 1969
Strathmore	P&O	23 428	1935	UK–Australia	*Henrietta Latsi*	Sold as hotel/pilgrim ship 1963, scrapped 1969
Strathnaver	P&O	22 547	1931	UK–Australia	*Strathnaver*	Scrapped 1962
Reina del Mar	Pacific Steam Navigation	20 234	1956	UK–S America	*Reina del Mar*	Cruising 1964, scrapped 1975
Reina del Pacifico	Pacific Steam Navigation	17 707	1931	UK–S America	*Reina del Pacifico*	Scrapped 1958
Alcantara	Royal Mail Lines	22 181	1927	UK–S America	*Alcantara*	Scrapped 1958
Andes	Royal Mail Lines	25 689	1939	UK–S America	*Andes*	Cruising from 1959, scrapped 1971
Asturias	Royal Mail Lines	22 071	1926	UK–S America	*Asturias*	Immigrant and troopship 1945–57, scrapped 1957
Dominion Monarch	Shaw Savill	27 155	1939	UK–New Zealand	*Dominion Monarch*	Scrapped 1962
Northern Star	Shaw Savill	24 731	1962	UK–Australia	*Northern Star*	Scrapped 1974
Southern Cross	Shaw Savill	20 204	1955	UK–Australia	*Ocean Breeze*	Sold for cruising 1973, in service 1999
Arundel Castle	Union Castle	18 980	1915	UK–S Africa	*Arundel Castle*	Scrapped 1959
Athlone Castle	Union Castle	25 564	1936	UK–S Africa	*Athlone Castle*	Scrapped 1965
Bloemfontein Castle	Union Castle	18 400	1950	UK–S Africa	*Mediterranean Star*	Sold 1959 converted to ferry 1978, scrapped 1987
Braemar Castle	Union Castle	17 029	1952	UK–S Africa	*Braemar Castle*	Scrapped 1966
Capetown Castle	Union Castle	27 002	1938	UK–S Africa	*Capetown Castle*	Scrapped 1967
Carnarvon Castle	Union Castle	20 063	1926	UK–S Africa	*Carnarvon Castle*	Scrapped 1962
Dunnottar Castle	Union Castle	15 007	1936	UK–S Africa	*Princesa Victoria*	Sold 1958, rebuilt, in service 1999
Durban Castle	Union Castle	17 388	1938	UK–S Africa	*Durban Castle*	Scrapped 1962
Edinburgh Castle	Union Castle	28 705	1948	UK–S Africa	*Edinburgh Castle*	Scrapped 1976
Kenya Castle	Union Castle	17 041	1952	UK–S Africa	*Amerikanis*	Sold for cruising 1967, scrapped 1995
Pretoria Castle	Union Castle	17 392	1939	UK–S Africa	*Warwick Castle*	Scrapped 1962
Pretoria Castle	Union Castle	28 705	1948	UK–S Africa	*Oranje*	Scrapped 1975
Pendennis Castle	Union Castle	28 582	1958	UK–S Africa	*Sinbad 1*	Sold 1976, scrapped 1980
Rhodesia Castle	Union Castle	17 041	1951	UK–S Africa	*Rhodesia Castle*	Scrapped 1967
Stirling Castle	Union Castle	25 550	1935	UK–S Africa	*Stirling Castle*	Scrapped 1966
Transvaal Castle	Union Castle	32 697	1962	UK–S Africa		
Winchester Castle	Union Castle	20 109	1930	UK–S Africa	*Winchester Castle*	Scrapped 1960
Windsor Castle	Union Castle	37 640	1960	UK–S Africa	*Margarita L*	Hotel ship 1977

USA

Atlantic	American Banner Lines	14 138	1953	US–Europe	*Universe*	Converted from cargo vessel, cruising 1967, laid up 1995
Constitution	American Export Lines	30 293	1951	US–Southern Europe	*Constitution*	Laid up 1998

Original name	Company	Launched	GRT at launch	Route	Final name/ 1999 name	Fate
Independence	American Export Lines	1951	30 293	US–Southern Europe	Independence	Converted for cruising, in service 1999
La Guardia	American Export Lines	1944	17 811	US–Southern Europe	Emerald Seas	Scrapped 1993
President Cleveland	American President Lines	1947	15 359	US–Far East	President Cleveland	Scrapped 1974
President Wilson	American President Lines	1948	15 359	US–Far East	Oriental Empress	Cruising 1973, scrapped 1974
Santa Paula	Grace Line	1958	15 366	New York–Caribbean	Ramada al Salaam Hotel	Sold 1972, hotel ship in Kuwait 1976, bombed 1991
Santa Rosa	Grace Line	1958	15 371	New York–Caribbean	Emerald	Laid up 1971–89, converted for cruising, in service 1999
Lurline	Matson Line	1932	18 021	California–Hawaii	Ellenis	Sold to Chandris 1963, laid up 1980–7, scrapped 1987
Malolo	Matson Line	1927	17 232	California Hawaii	Queen Frederica	Sold 1948, cruising 1965, laid up 1973–7, scrapped 1977
Mariposa	Matson Line	1931	18 017	California Hawaii	Homeric	Sold for cruising 1955, damaged by fire 1973, scrapped 1974
Monterey	Matson Line	1931	18 017	California Hawaii	Britanis	Sold 1963, cruising 1975, accommodation ship 1995
Monterey	Matson Line	1956	14 779	US–Australia		Converted from cargo ship. Sold 1990, still in service 1999
Argentina	Moore–McCormac	1958	15 257	New York–S. America	Enchanted Isle	Cruising for various companies from 1969, in service 1999
Brasil	Moore–McCormac	1958	15 257	New York–S. America	Universe Explorer	Cruising for various companies from 1969, in service 1999
California	Panama–Pacific	1928	20 325	East Coast–West Coast	Uruguay	Scrapped 1964
Pennsylvania	Panama–Pacific	1929	20 526	East Coast–West Coast	Argentina	Scrapped 1964
Virginia	Panama–Pacific	1928	20 773	East Coast–West Coast	Brazil	Scrapped 1964
America	United States Lines	1940	33 961	USA–Northern Europe	Alferdos	Sold 1964 to Chandris, cruising 1978, laid up 1979–94, wrecked en route for use as a hotel ship in Thailand 1994
United States	United States Lines	1952	53 392	USA–Northern Europe	United States	Laid up 1969

Bibliography

Archer, B. (1995). The impact of international tourism on the economy of Bermuda. *Journal of Travel Research*, **34**(2): pp. 27–30.

Argyris, C. (1960). *Understanding Organisational Behaviour.* London: Tavistock Institute, p.84.

Barr, A. and York, P. (1982). *The Official Sloan Ranger Handbook.* London: Ebury.

Belbin, M. (1981). *Management Teams, Why They Succeed or Fail.* Oxford: Heinemann.

Benjamin, W. (1973*). The Work of Art in the Age of Mechanical Reproduction, in Illuminations.* London: Fontana.

Boorstin, D. (1964). *The Image; a Guide to Pseudo-Events in America.* New York: Harper.

Bryden, J. M. (1973). *Tourism and Development.* Cambridge: Cambridge University Press.

Burns, P. and Holden, A. (1995). *Tourism: A New Perspective.* New York: Prentice-Hall.

CAA (1994). *ATOL Business – December 1994.* London: Civil Aviation Authority.

Cartwright, R., Collins, M., Candy, A. and Green, G. (1996). *In Charge of Yourself.* Oxford: Blackwell.

Cartwright, R., Collins, M., Candy, A. and Green, G. (1998). *In Charge of Resources and Information,* 2nd edition. Oxford: Blackwell.

Cartwright, R. and Green, G. (1997). *In Charge of Customer Satisfaction.* Oxford: Blackwell, p. 54.

Cohen, E. (1972). Towards a sociology of international tourism. *Social Research*, **39**(1), pp.164–82.

Croall, J. (1978). *Fourteen Minutes*. London: Michael Joseph.

Crompton, J. (1979). Motivations for pleasure vacations. *Annals of Tourism Research*, **6** pp. 408–24.

Dann, G. S. and Potter, R. B. (1997). Tourism in Barbados. In *Island Tourism* (D. G. Lockhard and D. Drakakis-Smith, eds). London: Cassell.

Davie, M. (1987). *Titanic – the Full Story of a Tragedy*. London: Grafton, p. 50.

De la Viña, L. and Ford, J. (1998). Economic impact of proposed cruise ship business. *Annals of Tourism Research*, **26**, pp. 204–7.

Dickinson, R. and Vladimir, A. (1997). *Selling the Sea*. New York: Wiley.

Dolby, J. (1962). *The Steel Navy*. London: MacDonald.

Doxey, G. V. (1975). A causation theory of visitor – resident irritants; methodology and research inference. In *Proceedings of the Travel Research Association Annual Conference*, San Diego,CA.

Dupuy, R. and Dupuy, T. (1960) *A Compact History of the Civil War*. New York: Warner.

Eddy, P., Potter, E. and Page, B. (1976). *Destination Disaster*. London: Hart-Davis, pp. 3, 87.

Emmons, F. (1972). *The Atlantic Liners*. Newton Abbot: David and Charles.

European Union (1998). EC Directive 93/104 Concerning Certain Aspects of the Organization of Working Time. Brussels: EU.

Fairlie, G. (1989). Steam days in eastern Scotland. In *Railway World Year Book 1989*, Shepperton: Ian Allan, p. 94.

Fisher, H. A. L. (1935). *A History of Europe*, vol. 2. London: Eyre and Spottiswoode.

Fodness, D. (1994). Measuring tourist motivation. *Annals of Tourism Research*, **21**: 555–81.

Fodor (1999). *Fodor's 99: The Best Cruises*. New York: Fodor

Gardiner, R. and Van der Vat, D. (1995). *The Riddle of the Titanic*. London: Weidenfeld and Nicolson.

Gibbs, P. (1912). *The Deathless Story of the Titanic*. London: Lloyds Weekly News, p. 2.

Green, W., Swanborough, G. and Mowinski, J. (1987). *Modern Commercial Aircraft*. London: Salamander.

Hall, D. (1992). Tourism development in Cuba. In *Tourism and Less Developed Countries* (D. Harrison, ed.). London: Bellhaven.

Hall, S. (1995). *Rail Centres – Manchester*. Shepperton: Ian Alan.

Hamlyn, J. (1998). *Explorer Caribbean*, 2nd edition. Basingstoke: AA.

Harrison, D. (1992). *Tourism and Less Developed Countries*. London: Bellhaven.

Haswell-Smith, H. (1996). *Scottish Islands*. Edinburgh: Cannongate.

Hastings, M. and Jenkins, S. (1983). *The Battle for the Falklands*. London: Michael Joseph.

Haywood, L., Kew, F., Bramham, P., Spink, J., Capenerhurst, J. and Henry, I. (1989). *Understanding Leisure*. London: Hutchinson, p. 87.

Hoffer. W. (1980). *Saved*. London: Macmillan, p. 206.

Holbrook, E. (1947). *The Story of American Railroads*. New York: Crown.

Honey, P. and Mumford, J. (1986). *A Manual of Learning Styles*. Maidenhead: P. Honey.

HMSO (1938). The Holiday with Pay Act. London: HMSO.

Isherwood, J. H. (1977). Steamers of the past – Duke of York. *Sea Breezes*, July 1977.

Jones, T. O. and Sasser, W. E. Jnr (1995). Why satisfied customers defect. *Harvard Business Review*, November–December 1995, pp. 88–99.

Kludas, A. (1992). *Great Passenger Ships of the World Today*. Sparkford: Patrick Stephens.

Kotler, P. (1980). *Marketing Management*. New York: Prentice0-Hall.

Krippendorf, J. (1987). *The Holiday Makers*. London: Heinemann.

Lavery, P. and Van Doren, C. (1990). *Travel and Tourism – a North American–European Perspective*. Huntingdon: Elm Publications.

Laws, E. (1997). *Managing Packaged Tourism*. London: International Thomson Business Press.

MacIntyre, D. and Bathe, B. (1974). *Man-of-War*. Gothenburg: Tre Tryckare AB.

Maddocks, M. (1983). *The Great Liners*. New York: Time-Life.

Maslow, A. (1970). *Motivation and Personality*. New York: Harper and Row.

Mathieson, A. and Wall, G. (1982). *Tourism, Economic, Physical and Social Impacts*. Harlow: Longmans.

McAuley, R. (1997). *The Liners*. London: Boxtree.

McCannell, D. (1973). Staged authenticity: arrangements of social space in tourist settings. *Journal of Sociology*, **79**, pp. 589-603.

McGregor, D. (1960). *The Achieving Society*. New York: McGraw Hill.

Mill, R. C. (1990). *Tourism: The International Business*. New York: Prentice-Hall.

Miller, W. H. Jnr (1992). *Modern Cruise Ships, 1965–1990*. Toronto: General Publishing.

Miller, W. H. Jnr (1995). *Pictorial Encyclopaedia of Ocean Liners, 1860–1994*. Toronto: General Publishing.

Nelson, L. D. and Kuzes, I. Y. (1995). *Radical Reforms in Yeltsin's Russia: Political, Economic and Social Dimensions*. New York: M. E. Sharpe.

Nuñez, T. (1989). Tourist Studies in Anthropological Perspective. In *Host and Guests* (V. L. Smith, ed.). Philadelphia: University of Pennsylvania Press.

P&O (1995). *Oriana: From Dream to Reality.* London: P&O Cruises, p.27–8.

P&O (1995). *The Ballad of Oriana* (video). London: P&O Cruises.

Parker, S. (1983). *Leisure and Work.* London: Allen and Unwin.

Pearce, P. L. (1988). *The Ulysses Factor: Evaluating Visitors in Tourist Settings.* New York: Springer Verlag.

Peters, T. (1987). *Thriving on Chaos.* New York: A. Knopf Inc.

Peters, T. and Waterman, R. (1982). *In Search of Excellence.* New York: Harper and Row.

Phipps, R. and Simmonds, C. (1995). *Understanding Customers.* Oxford: Butterworth-Heinemann.

Pi-Sunyer, O. (1989). Changing perceptions of tourism and tourists in a Catalan resort town. In *Hosts and Guests: the Anthology of Tourism*, 2nd edn (V. Smith, ed.). Philadelphia: University of Pennsylvania Press.

Plog, S. (1987). Understanding psychographics in tourism research. In *Travel and Hospitality Research: A Handbook for Managers and Researchers* (J. R. B. Ritchie and C. R. Goldener, eds). New York: John Wiley and Sons.

Porter, M. E. (1980). *Competitive Strategy.* New York: Free Press.

Porter, M. E. (1985). *Competitive Advantage.* New York: Free Press.

Price Waterhouse (1996), *The Economic Impact of the Passenger Cruise Industry on the Caribbean 1995.*

Readers Digest (1972). *Great World Atlas.* London: RDA.

Ryan, C. (1991). *Recreational Tourism.* London: International Thomson Business Press.

Sabbach, K. (1995). *21st Century Jet: The Making of the Boeing 777.* London: Macmillan, p. 5.

Sea Breezes (1977). Veteran of the Seven Seas. *Sea Breezes*, July: 412–14. Liverpool: JOC Publications.

Shackleton, L. (1976). *A Report into the Future of the Falkland Islands.* London: HMSO.

Shaw S. (1990). Where has all the leisure gone? The distribution and re-distribution of leisure. 6th Canadian Congress on Leisure Research.

Toffler, A. (1970). *Future Shock.* New York: Random House.

Urry, J. (1990). *The Tourist Gaze.* London: Sage.

Ward, D. (1994). *Berlitz Guide to Cruising and Cruise Ships – 1994.* Princeton, NJ, and London: Berlitz, pp. 18, 202.

Ward, D. (1997). *Berlitz Guide to Cruising and Cruise Ships – 1997.* Princeton, NJ, and London: Berlitz, p. 46.

Ward, D. (1998). *Berlitz Guide to Cruising and Cruise Ships – 1997.* Princeton, NJ, and London: Berlitz, p. 571.

Ward, D. (1999). *Berlitz Guide to Cruising and Cruise Ships – 1999.* Princeton, NJ, and London: Berlitz, pp. 281, 323–4.

Wilkinson, P. (1997). Jamaican Tourism. In *Island Tourism* (D. G. Lockhard and D. Drakakis-Smith, eds). London: Cassell.

Wille, E. (1992). *Achieving Business Excellence.* London: Century, p. 1.

Woman's Own (1998). *Woman's Own,* December 21–28, p. 9. London: IPC Magazines.

World Tourism Organization (1991). International Conference on Travel and Tourism Statistics (Ottawa), 24–28 June 1991. Resolutions, Madrid: WTO, p. 4.

Yearsley, I. (1962). *The Manchester Tram.* Huddersfield: The Advertiser Press.

Zenfell, M. E. (ed.) (1995). *Insight Guides: Greek Islands.* London: APA.

Zuzanek, J. and Mannell, R. (1983). Work leisure relationships from a sociological and social psychological perspective. *Leisure Studies,* **2**, September: p. 327.

Index of ships

Appendix 3 lists main liners in operation post 1945. Where an entry has a number in brackets after the ship name e.g. *Sea Princess (1)*, *Sea Princess (2)*, the highest number relates to the latest vessel with that name to be put into service. Where there is a number not in brackets after a name e.g. *Sea Goddess 2*, then this is the official name of the vessel

Author index

Subject index

Swan Hellenic, 99, 117, 149
  Fleet 1998–99, 276

TFDS, see Norwegian Coastal Voyage
Theme cruises, 236–7
Thomas Cook, 3
Thomson Cruises, 32, 44–5, 57, 64,
    66, 87, 98, 116, 133, 135, 260
  'Fortunate Isles' itinerary, 166
Thornton's Cruise World, 46, 114
Tillberg, R. (designer), 179–181, 194
Tips See Gratuities
Tompkins, Capt., *xxiv*
Topweight, 174–6
Tourist Career Ladder, 15–17
Tourist Gaze the, 15, 19–20
Trade-Off Hypothesis, 9,
Transocean Tours, 72
Travel Savings Association, 8, 29
Typology:
  of tourists, 13–14
  of cruisers, 94–103, 116, 119, 215, 241
Travel Savings Association, 8

UK industry growth, 42–5
Union Castle, 8, 27, 29
Unique Selling Point (USP), 86

Vacations, 2, 12
  See also Holy days
Virgin Atlantic, 66

Wakes Weeks (UK), 4
Watchdog (BBC TV), 61, 131
Webster, C., 231–2
White Star, 23
Wilson, D. and M., 91
Windjammer Cruises, 241
Windstar, 39, 117, 238
  Fleet 1998–99, 276
World City, 264–5
World Tourism Organisation, 11
World War I, 23–4
World War II, 25
  Tonnage post WWII, 27
World Wide Web (WWW), *xxiii*